From the

Dust Bowl

to the

Corn Fields

From the
Dust Bowl
to the
Corn Fields

*For my friends (Ron & Leanne Schartz
Best Wishes,
D Paul Miller*

D. Paul Miller

RPM ▰ Publishers
Evanston

RPM ▲ Publishers
Evanston

THIS IS A MEMOIR
PUBLISHED BY RPM PUBLISHERS

Copyright © 2011 by D. Paul Miller

All rights reserved. Published in the United States by
RPM Publishers, Evanston, IL
http://rpmpublishers.com

Library of Congress Control Number: 2011913786

ISBN 978-0-983-36420-7

Water color painting on the front cover by Brenda McCasland
Book cover design by Richard Miller

Manufactured in the United States of America

First Edition

Acknowledgments

It would not be possible for me to complete this project without the efficient help with the editing and production work of my son Richard. He has spent many hours on the computer with the editing and layout of the book into its final format. My daughter, Brenda has exercised her artistic skills in designing the cover. She too, has spent hours of time and energy, and I appreciate what she has done. I have had occasional conversations regarding my project, with my son, Don and always appreciate his input and support. So congratulations and thanks to my kids. Although my grandchildren have not been personally involved, I feel and appreciate their relentless support. The only thing more important than friends is family. And I appreciate my family.

CONTENTS

Preface

"My Story" is about events and activities I've experienced in the process of living. It is not an easy matter to decide what to include and what to omit. Obviously, some of my *living* detail is not included. To remember all is impossible, and it's also impossible to include all that I do remember. In some instances some of the trivia I do include will probably seem trite and bore some readers. But lines have to be drawn someplace and I have tried to do that, so that materials included relate closely to actual life. I've started at the point of my earliest memories in childhood, and worked through a complex maze of a long life, down to the present time.

One of the problems I'm facing is that most of the manuscripts listed in the table of contents were originally written as independent documents, and at the time of the writing were not intended to be combined into one major project. Consequently, quite frequently I find some of the stories, or events of my life being repeated in more than one of the chapters. I've tried to eliminate these repetitions as much as possible, but find that some still remain. The reader will just have to forgive or ignore the repetitions.

In the first chapter "Life at Protection," I include some early history of my grandparents moving into the Protection area, along with some of their pioneering experiences. I then recall some of my earliest childhood memories, then move into grade school, and high school, some early college experiences, and rural school teaching.

Beyond Protection, Chapter II, begins with my parental family leaving Protection and moving to Berlin, Ohio, in 1941. Activities beyond this point include finishing college, CPS experience (which is detailed at some length in a separate chapter), finishing college at Goshen and graduate work in Nebraska, marriage, and the many activities of the D. Paul & Anne Miller family as they developed in the ensuing years.

"Civilian Public Service" includes details of the four years spent as a draftee of Uncle Sam, in work that was considered to be "work of national importance." I also include events leading up to that service. In response to a request from a number of Farnhurst CPS fellows I wrote an eighty-one page document and distributed it in bound form to the members of the unit at the Farnhurst CPS 50th Anniversary Reunion, in Bluffton, Ohio, 1992. Several years later I was asked to discuss my CPS experiences at our Saturday Morning Roundtable, a small group, mostly church friends, that meets for discussion and breakfast at our local hospital cafeteria. For this I prepared a more general manuscript to include not only Farnhurst experiences, but all CPS, but in an abbreviated form. For this present volume I have tried to combine these and add the story of the Farnhurst quilt which has come into the picture just recently, 2010. This quilt was planned and put together by the wives of the men in our CPS Unit. Our minister at the Mennonite Church of Normal, requested to use the quilt in a church service Memorial Day, May 30, 2010. It was on display in the front of the church May 23 and 30. It was then delivered to the Goshen College archives the first week in June.

The "Senior Olympics" chapter describes in detail a program that has become an important part of my later life. It has become a strong motivation for me to keep in good physical condition, which in turn has enabled me to engage in ardent physical work such as gardening, cutting down big trees, cut firewood, keep and continue to use our Four Seasons membership well into old age.

We had family membership to Four Seasons from 1962 to 2007. I told my friends at Four Seasons that I have tenure here.

In addition to the good friends we meet in our Four Seasons activities, it is important to me, that Anne and I have developed a lifestyle, arising at 4:15 am, dress and put on the cereal to start cooking, (then turn off before leaving), arrive at Four Seasons by 5:00, when the doors open, spend two hours divided among the weight room, stationary bike or tread-mill, gym, and pool, and leave for home at 7:00 am, eat breakfast and be ready to start the day at 8:00 am.

We've been following this schedule since we retired in 1982, to the time when Anne was no longer able to negotiate the steps at Four Seasons, and we terminated membership in 2007. It is amazing how Anne would hang right in there, moving slowly from weight machine to machine using (what she calls) her stick (but which is actually a nice cane) for walking. The important thing is that she still keeps at it, (January, 2006). We are recognized by participating members at the club as the oldest participants, and friends there contribute a great deal to our social life. This program of exercise and vegetarian diet appears to pay off. We were both in good health in 2006, and besides we seem to enjoy it.

An update here is that after Anne had her fractured vertebrae problems, had difficulty walking, and became dependent on me, we reluctantly discontinued membership at Four Seasons, and I began using Shirk Center, the IWU Fitness Center, since January 2007. After three years plus, in this condition, Anne passed away February 5, 2010. This information will be detailed in the pages describing our downsizing and retirement, in the chapter "Beyond Protection."

"Rocky Branch" and "Hedgewood" reflect my deep interest in woods and forest management. We acquired 127 acres in Clark County, Illinois, 120 miles south east of Normal, in 1981, and seven acres, Hedgewood, in Woodford County, Illinois, in 1997, which is fifteen miles from home. The Clark County woods has a primitive cabin, and a trip there often involves staying overnight, although quite often wc drive down spend several hours of intense work and return home the same day.

I describe Hedgewood as my "playground." I can go out, work a few hours or all day, and come home to eat and sleep well. I am working both areas under the supervision of the State foresters. I have planted many trees in both areas. This experience provides opportunity for many hours of rigorous physical activity along with the satisfaction of the pure joy of the out-of-doors and nature in the rough.

Another chapter describes my experiences in Haiti. A group of seven people from our church volunteered to spend ten work days in Haiti, January, 1994. My experiences and reaction to that are written up in this chapter.

"My Spiritual Journey" is an honest attempt to walk the reader through my experiences which I define as spiritual. I describe my spiritual life in a framework of three "conversions." The last two are somewhat complicated and have involved some mental conflict along with the inevitable philosophical and theological adjustments that were inevitably made. This chapter includes some of my dilemmas and frustrations experienced in my philosophical adventures.

I have a chapter titled "Believing Man: A Sociological Perspective of the Origin and Development of Religious Behavior." This statement relates closely to the "My Spiritual Journey" chapter. It, the "Believing Man," chapter has proven to be useful in my teaching of religious institutions, and is useful to me personally in relating to some of the imponderables in life. Actually I have gotten a lot of mileage from this statement and it is sufficiently important to me that I am including it in this project. I added a statement "A New Revelation: Nature Offers a Dilemma," as a sort of "tack on."

I have written a couple of other manuscripts reflecting my research and teaching experiences. These are titled "The Sociology of Creativity," and "A Primer of Sociological Theory." These were both rather important to me in my academic pursuits, but they were never published. I have decided not to include these in this "story" because they are more or less distant from actual "living experiences," and also, they are available in individual manuscripts.

My on-going activities continue. They remain in "the active tense." They begin at birth and I hope will continue to the "dead end." Consequently, in that sense, it is impossible for me to complete "My Story." However, the story I write will end. I will conclude it at the point where I submit it to the printer. Even though not complete, it will be the major part of the complete story. That, I guess, is the best we can hope for.

I - Life at Protection

The Beginning

"The Eighty," an eighty-acre farm twelve miles south of Protection, Kansas, is where it all began for me. I was born at home on the Eighty. The nearest hospital was in Ashland, twenty-five miles away. My siblings, two brothers and two sisters and I, were all born at home, with an attending physician in the home, rather than in a hospital.

It appears that "the eighty" where I was born, was land that was part of the inheritance referred to in the Judgment Awarding Partition that

Picture 1 - D.D. Miller family, from left to right, Emerson, Dennis, Dad, Ruth, Mom, Paul and Ethel c.a. 1937.

my grandma, Sophronia Miller, had registered in the county records, dated March 13, 1908. Grandma gave each of her fourteen children a parcel of the real estate known as "the ranch." According to that record, David D. Miller was awarded a total of 169.76 acres.

Family lore has it that, by law, the State of Kansas could not incorporate a village until it had a population of one hundred. In the early 1900s, the village of Protection had a population of 89. In 1908, Noah E. Miller bought the 2000 acre ranch south of Protection. He moved his family into Protection while the home

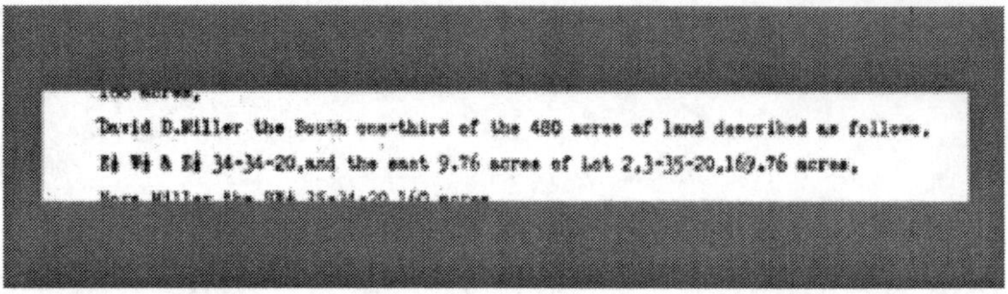

David D.Miller the South one-third of the 480 acres of land described as follows, E½ W½ & E½ 34-34-20,and the east 9.76 acres of Lot 2,3-35-20,169.76 acres,

Picture 2 - From the original deed of the 2,000-acre ranch filed March 13, 1908. David D. Miller family is Paul's father. (See Appendix VI for the entire two-page deed).

was being built on the ranch. This boosted the population to over 100, and as a result of the Miller family moving into the village, Protection became an incorporated town.

I do not know how it ended up being "the eighty," but I am aware that some trading, buying and selling, transpired among the children and years later at the time when I was old enough to become aware of what land possessions meant, the three youngest boys, my uncles Billie, Levi, and Harold, each had "a forty" in that area.

Dad sold our "eighty" to Curt Lindsey in 1924, and according to Ralph Sanders who lived in the area all his life, the buildings and trees were torn down in 1935. When our family visited Protection April 14, 15, & 16, 2001, the area that was once our homestead was all farmland.

My birth date was August 30, 1917. I have a few specific recollections of events in my early life, at age four. Two are very real to me. One, I injured the little finger on my left hand so that the tip was taken off at the first joint. All my life since the accident, I've been told that this happened when I was four years old. The second event is my brother, Emerson's birth. Since Emerson was four years younger than me this event would put me at four years of age.

Regarding the finger accident, my sister, Ruth, and I were pumping water to wash our feet. We always went barefooted in the summer time and our mother instructed us to wash our feet before we came in for supper. I was pumping water from our well, a little four-year old pulling up and down on the handle when the bolt holding the handle slipped out and the handle came down hard with my little finger between the handle and the extended piece of metal designed to catch the handle at the bottom of the stroke. It smashed the finger severely, blood was running from the wound as Ruth and I ran to the house to tell mamma, both crying at the top of our lungs. Mom always said Ruth was crying harder than Paul. Dad was not at home at the time, so Mom called my Uncle Howard who lived a mile away. In the meantime Mom wrapped the finger to stop the bleeding, and Howard arrived and took my mother and me to the doctor in Protection.

Apparently they did not give me any anesthesia. I recall vividly having severe pain. I screamed and fought while the nurse held me, and the doctor worked on the finger. I thought this nurse was the strongest woman I ever encountered. The doctor cleaned up the wound and took the tip completely off at the first joint, nail and all. I was relieved when we could leave the doctor's office. To console me, my mother bought me a pocket knife as a reward for going through the ordeal and, as she said, being brave. The knife had a chain that would attach to my jean button. It cost twenty-five cents.

The second event that I can recall vividly as a four-year old was the time my younger brother, Emerson, was born. Our father took Ruth, Dennis and me to stay with our relatives who were living on the ranch home my grandfather had purchased when they moved to Protection in 1908. Some of my uncles were still at home with Ma (my grandmother) at that time. My Uncle Levi brought us home to see the new baby. He, baby Emerson, was in his little crib and Mom was still in bed, not too well yet from the delivery. As I stood next to the bed looking at baby Emerson, he wrinkled up his face and made a snoot. At that point my Uncle Levi made a comment which I remember to this day, "When he does that he looks just like you."

At a very young age my sister Ruth and I got into the philosophical discussion of how people can tell right away whether a new baby is a boy or girl. We were probably five and seven years old, discussing this while washing and drying dishes one day. We agreed that after a baby gets older you can tell a girl because she wears dresses and a boy wears trousers, also a girl has long hair and a boy short hair. Boys and girls bottoms look alike, but the "pee'ers" don't. But, we mused; you wouldn't think they'd look at that right away, would they? This was a very important issue with us at the time. It wasn't until some years later we realized the facts in the matter.

Another landmark story: In our home as youngsters growing up, we had two terms commonly used, "poo-tink" and "pee" to describe the two bodily eliminations. I learned that "pee" is a concept used pretty much universally. "Poo-tink," I later found out was not commonly used. In my early days I couldn't understand why people didn't know what I was talking about when I'd say "poo-tink." A friend at school called it just "poo." I knew then that he wasn't saying it right. Even to this day I feel that the term we used for "number two" in my childhood was a good one even though we did not use it with our children. We'd simply say "b.m."

Picture 3 - My fourteen aunts and uncles - oldest to youngest, seated left to right; Ursula, Elias, Alfred, Lewis, David, Howard, Baldwin; and standing right to left, Tucson, Mary, Nora, Billie, Levi and the twins, Christina & Harold in 1949.[i]

Another incident I can recall as a small child, but which I can't date in time occurred during the Christmas Season. My judgment is that this incident occurred a year or two earlier than the incidents described above. It was probably when I was a late three-year-old or early four. We had a bedroom upstairs which was closed and not used during the winter. I was upstairs alone and opened the door and saw a big box on the bed. I crawled onto the bed and looking in it I saw a number of new things, things I had never seen before and didn't know we had. One was a big red ball. I bounced it a few times. Then also in the box was a big butterfly with wheels and a stick-handle which, when you pushed it, the butterfly would flap its wings. I was all excited about it and ran downstairs to tell Mamma what I had found. In my innocence I was sure this would be news to her. She, however, didn't seem too surprised, tried to make little of it, and told me I shouldn't go into that room when it's so cold. The things disappeared and I had forgotten about them, but interestingly they appeared at our family Christmas celebration on Christmas day. Even at that age, I was beginning to put things together.

It was several years later during a summer rainstorm, mom and dad were out in the shed oiling the harness for our work-horses. It was lightening and thundering hard. I was sitting by the window with my feet on the "slop bucket," which we kept in the house to put our scraps and dish water which was later fed to the pigs. Suddenly we heard a bang and I saw a bolt of lightning flash by the window outside, close to where I was sitting. It apparently came on the telephone line, knocked plaster off the wall, I felt a big shock, and the room was all smoky. It frightened me and I began to cry. Mom and dad heard the bang and came running through the rain to the house. Dad noticed that the lightning had struck the corner of the house and had splintered some wood in the roof and rafters. He said if it hadn't been raining so hard the house might have burned.

Regarding my fourteen aunts and uncles on my Dad's side, when I was growing up, I always heard that his parents "…ended up with twins in order to miss the unlucky number '13.''

Picture 4 - Left to right, Ruth (5), Paul (3) and Dennis (1), along with our new 1920 Model-T Ford purchased at the time for $495.

Another vague but nonetheless definite recollection I have which today I'd judge to have occurred at about age three is my Aunt Mary Baker coming to our place in a horse-drawn carriage while we were living on the Eighty. My recollection is that the carriage was sitting in our yard and when she was ready to go home she had to untie the horses and climbed into the carriage. It's the sight of the carriage in our yard that is still set in my mind. Aunt Mary was the sister of my grandfather and the wife of Henry Baker who lived five or six miles away. These were the days of transition, buggies to automobiles

I can recall when we sold or traded our old Model-T for a new one. The cost for the new Model-T was, I think, four hundred, ninety-five dollars. Our first Model-T had a windshield wiper with a lever on the inside at the top of the windshield that the driver would operate by hand while driving. They did not have self-starters. We had to crank them to start the motor. It was in the nature of the beast that they would often start to move forward as soon as the motor was running. I think the oil in the gears was stiff enough to cause it to start moving.

If we kids were around when Dad was cranking the car, he would sometimes tell us: "When it starts, put your foot on the brake," and we always felt important doing that. In the Model-Ts, there were three pedals. Left side was the clutch. Different from our modern cars, you'd push the clutch in to start the car moving. The middle pedal was reverse, and the right side, the brake. Then there was a lever on the left side that once the car was moving, you'd push forward and be in high. It had no foot accelerator. The speed was regulated by hand with a gas lever just below the steering wheel.

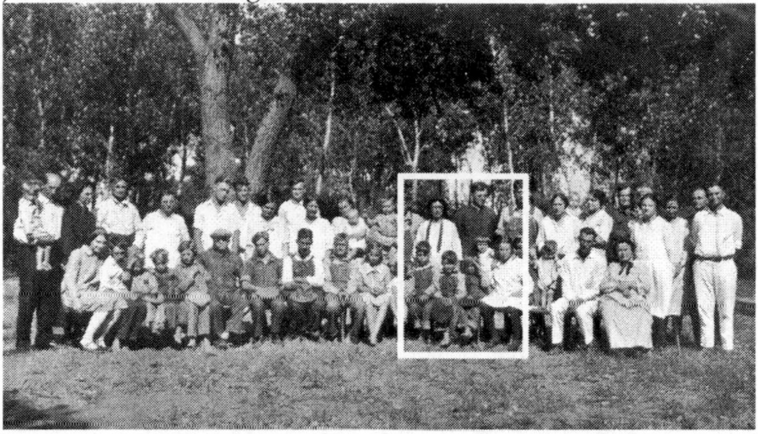

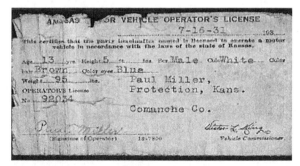

Picture 5 - Miller family reunion in 1928. The DD Miller family is outlined by the white box in the picture, with the parents in the back row, along with the five children in front.

In this instance, the car was sitting near the closed garage door, Dad was cranking, and I was told, "Put your foot on the brake when it starts." Dad cranked, it started, and mistakenly, I put my foot on the wrong pedal, the clutch. It started forward and Dad had to scramble to get out of the way before it pinched him between the car and garage door. Dad cleared the car and it hit the door and stopped. It was my mistake, and we were lucky that Dad got out of the way before the car hit him.

VEHICLE OPERATOR'S LICENSE

7-16-31 193

Age 13 yrs. Height 5 ft. ins. Sex Male Color White Color hair Brown Color eyes Blue

Weight 95 lbs.

OPERATOR'S License No. 92034

Paul Miller,
Protection, Kans.

Comanche Co.

(Signature of Operator) 13-7800 Vehicle Commissioner.

Picture 6 - D. Paul's original driver's license issued by the state of Kansas on July 16, 1931, when he was 13 years old.

I learned to drive the Model-T and at age ten Mom sent me to the neighbors, Clay Woolfolks, in our Model-T to borrow something for her cooking, some sugar or flour. That was a real thrill for me. I made the round trip and felt like a grown-up. I received my first state-issued driver's license at age 13. I still have the original in my possession at this writing. It states "13 years old, 5 feet tall, brown hair, blue eyes and weighed 95 pounds." Having located this license among my stored possessions a few years ago I was interested in the background of auto-licensing in Kansas so sent a copy of this license to Wilburn Dillon, our niece Evelyn Wiebe's husband who is an attorney in Topeka, Kansas. He did some research and sent me a copy of the law relating to "automobile and motor vehicle operator's license" in the state of Kansas. I learned from Wilburn's research that the first statutory requirement for operator's license in Kansas was enacted June 30, 1931, with licenses granted at the minimum age of 13. My license is dated July 16, 1931. So it was issued just 16 days after the first law requiring operator's license in Kansas became effective and at that time I was at the minimum age.

Picture 8 - "Ma" and "Pa," my grandparents Saphrona & Noah Miller c.a. 1879.

Another recollection which reflects what I later learned in psychology class to be conditioned response occurred in our farmyard. We had an old tin granary where we stored our chicken feed. It was usually my job to feed the chickens. When I'd open the old and rickety tin granary door it'd make a lot of noise and the chickens soon learned that that noise was associated with feeding. It wasn't long until as soon as I'd open that door and they'd hear the noise, the chickens would come running from all over the farmyard to get the feed. I'd simply scatter the grain on the ground and they'd pick it up as they ate. A few chickens would usually remain and scratch to find the last grains. It was interesting to watch the chickens scratch in the loose dirt, peck at a kernel then scratch some more until the grain was cleaned up.

An interesting sidelight about our milking is that in the summertime, we'd go get the cows from the pasture, herd them into the corral, close the gate, then take our milk bucket and stool, sit down and milk the cows in the open without them being tied down or otherwise controlled. Many people who always put their cows in the barn or in stanchions would hardly believe that cows would stand still for such an operation. Also, we had cats which came to the corral at milking time and we'd squirt milk into their mouths. As well as giving the cats their milk, it was entertainment for us although it did waste milk, and I confess, sometimes I would squirt milk into my own mouth.

Usually two or three of us kids would milk. We'd have maybe six or eight milk cows and each would have his/her one, two or three cows to milk twice a day, morning and evening. After milking we'd take our buckets of milk to the milk-house, strain it into the bowl of our "separator" where we'd separate the milk. The separator was a machine with a crank we'd turn by hand. It had a little bell on the handle which would jingle with each revolution of the crank until it had enough speed that the centrifugal force would stop the jingle. At that speed it'd be fast enough to turn on the faucet so the milk would flow into the separator to separate the milk from the cream. Cream would come out of one spout and milk from another. Before separating we'd usually save milk to be used for family meals into another container. Cream would be saved in a cream-can which would be taken into town periodically to sell. The skim milk would be fed to the livestock. If we'd have small calves still drinking milk they'd

Picture 7 - "Ma" (1934), my grandmother and the mother of the fourteen aunts & uncles, a year before she died.

get their portion of the separated milk. Aged milk would clabber. We'd often feed the clabber milk to the chickens and the remaining whey to the pigs.

Grade School

A year or so before I started to school, Dad was teaching at West Creek country school, five or six miles east of where we lived. Dad would ride horse back to school some days, and sometimes Mom would take him in our new Model-T Ford. She'd take him, drive home then go back and get him after school. It was done this way because Dad didn't want the new car to sit out in the sun all day. He thought the sun was hard on the paint.

Picture 8 - Dad's school at Pleasant Valley one-room school in 1924. D. Paul is in the front row, right end, while his older sister, Ruth, with braids, is in the middle of the front row & Dad, our teacher, in the upper-right corner.

When I started to school at age six, Dad was teaching at Pleasant Valley School about a mile east of our home on "the eighty". He was my teacher grades one through four. The first two years were at Pleasant Valley, we then moved into the Collier Flats District about seven or eight miles north where Dad was hired to teach. The next two years I, along with Ruth and Dennis, attended Collier Flats, which was often referred to as the

Baker School because Uncle Henry Baker lived on a farm close to the school.

Those were the days when in our country school we had anywhere from twenty to thirty students, representing all eight grades. The school house had low windows, we could look out and see cars drive by or farmers working in the field with horses or tractors, cows in the pasture, and even kids who had asked "to leave the room," go to the outdoor privy.

Apparently, Dad was competitive in his athletic interests. He had good ball teams at Pleasant Valley School and arranged matches with other schools in the area I was not old enough to play on his teams at Pleasant Valley, but as a fourth grader I did play on the baseball team.

When I was in the fourth grade, I recall Dad took me aside and explained that he was going to have me play on the baseball team rather than Walter Christopher who was a third grader but taller and bigger than me and was considered a possibility to play on the team, but when we play basketball, Dad said he would have Walter play on the team. It all made sense to me and I was happy to play baseball.

Dad was a strict disciplinarian. He always had good order in the classroom. An event that Dennis and I often joked about later was that he, Dennis, and a classmate, Cleo Stewart, were working at the blackboard, and something funny happened with Dennis and Cleo and both of them snickered and couldn't hold themselves and laughed out loud attracting the attention of the whole room. Dad walked over to the boys, took each of them by the hair and led them down to their seats, plopped them down, and told them to get to work. It was a tense moment and the whole room caught the message.

In 1927, the folks bought another farm north and a little west of The Eighty, less than a mile north of the original ranch or home place of Dad's father, my Grandpa, whom I never knew. My grandfather, always called Pa, had died at age 49 and Ma took over the ranch and according to reports I've heard many times, did a good job of managing the financial affairs paying off the mortgage on the ranch the second year after Grandpa's death. I was ten years old when we moved to this newly acquired home. Dad had retired from teaching and planned to focus on farming and his ministerial work. This home is where our family really grew up and all of my siblings and I remember it as the home place.

Picture 9 – The family 'home place' where D. Paul grew up, a photo he took in 1935. Brenda's artwork on the cover of this book is designed from this photograph.

We attended Cimarron School, and for the first time, as a fifth grader, I had a teacher other than my father.

The first year at Cimarron was not a happy one for our family. It seemed that the teacher, Lela Risley, was always sort of antagonistic toward us. We did survive the year and interestingly, Dad was voted in as a school board member the following year, and Miss Risley, took an entirely different attitude toward us kids. I think Dad being on the board was an important factor, although looking back, I feel that part of our problem was simply making the adjustment to another teacher and another community. After Lela Risley's second year, the board hired a different teacher, Alice Toothacher. She was my 7th and 8th grade teacher and we liked her very much. (Alice Toothacher later married our cousin Chester Baker and became a very good friend of our family.) This takes us up to my high school experiences.

It was custom at that time that all 8th graders go to a central place, the high school in town, and take the 8th grade examinations. I recall that, even though I was worried about passing, I passed with good scores.

High School

Dad wanted his children to have a good education. He was particularly conscious of this and occasionally made comments about it, I think because he had not yet finished high school. Two of the stalwart families in our church, Selzers and Bakers, did not favor educating their children beyond 8th grade. Dad, however, always said he'd like to see his children have a high school education, and then beyond that they would be on their own. He and Mom made great personal sacrifices to see that all five of their children did get through high school, and even after high-school our parents did all they could to encourage and support them in college. Somehow they all got bachelor's degrees in College, the three boys went on to complete doctorates.

When I was ready for high school, our home was eleven miles south of Protection, where our nearest high school was located. The year earlier, Ruth had driven our Model T Roadster (a one-seated Ford) to high school alone. In my first and second year, Ruth, our cousin Sanford, who lived just a quarter of a mile west of our place, and I, drove the Roadster. In my Junior and Senior years, the folks arranged for us to drive and pick up passengers along the way. We had acquired a two-seated, two-door Model A, and the folks arranged for us to pick up passengers along the way who paid a fee, all of which helped with transportation expenses. One year, we had so many passengers that dad had made a little wooden stool to sit in front of the rear seat for the 7th passenger to sit on.

Because we had passengers, we always had to come home right after school that prohibited any of us from participating in after school activities. I was particularly conscious of this since I would like to have participated in athletics. I always had the feeling that Dad really objected to his boys participating in athletics and the car pool leaving right after school was a good way to handle that matter diplomatically.

Ruth told me later that Dad did not permit her to participate in Glee Club because the girls were required to wear long formal dresses for performances and this was not acceptable in the conservative Mennonite tradition. I think mainly because of Dad's objection to formals, Ruth was permitted to attend and graduated from Hesston Academy her senior year. By that time I was permitted to participate in Glee Club. The music classes were during school hours so I participated in Boys Glee Club and the mixed chorus.

One year I was chosen to sing in the boy's sextet. One of the instances I'll always remember was that the boy's sextet was scheduled to sing in a minstrel show. We did our practicing during school hours, but the show was at night. I went home the night of the show and for some reason told dad that the members of the sextet were to have blackened faces. We were to be Negroes. For some reason Dad did not approve of this and said I could not participate. I said, "But I'll have to. The show is tonight." Dad said he'd take care of that. He then drove eleven miles into town, spoke to Mrs. Dale, our music teacher, and that night at the show a quintet, rather than a sextet, sang.

As a high school student I was very conscious of and frustrated because of things we were permitted to do and not do. I wanted so much to be like the others that in my freshman year I put motor oil on my hair so I could have "slick" hair like the other boys in school. We were not permitted to go to our class parties, dances, and picnics after school and evenings. I was, however, permitted to go to the Fine Arts Contests where our music groups sang in the competition.

On one of these occasions our school was to go to Ford, Kansas, one of the schools in our Iroquois League, where the Fine Arts Contests were held. I was particularly self-conscious because we as young boys in the church were not permitted to wear neckties. Also, we never could wear ties to any of the school functions. However, on this school function, in my senior year, I decided to take matters into my own hands. I bought a necktie, a brown silk tie at the dry goods store in Protection, for twenty-cents, all unbeknown to Mom and Dad. I was on my way to the Fine Arts Contest with a group of my high school friends with the tie in my pocket. I had no knowledge of how to tie the tie. My friend, Harold Newton, tied it for me; I put it on, wore it all day and really felt good. I had it made. I took the tie off, however, before I went home that evening and kept it hidden from my parents.

Weeks later, a group of our church young folks were riding around, on a Sunday afternoon. I had the tie in my pocket, and for some reason was still wearing my Sunday suit. I put the tie on. (By this time I was able to tie it myself.) At our high school building I stood in front of an evergreen tree and had one of my friends take my picture. It was developed and my friend gave me a copy. I carried it around for a while and eventually had the nerve to show it to my mother at a time when Dad wasn't at home. Mom always seemed more lenient on matters of this kind than Dad. And, I recall so vividly her comment when she saw the picture. She said, "Paul, that doesn't look like you."

Picture 10 - D. Paul wearing his first necktie.

Anyway for me the ice was broken. Mom said, "I'm going to show it to Papa." Of course that's precisely what I wanted her to do. Dad didn't reprimand me or say or do too much about it and before long I started wearing the tie to church. At that time I thought my brothers should wait until they were as old as I was before they would be permitted to wear ties. And, you guessed it, Dennis was wearing a tie a month later and when Emerson wanted to he also had a tie.

Later I realized why Dad didn't reprimand me for what I did. After he had died and one of my cousins was working on the Miller genealogy, I discovered a letter from the genealogy material indicating that my grandpa, Noah Miller, had written to some church conference officials defending the action of three of his children. One of them was Dave, my Dad, who was disciplined by the church because he wore a tie. Another was disciplined for joining a literary society; the other would be disciplined if she were home, for having a piano.

Along with the letter we somehow got hold of a picture of Dad, yes, my father, wearing a sporty tie. How this all happened that somehow we never got this information of Dad wearing a tie while he was living is hard to explain. Whether he deliberately tried to keep his own tie experience from his boys or whether it just coincidentally happened that I never got the information, I'll probably never know.

After my senior year in high school Dad was scheduled to hold a series of evangelistic meetings in Oregon and Idaho. The folks asked me to stay out of school the year following my high-school graduation to help Mom harvest our row-crop and do chores. Our main job was to "top" our row-crop. (The topping process was to take a kitchen paring knife and cut off each individual head of grain and throw it into the wagon.) Mom and I would go to the field with a team of horses hitched to a wagon with a high side-board. We would top a wagon load, then unload it in narrow stacks near our house, and go back to the field to top more grain. The crop was unloaded in narrow rows so the heads of grain would dry out, and when the crop was in, we would engage someone to come in with a combine to thrash the grain from the head. The fall harvest, as I recall, took several months, but we got it all done and the harvest was completed by or near Thanksgiving time. We also had cows to milk, pigs and chickens to feed and care for.

As a reward helping while Dad was gone, I was permitted to attend Hesston College for a six-week "short term" that winter. It was the first time I had been away from home and out from under of the influence of my parents. I developed many good and lasting friendships. One was 'Rip' Stehman, a relationship we kept alive until his death a few years ago at age 80. Another was Bob Garber, who became my roommate the following year when I attended Hesston College. Incidentally, his dad and my dad were roommates when they were students at Hesston years earlier.

Someone had told me that if you pick up a skunk by the tail it couldn't spray on you, that is unless it got it's front feet propped up on its body, then all you'd have to do if you had it by the tail is shake it so the front feet came loose then you'd be OK on the spraying deal. So one evening when our family was driving to visit our neighbors, a skunk ran across the road. I asked dad to stop and I hopped out and took out across the field after him. I'd catch up with him and he'd dodge, I'd catch up again and he'd dodge again. This kept up a while and in the meantime he was spraying whenever I'd get close to him. I finally got him by the tail and I do not know if that stopped his spraying but by that time I was well sprayed anyway. I took him, still alive, over to the car to show the family. I told dad to give me the hammer. I gave him a few blows on the head. That's the only way we had to kill our trapped animals at that time.

Later I got my .22 rifle and that simplified the process. But here, each time I'd hit him with the hammer, he'd spray. I finally got him knocked out and put him in a gunny-sack. We went on to the neighbors but our visit was short. I stayed outside the house all evening. The next day I skinned and stretched the hide and this was

Picture 12 - Result of a Comanche County rabbit hunt.

another pelt added to my collection. It fetched another one-and-a-half dollar which I added to my spending money but it took several days to wear off the odor. I had been pretty well saturated.

I did a lot of trapping as a young boy. My Uncle Billie taught me how to skin and stretch the hide, along with various techniques of successful trapping. On one occasion I used the blood I had collected from the family butchering to kill the human scent on my gloved hands and shoes. In one setting I placed two traps for coyotes, with some of the scraps from butchering, and the second night I had a coyote. I was riding our horse, named Short, and by this time was carrying my .22 rifle. The coyote was caught by a front foot and a back foot in the two traps I had set.

It hurts me to say it today, but in those days I was so conditioned that I could kill an animal with a club or shoot it with no thought of being cruel to the animals. Times have changed. I shot the coyote, loaded it on my horse and took it home. The hide brought $2.00. I thought that was a low figure. Prices varied considerably from year to year and even varied during the season in a given year because of the supply/demand situation. One year I caught a badger which I sold for $4.00. That's the most I ever received for any one pelt.

Trapping was the major way I had of getting any spending money. During trapping season, my routine was to get up early and run my trap-line before choring, usually riding Short, then chore, eat breakfast, change clothes and go to school. Many days I went to school with strong skunk odor. You don't remove skunk odor by simply bathing and changing clothing. It has to wear off. Friends and classmates were well aware of the odor and would talk about it but simply accept it. Kids did not get monetary allowances in those days. At least we didn't in our family nor did the families of our friends. We have to remember that most of these early days were during the depression years, late 20s and early 30s.

The purchase of my first rifle used for shooting the animals in my traps, was quite an important event in my young life. I was about an 8th grader, I had saved enough money and bought a Stevens, .22, bolt action single-shot rifle. After this acquisition I felt that I was an accomplished trapper. I had reached the top in the trapping world. On butchering day I sometimes was permitted to shoot the hogs. At that time, that was a special privilege for me. My comment today is "what a perverted sense of values!"

As kids at home, we were permitted to do whatever we wished on our birthdays. Sometimes we'd just play or do as nearly nothing as possible, not even have to do our chores, wash or dry dishes or whatever. Usually, however, I chose to go fishing. I would take my fishing poll, dig some worms, and start south across the pasture to the creek three-quarters of a mile away. I'd catch grasshoppers on the way for bait. With grasshoppers and worms for bait, I'd usually come home with a string of fish which we would clean and eat for supper.

Rabbit Drives

During the depression days of the 1930's, I participated in two Jack Rabbit Drives. In those days we had lots of Jack Rabbits and considerably less Cotton Tails. Cotton Tails were smaller and good to eat, but we'd eat only young Jack Rabbits. The folks always said the old ones were too tough. It was common to see Jack Rabbits in the fields, and often they would run out into the roads as you'd drive along. If we'd get one in the road ahead of us in the car, we'd follow it and try to run over it. They could run sometimes thirty to thirty-five miles per hour. Usually, just before we'd catch up with it, it would dodge off into the ditch or field.

Our dog, Jubilee, would follow us to the field when we were cultivating the row crops with the four-horse team, and he'd quite regularly scare up a jack rabbit and chase it until they were both played out. He'd often times catch it and after he got rested, eat it on the spot.

Rabbits were so plentiful that they would often damage our crops to the point that it would reduce the harvest. They did so much damage, that the community organized drives to get rid of them in order simply to protect the crops. For the drives hundreds of people, men, women, boys, and girls, anyone old enough and able to walk several miles would participate. Schools were dismissed in order to increase the number of people to cover a larger area of the rabbit-infested country.

The drive corral would include approximately half a mile or more of snow fence set up to funnel the rabbits into a smaller enclosed area To start the drive, neighbors with trucks and cars would distribute people a mile or two in front of the enclosure. The drivers would walk, spacing themselves perhaps fifty to a hundred feet apart at the start, far enough apart to cover a larger space but close enough to keep the rabbits running forward. All would then start marching toward the corral. At the start the line would probably extend a mile or two along the section line with everyone instructed to walk toward the corral. As we marched the line would close in so that the people at the ends of the line would come in to meet the ends of the snow fence.

No guns were allowed. Almost everyone carried a sturdy club. The rabbits would run ahead of the drivers and occasionally we'd have a coyote among the rabbits. The coyote usually got back through the line before going into the funneled enclosure, but the rabbits would work in the funnel to the corral at the end. The corral would enclose perhaps an acre of space, and at the end it'd be literally filled with rabbits.

One drive I participated in we bagged over two thousand Jack Rabbits. At the end with the corral full of rabbits, the organizers encouraged us younger kids to get in and club the rabbits to death. Sometimes when we were chasing them in the enclosure they would pile up on top of each other almost as high as the four-foot fence. On this particular drive there were several trucks from the "meat-scraps" company in Wichita there to take the dead rabbits to process into meat scraps which were sold for livestock feed. I can recall when my father would purchase a gunnysack of meat scraps to mix with the chicken or hog feed.

The large number of rabbits thus didn't go to waste but can you imagine what the animal rights people would say today. It is obvious that in those days, the depression, and dust bowl days, a different value was placed on the life of an animal as compared with today. When a horse or dog needed to be destroyed, we'd lead it out to the far corner of the pasture and shoot it with little or no thought of the value of an animal's life, and in the case of a horse, leave it lay for the coyotes to clean up. And in a few days nothing would be left except bones and probably the hide.

Our Family Dogs

While living at Protection in the 1930's, we had only one dog that we really considered a good family dog, Jubilee. We called him Jubbie. We had a brown dog that somehow appeared on the scene but we did not keep him long. And I don't remember how we got rid of him. He does appear on the picture with our skunk picture, but wasn't with us very long.

Jubbie would follow us to the field when we were cultivating our crops, and would quite often scare up and run down a rabbit. He would then eat it, and enjoy a good meal. Contrary to how we care for pets today, we never bought dog food for Jubbie. His meals consisted of table scraps plus what he could scrounge. But he always seemed to be reasonably well fed and it good shape.

As I recall, in those days I never saw a house-dog. None of our friends kept their dogs in the house. Dogs always lived outside. In cold weather, Jubbie would find the warmest spot in one of our sheds or the barn. In warm weather, he would invariably be lying at the door to greet whoever came out of the house first in the morning.

I recall one of his rabbit chases where both Jubbie and the rabbit had run so long, and they were both so tired that the pace of both had slowed down to a very slow run. Suddenly, the rabbit stopped, it was apparently so tired it couldn't run any more, and it surprised Jubbie. He also stopped, and looked at the rabbit. In a few seconds the rabbit started running slowly, and then Jubbie grabbed it, and soon enjoyed his good meal. I left home to do my country school teaching in near Peabody, Kansas, my siblings also left home before long, and none of us remember what actually happened to Jubbie.

I had no further experience with family dogs until we moved to Mankato. Our kids were small and wanted a dog so we bought a little Beagle, and also called him Jubbie. He was still with us when we moved to Illinois. For some reason he got a sore that developed into a condition of distemper. We took him to the vet. The vet said it was such a serious case that it was impossible to cure, so we had him put to sleep. That was a sad day, particularly for Don, who was with us at the vets. We took him home and gave him a respectful burial in our back yard.

As you might imagine, we all missed a dog, the kids were still at home, and all wanted another dog. So we bought another cute little beagle. Don named him Kon-Tiki. He developed into the most ideal little dog I've ever known. He was a combined out-door-indoor dog. He was house trained. We had a comfortable basket with bedding for him in the kitchen, and he was trained to not go into the living room on our rug. He was tied up outside during the day when the family was gone, had a nice dog house outside, and when the kids came home from school, we'd bring him in; he'd go to the basement with the kids as they played or watched television. Even in winter time Kon-Tiki would sleep outside in his dog house. By that time we bought dried dog-food, and we'd feed him table scraps, including chicken bones. In fact when we'd have a chicken meal, that would also be Kon-Tiki's best meal of the day. When we asked him to beg, he'd stand up on his hind legs and wait for the food.

We all loved Kon-Tiki. We had him even after the kids were away in college. Almost daily, when I'd get home from school, I'd get on my bicycle, turn Kon-Tiki loose and we'd go for his workout. He was good at dodging cars, and like all of our dogs, would chase rabbits, and often catch one and eat it.

On our final run, Kon-Tiki and I were out in the country, I on my bike, he running loose, west on College Avenue, at that time relatively undeveloped, when he scared up a rabbit out in the field. He chased it across the road when a car was coming. The car missed the rabbit but hit Kon-Tiki with both wheels, and killed him instantly. I took off his collar and tags, rode home, broke the news to Anne who was sad, took a shovel, went back and buried him on the bank of the stream near the corner on West College. Then it was difficult but, I had to break the news to all of our kids who were away from home at the time. Our whole family was saddened, but we all had to accept and adjust. That was our last family dog.

The Great Depression and Dust Storms

My last years in grade school and all through high school were the heart of the Great Depression. Memories of that are vivid. I was driving our Model-A Ford to high school and one day we had planned to do some business in town before coming home but couldn't because we were told the banks are closed. It was the "bank holiday" President Roosevelt had called for banks in the entire nation. This was one of the many moves President Roosevelt made in the attempt to bolster the economy to get us out of the depression.

One afternoon it was announced that the schools were going to be dismissed at noon because of the severe dust storm rolling in. The storm had started before we left school. As we drove home it was so dark at one o'clock in the afternoon, that at times we literally could not see the radiator cap on our car. We simply pulled over to the right side of the road and crept along very slowly, finally arriving home.

Many days in the storms you could not see our granary, washhouse or barn, from our kitchen window. Dust drifted like snow. Some of the fence of the pig-pen along the road west of our mailbox was drifted so that the fence, four or five feet tall was completely covered, and later had to be dug out by hand.

After a night's sleep we would wake up in the morning many times with a white spot where our heads had laid during the night. The sheet and pillow would be covered with dust. We would use a scoop and broom to clean up the dust on our kitchen floor. Some of these stories seem unbelievable today, however, I have a documentary video of the dust bowl which my cousin, Ralph Miller, Uncle Harold's son who lives in Eastern Colorado, showed at a recent Miller Reunion. It shows scenes of the dust bowl stories in a very realistic fashion.

In those days prices of farm produce were unbelievably low. This was during the time when the government was paying farmers to burn cotton crops, plow under wheat, kill little pigs, and pour milk down the gutter in order to reduce the supply and hopefully increase the demand and ultimately the price. I helped catch some of our shoats, (young pigs), put them in a gunny sack for our neighbor who paid dad twenty-five cents per pig. Wheat was 25 cents a bushel, and when I was in College at Hesston, I bought gas for my car for eleven cents per gallon at the Unruh

Station at the north end of Newton. Ice cream cones were a nickel and malts when I was in Hays State College, 1937, ten cents. The waiter would fill our glass, and then give us the remaining malt that was in his metal cup used for mixing.

Picture 13 - Sunday-school picnic at 'the Slab,' one mile south of our home c.a. 1927.

Dad registered for the WPA (Works Progress Administration), a government program designed to help poverty families during the depression. He had me be responsible for and drive our four-horse team, pulling a slip, working on the new bridge over the Cimarron River couple miles south of our home. I never really liked this job. First, I had to drive couple miles to the project, then worst of all, our four-horse team was not one to be proud of. We had one horse, Short, that was extremely lazy, and another that was somewhat crippled. With these handicapped horses it was not always an easy job to keep up with the other teams on the job. But dad always got his welfare check for the time we spent with our four-horse team and that was important to our family.

Dad never really had his heart in his farming. He was more interested in his pastoral work and holding evangelistic meeting. The congregations where he'd hold meetings would always take one or two free-will offerings during his week or ten days of meetings. It was not uncommon for him to bring home checks of one hundred dollars or more from one congregation, all of which proved to be important to our family income.

I do not recall of ever seeing dad work a full day in the field with the horses. I was ten years old when he bought the farm mentioned earlier as our home place. Although I do not recall him doing it, he must have spent some time doing field work. Dad started farming after he retired from teaching and we moved to the farm. At that time I started working in the field with a four-horse team pulling a lister. My first job was in the field east of our buildings. This was a new experience for me and I welcomed it. It made me feel grown-up. A few years later Dennis and Emerson also got involved in working in the field with the horses. Dad would go to the field with us to get us started with the cultivator or planter, and then he'd go home and work around the house or go to his study. He spent a lot of time reading and preparing for his preaching and church work.

To show the degree of religious devotion my mother and father had, I never saw them get into bed before they had kneeled down beside the bed and said their long but silent prayers. To observe the biblical principle of the "the woman having her head covered when praying," Mom would always cover her head with the sheet or blanket.

Dad was never one to play. He would never play ball or go fishing with us in our free time. We were always happy when our Uncles Billie, Levi and Harold would come and a bunch of us would go fishing, or swimming. We spent a lot of our recreational time at the creek, Bluff Creek, which was less than a mile south of our home. Occasionally we'd go to what we called The Lake which was merely a swimming hole, perhaps couple hundred feet long and twenty to thirty feet wide, next to Cimarron River. It was in this lake where I first proved to myself that I could swim. It was deeper than I could wade, but after working at it for a while, I could swim across it, a distance of probably 20 or 30 feet. That was a big accomplishment for me, although I would only "dog-paddle." I never learned the four swimming strokes until I took swimming lessons at Four Seasons after I was 60 years old.

We could usually get some pretty good swimming and fishing at Bluff Creek. Periodically the creek would flood. The water would come up over the slab (the concrete bridge over the creek) and cover the road so that traffic would be shut off. I recall one time several of us waded in to the slab and with inner tubes, jumped off the slab into the rushing water and floated several hundred feet to a landing, then come back to repeat.

I also recall when a deep pond would be washed out along the creek in Billie's pasture. Billie and his brothers put up a diving board on an old buggy frame. The springs on the buggy frame would give us a spring on the diving board, and we had a ball diving off that. After the water subsided we'd often go hand-fishing and sometimes come home with tubs full of nice cat fish and usually some carp, fish 15 to 18 inches long and weighing five or six pounds.

After I left home and started teaching in McPherson County, near Canton, I became good friends with some former grade school students in the community, who were graduated, and who did a lot of rabbit hunting. I often joined them. These experiences help to explain my current interest in deer hunting and even beaver trapping, which I did at "Rocky Branch" just a few years ago. It was a sort of carry-over from my youth.

Harvesting

Another important segment of my early experiences was harvesting with Uncle Henry Baker and his three sons. They always needed hired help during harvest and for the plowing after harvest. All three of us boys hired out as soon as we were old enough to run the tractors. I think we started working for Bakers at about age 13 or 14. Those were the days when the tractor, with lugs rather than rubber tires, pulled the combine and everything was out in the open, no self-propelled equipment, no enclosed cabs.

I was always the tractor operator, and one of the Baker boys was the combine man. I would stay at Uncle Henrys during the week. We put in really big days, get up early, I'd help milk the cows, eat breakfast, and be in the field as soon as the dew was dried up so the wheat would be dry enough to thrash. Then we'd work as late as we could see assuming that it wasn't too damp for the wheat to thrash out of the heads. In Kansas it was usually dry early and late. Sometimes we wouldn't get in for supper 'til 9:30 or 10:00 o'clock, eat and fall in bed only to get up at 5:00 for another day. Sometimes I was so tired that I welcomed a break-down or a rain to give us a break. In case of a break-down, if I'd get the chance, I'd lay in the shade of the combine while one of the bosses would go to town for the needed repair part. Usually, however, there was work to be done taking things apart to make the needed repair.

One day I had an interesting experience while driving the tractor for Ralph, the middle of the three Baker boys, who was my favorite of the three Baker boys. Riding the tractor hours on end my lips were chapped from the dry winds and dust. Ralph told me he had a cure for that: take a good chew of tobacco. Tobacco, he said, is healing. The Baker boys usually had chewing tobacco on hand and the oldest one, Orie, smoked cigarettes but kept that hidden from his dad. (Sometimes he would put a lighted cigarette in his pocket if his dad appeared unexpectedly on the scene.)

I was concerned about my chapped lips so I took a good chew from Ralph then we got on the tractor and combine and started harvesting wheat. All went well for a short time, but soon, I began feeling nauseous. I got sick, was dizzy and finally had to stop the tractor, get off and tend to my illness. I vomited, and had what the dictionary defines as "abnormal flow of intestinal discharge," (diarrhea) which describes well my condition. I was extremely uncomfortable for a period. Ralph stood on his combine and virtually cracked up laughing at me. In twenty or thirty minutes, I was feeling better and we got back on our machines and continued harvesting wheat. In the ensuing years, right up to his death, whenever I'd see Ralph we would get a good laugh recalling this experience.

Harvest time would usually bring us good wages. Top daily wage at that time for me was $4.00 a day. Most of our harvest work was with the Bakers. One year I hired out to a Pletcher family in Texas which dad got acquainted with when he made trips to Perryton, Texas, for church services. That year in Texas I helped harvest 2000 acres of wheat and we used a combine with a 20-foot swathe. That was an unusually big combine for those days. The year after I attended Hesston College, 1936-37, I stayed in the Hesston community and worked for Ralph Vogt a good friend I had gotten acquainted with while in school that year. Wages weren't as good with him (he paid only $2.50 a day) but I enjoyed being in the Hesston community and he was a good man to work for.

I had another experience related to harvest but it occurred in a later period in my life. After I was discharged from CPS, and returned from the cattle-boat trip, (described in my CPS Story) Elmer Ediger, working for MCC, contacted me asking if I could go to Houston, Texas to do some trouble-shooting. A group of cattle-boat attendants were in Houston waiting for their load of cattle to ship out. They had been waiting there for a week and were becoming disgruntled and he wanted me to go there to (I guess) console them. Earlier I had contacted Ralph Baker asking if he would have a harvest job for me that summer, so I could earn some money before attending Goshen College in the fall. He had a job for me so I decided to stop and help him harvest before returning home to Ohio.

MCC paid expenses for my Houston trip but at a low rate. I traveled to Houston by bus, stayed in the hotel with the boys, at MCC's expense, until their ship was ready to sail, then having already received my pay from MCC, I decided to save money so started hitch-hiking to Protection, Kansas to start my harvest job with Ralph. I got a ride that dropped me off about one hundred miles north of Houston. It was raining. I was very uncomfortable and it was getting dark. At that stage in my life I would not consider paying for an overnight hotel bill. I was at a filling station when a car with a young man drove in for gas. I asked him for a ride. He said sure. After we were on the road I asked how far he was traveling. He was on his way to New

Jersey, and planned to travel the interstate through Columbus, Ohio. Earlier my folks had moved from Protection to Berlin, Ohio, which will be detailed later. I had planned to live with the folks in Berlin until I go back to college, so Columbus was just a 90-mile bus trip from home. With my dislike of hitch-hiking, and with this opportunity of traveling from Texas to Ohio, I had some decisions to make. Should I travel with this fellow a few hundred miles north, then get off and head for Protection for the harvest, with more of the uncertainty that goes with hitch-hiking, or should I change my plans of harvesting in Protection and take advantage of this ride home.

I liked this young man I was traveling with. He was a discharged marine and was having some mental adjustment problems, just returning from some harrowing experiences on the battle-field of World War II and was traveling, just driving somewhat aimlessly through the country just to try to, as he stated, "find himself."

After considering all angles, I decided to call Ralph and tell him I was changing plans. I then stayed with my ride to Columbus. This worked out real well. The marine stopped for the night, I think in Dallas, and he, like me, did not want to spend much money for a motel. He stopped at a cheap hotel which might well be called a "flop house," one dollar a night. It was a sort of dormitory. We had only one sheet to sleep on. The sheet looked clean and it was a place to sleep and get in out of the rain. The sleeping quarters suited me okay; we spent the night, were well rested, and drove on the next day. At Columbus, he took me to the bus station. I caught the bus to Berlin and was happy to get home.

My harvest job in Protection was abandoned. Instead, I worked at the pottery factory in Fredericksburg, near Berlin until summer school started in Goshen. I worked six weeks in the pottery factory where I earned about the same as I would have in the harvest job. Also, to be at home with the folks gave me a sense of security I needed after having been away from home so long. I had been in CPS for four years, then on the cattle-boat trip to Germany and my Houston trip and was anxious to be home.

Home and Family Life at Protection

We always had a strong family relationship between siblings and parents. I feel that growing up during the depression period actually strengthened the bonds among us. We were hard up financially, but so was everybody else. We didn't feel particularly persecuted for the sacrifices we were forced to make because others, generally speaking, were having similar experiences. We kids all worked hard to help survive the difficult times. When Dad was away holding revival meetings or involved with other church business, we would all pitch in and it seems we'd get done what needed to be done. When we worked out of the home, the wages, at least most of it would go to provide for family needs. In those days and under the difficult conditions, we children never considered keeping the money for ourselves.

Shortly after Dad quit teaching and we moved to the farm, our neighbor, Clay Woolfolk, asked Dad if they could get Paul to run their team of horses cultivating row crop with a "sled knife," in their field just north of our home. As a youngster eleven or twelve years old, I was anxious for the new experience, and Woolfolks agreed to pay me one dollar a day. In those days that was good pay for a kid my age. That summer as I recall, I worked, seventeen days, and was paid seventeen dollars.

To reward me, the folks offered to use part of the money to buy me a new suit, a suit with long pants. The young kids in our church, up to a certain age, always wore knickers or short knee pants. Long pants were a sort of puberty rite. So for me long pants were a sign that I was growing up and I was really pleased to get personally that much with the wages I had earned.

A big part of our family life included singing. Quite frequently our family would provide special music for the Sunday evening church service. I can recall when Ruth and I sang duets. We did this when we were so small we stood up on the church bench while Dad who sometimes sang with us stood beside the bench. After we were grown up, we had a male quartet, we three boys and Dad. Dad sang the first tenor, usually Dennis the bass and Emerson and I the middle parts. We also had mixed voices with Ruth and Ethel singing. I don't recall that Mom ever helped with our family singing.

On one of our trips to Ohio and east, when our family was still together, Dad was scheduled to have a church service in a Pennsylvania congregation. We spent some time visiting friends and relatives in Holmes County, Ohio, before going on to Pennsylvania. We three boys were dating some of the Berlin girls at the time. We were out late at night, got to bed about two o'clock, and it seemed, had hardly gotten to sleep when dad called up the stairway, "Boys, it's time to get up and start traveling." We drove to Pennsylvania that next day and were on the program to sing couple special numbers in the evening. The singing really didn't go well that night. I told someone later that I nearly went to sleep between verses in the song. With very little sleep the night before we simply were not up to concentrating on singing.

It was on this trip that we went east to Washington D.C., and visited the White House, the Washington and Lincoln Monuments. We kids literally raced up the steps to the top of the Washington Monument, on that trip visited Mount Vernon and other places of interest. Our entire family of seven, traveled to the east coast in our 1935 Ford V8. It was on this trip, on the way home, coming across Missouri, Ruth got sick, so car-sick that we had to stop frequently for her to vomit. We have pictures of her on one of those stops.

At one of our recent D.D. Miller reunions my sister Ruth reminded me that on our trip east in our 1935 V8 Ford, when I'd get a head-ache rather than taking an aspirin, I'd get out and run it off. I had almost forgotten the incident but I have always been reluctant to take aspirin or any drugs or medicine. I figured it was better to let the body heal on its own.

When I was about eighteen or nineteen years old, Dennis and I both became aware that we needed to be circumcised. The folks had not had that done at birth. Ruth was in nurses training in La Junta, Colorado. She arranged to have our operations done there by Dr. Stickles, the doctor she liked at the hospital. In

order to save expenses for Dennis and me, Ruth arranged for us to stay in the basement of the hospital rather than a regular hospital room. The operation was done. We were recuperating, spending most of our time in our basement room. In the healing process our penises got black and blue, part red and part blue. I became concerned and asked Dr. Stickles if it might be blood poisoning. He became very serious and said, "I suggest you get a can of white paint, paint it partly white, then you'd have a red, white and blue flag." That answered the question of blood poisoning.

Picture 14 - Grandma Varnes, mother of Elizabeth Gonser and a full-blooded Cherokee Indian, born in 1800.

Mom and Dad's Background

Both our mother and father have had some relationship with the Cherokee Indians which have been not only interesting for our family, but in my opinion somewhat noteworthy.

Dad had a grandmother four generations back who was a full-blooded Cherokee Indian. Our genealogical records show that she was the mother of Elizabeth Varnes, and was born "around 1800." Her Indian name and exact birth date are not known, at least according to our genealogical records. That line of ancestry goes Varnes to Gonser to Hummel to N. E. Miller to D.D. to D. Paul Miller. Varnes and Gonser were from England. Accordingly my own grandmother five generations back was a full-blooded Indian.

In the early part of the 1800s the Cherokee Nation existed in the Southern Appalachian Highlands (parts of Georgia, N. Carolina, Virginia, Tennessee, and Kentucky). Because of pressure from potential settlers, the U.S. Government was attempting to get the Cherokees to abandon their nation and move west. When their chief William P. Ross returned from Washington, D.C. where he was attempting to work out a treaty with President Andrew Jackson for the very survival of their Cherokee Nation, he found many of his people "penned up in camps like

Picture 15 - My Dad in clerical garb, c.a. 1916.

cattle, many sick, discouraged, and grief-stricken." (See Grace Steele Woodward, *The Cherokees,* University of Oklahoma, Norman, 1963).

The U.S. Government offered the Cherokees land in Oklahoma and eventually ordered them to leave. Following orders, a large number trekked to Oklahoma, 1838-39, in what is known as "The Trail of Tears." They were promised supplies and general support along the way, most of which was never provided. It is estimated that 4,000 Indians died along the way of starvation and illness before reaching their destination in Oklahoma. In honor of the Cherokee Indians, museums have been established in Cherokee, North Carolina, and in Tahlequah, Oklahoma. I have personally visited both museums.

My brother Emerson and Ruth, his wife, along with Anne and I took a trip to the Southern Appalachian Area in the late 1980s, to visit the Cherokee area. A few years later the N. E. Miller reunion was held in Prior, Oklahoma. At that time Anne and I visited the Tahlequah Cherokee country in Oklahoma and it becomes increasingly obvious to me that the U.S. Government and early settler's treatment of the Cherokees, is just one of the many injustices that the Native Americans have experienced.

Picture 16 - My mother, Maggie May Kuhns c.a. 25 years old in 1916.

The story goes that rather than joining what became known as the "Trail of Tears," our Cherokee grandmother with some others of her tribe escaped north across the Ohio River, settled in Ohio, and later married a white man and had a daughter who was the Elizabeth Varnes in our line of ancestry.

Another story relating to our mother, Maggie May Kuhns is that she was born out of wedlock, April 6, 1890, to Susan Kuhns. Later Susan married Ben Hostetler and we learned to know her as Susan Hostetler. Our mother, Maggie, was then raised by Susan's parents, Sam and Magdalene Kuhns, who had a young daughter, Emma, only 3 years old. Maggie and Emma were then raised as sisters, although Emma was actually Susan's younger sister and Maggie's aunt.

Picture 17 - Susan Hostetler, Maggie's mother and my grandmother, c.a. 1938.

In those days people were reluctant to talk honestly about children born out of wedlock, and although Mom was raised by her great aunt, she was left with the impression that Emma was her sister rather than an aunt. In fact, my brother Emerson interviewed Emma before she died and Emma told Emerson and his wife that she was not aware of the truth of the matter until quite late her life.

With these facts on the table let's go to another experience in my life, which has become increasingly meaningful to me as time passes. I was attending college at Hesston. During the fall term at Hesston, a friend, Gideon Yoder, invited me to go with him to his home at Chrystal Springs, near Harper, Kansas, one week-end. Students who are generally confined to the campus usually welcomed such invitations. I went and on

Sunday we attended the Crystal Springs Mennonite Church. In the service an old minister by the name of Jacob Zimmerman preached the sermon. After church he was in the back by the door shaking hands with the people of the congregation as they walked out. When he met me and shook hands he asked my name. I told him Paul Miller. He said, "Paul Miller, who is your father?" I said, "D.D. Miller from Protection." I noticed tears began rolling down his cheeks. I didn't think much more about it, just figured he was a senile old man who sometimes expressed emotions with tears. A later turn of events explained his tears.

Dad had come to Hesston to get me for Christmas vacation that year. We were traveling alone, visiting about various things when, out of the blue, he said, "Paul, I guess you've heard about Mom." I couldn't imagine what he was referring to. I said, "Heard what?" He said, "That Mom was an illegitimate child." This knocked me for a loop. It was all news to me. For some reason, here I was, 19 years old and had never heard anything about this. Dad went on to explain who Mom's biological father was. He said, "Old Jake Zimmerman who is now a preacher at the Crystal Springs Mennonite Church is mom's real father."

Things began to turn in my mind. I recalled Jake Zimmerman's reaction when he shook hands with me walking out of his church the Sunday I was visiting with Gideon Yoder. At that service when I told Jake Zimmerman I was D.D.'s son, his thoughts no doubt were, "Here is my grandson." And this explained the tears rolling down his cheeks.

I recall some follow-up comments Dad made in that conversation while traveling from Hesston to Protection. He said, "I think we have better blood in our genes with Jake than it would have been with Ben Hostetler," (Susan's present husband).

Growing up, we kids were left with the impression that Susan was Mom's sister while she was actually Susan's daughter. Susan, a young 19-year-old woman, was not able to provide a home for her new-born daughter, so Susan's parents raised her. (Emerson & Ruth, in their book on Mom's background and genealogy describe in some detail these relationships.)

I remember Susan would always remember us kids sending us a quarter on our birthdays. Later it was increased to one dollar. She would always sign her name, "Grandma Hostetler." It was a sort of mystery. I "knew" she was our aunt, being Mom's sister but figured she just liked to be called grandma. When the facts in the case were revealed to us I then realized that the "grandma" signature was literally correct.

Dad told me that at the time he was dating mom, he raised some question about marrying her because of this background. He said he had asked different people for advice on this and without exception, everyone he asked told him he should never let something like being born out of wedlock stand in the way.

After we kids were aware and the facts were out in the open, I tried to discuss this with Mom. It seemed to me that, unfortunately, she always seemed to have a sense of guilt about her background. I told her very candidly that it was nothing she had chosen to do and that she had done nothing wrong. I assured her that she certainly should not feel bad or guilty about it. Strangely, however, she would never discuss the issue. I brought up the subject, hoping to clear things up and give her a sense of liberation. These discussions took place not many years before she died. But I always got the same reaction. She would just clam up and not say anything, never a comment; she just would not talk about this matter. My sisters, Ruth and Ethel both say that they too had tried to discuss this with Mom and they received the same response. I always felt sorry that we could not discuss it openly, but it just didn't happen.

Hesston College and Grade School Teaching

I attended Hesston College for one year, 1936-37. That year was extremely enjoyable. Hesston at that time was non-accredited but had arrangements worked out with Hays State Teachers College that Hesston students could attend Hays for one summer and upon successful completion of a summer term, they recognized Hesston credits and issued a teaching certificate based on one year of college work. Seven fellows from Hesston attended Hays summer school in 1937, Allen (Rip) Stehman,

Gideon Yoder, Reuben Yoder, Daniel Diener, Walter Marner, a blind man whose last name was Zimmerman, who had not been a student at Hesston, but for some reason joined our group, and D. Paul Miller.

Allen Stehman and I were close friends at Hesston and at Hays summer school. At Hays we played a lot of tennis. We did OK but didn't take our school work too seriously. We frequented the Dairy Queen with a high degree of regularity. Ten cent malted milks were the big specialty for us at that stage of life. We also dated quite a bit.

It was while at Hays that I attended my first movie. The girl I took out (last name Sucksland) gave me the shock of my life when after the movie, we got in the car she opened up her purse took out a cigarette and lighted up. I was baffled. Here I was, a young, conservative, Mennonite farm boy out with a girl that smokes. Walter Marner, our friend with a car, was the driver. He explained to me later that he was sitting in front about to crack up because of the embarrassment he knew the smoking was causing me. Needless to say, that date didn't last long that night.

Later I got acquainted with a fine young Spanish girl, Virginia Richardson, a teacher at McPherson, Kansas, and Rip got acquainted with another girl and we double dated a lot that summer. My relationship with Virginia continued into the school year while teaching at Peabody, mostly by correspondence, but I realized that it would be impossible for me to carry out my financial goals of paying off my car debt if I did a lot of dating. Also important for me was the fact that I knew my folks would be very disappointed if they knew I was dating a non-Mennonite girl. So I wrote Virginia suggesting we discontinue our relationship.

For me to get away from home to attend Hesston College, then Hays, and to begin my teaching career away from my sheltered home environment was the beginning of a new era for me. It was a new life, free, exciting, and full of adventure and joy that I heretofore did not know. At college I was on my own except when attending class. It was hard for me to believe that I was not required to be in the study hall under supervision. I never knew there were so many neat people to be my friends. The whole world was out there ready for me to jump in.

It was at Hesston where I was first permitted to participate in athletics. I made the college basketball team. I was fifth man but still I was on the team and played most of the time. It was an intramural program with each academy class (high school) having a team and the college freshmen and sophomores combined having one team.

The most serious rivalry was between the college team and the "Juniors." The "Junior" team had two very good players, Ralph Shetler, a good all-around athlete, and "Chick" Roupp, another good player who I find out in recent years

Picture 18 - D. Paul (left) and his first car, a 1926 Model-A Ford sedan, along with his friend 'Rip' Stehman (right) and his car, 1938.

was the father of Elaine Harms (Jim Harms' wife. Jim is Anne's sister's son). In my old photograph album, I have pictures of both teams, the academy Juniors and College team. They are listed as co-champs. In the spring, track meet was important. It provided a new chapter in my life which I will discuss later.

My First Car

After my year at Hesston and summer at Hays State Teachers College, I contracted to teach at a country school near Peabody, Kansas. Dad went with me to the bank and signed a note to help me buy my first car so I was all set to launch out into the cold world on my own. I had bought a 1926 Model A 2-door sedan for $75. We worked out the plan that I was to pay ten dollars a month and have the car completely paid in the eight months.

The first year of teaching I stayed with a patriarchal German family which had a registered herd of Holstein cows. Those were the days before milking machines. This family lived about one-half mile from school. He offered me the opportunity to board at their place, help milk the cows morning and evening and he would allow me wages (I think 35 cents per hour) to be applied to my room and board bill of $18.00 a month. I worked as much as feasible along with my school work, and never paid more than six dollars a month in cash for room and board. With this program I paid more on my car debt than was scheduled and had it completely paid by January.

The second year at the same school I received a salary of $70.00 a month and stayed with a family that lived one-and-three-fourth mile from school. With this family I paid only $12.00 a month for room and board and didn't have to milk cows.

Picture 19 - D. Paul's school during his first year of teaching at Pleasant Hill (Peabody, KS), 1937-38.

I changed schools the third year. Contracted to teach at Bunker Hill, near Canton, Kansas about twelve miles north of Hesston, another 8-month school, grades one to eight. It was a school my Uncle Billie had taught at for the previous eight years.

I was offered $90.00 a month, with 27 students. I considered this a real promotion. Billie had been a good disciplinarian and these students all knew how to settle down and study. It seemed to me that this was never possible with my Peabody school. My Peabody school was always more "free-wheeling." In this new school, my salary was increased to $100.00 a month the second year and I felt I was really in good money.

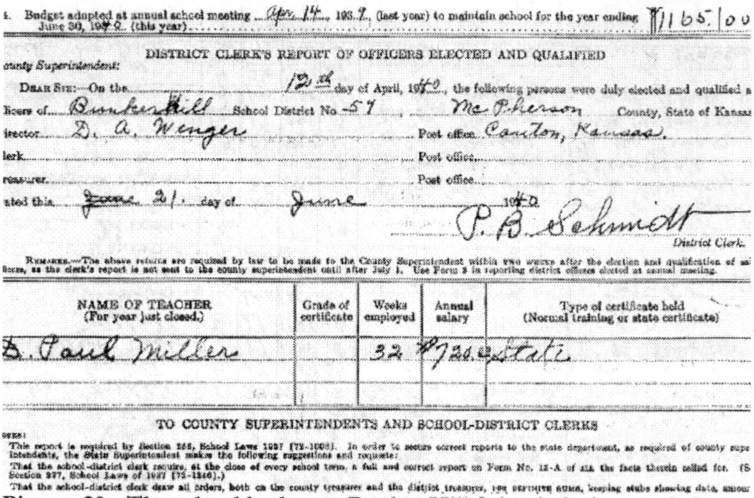
1. Budget adopted at annual school meeting Apr. 14, 1939, (last year) to maintain school for the year ending June 30, 1940 (this year) $1165.00

DISTRICT CLERK'S REPORT OF OFFICERS ELECTED AND QUALIFIED

County Superintendent:

Dear Sir:—On the 12th day of April, 1940, the following persons were duly elected and qualified as officers of Bunker Hill School District No. 57, McPherson County, State of Kansas

Director D. A. Wenger Post office Canton, Kansas.

Clerk Post office

Treasurer Post office

Dated this June 21. day of June 1940

P. B. Schmidt
District Clerk.

Remarks.—The above returns are required by law to be made to the County Superintendent within two weeks after the election and qualification of said officers, as the clerk's report is not sent to the county superintendent until after July 1. Use Form 3 in reporting district officers elected at annual meeting.

NAME OF TEACHER (For year just closed.)	Grade of certificate	Weeks employed	Annual salary	Type of certificate held (Normal training or state certificate)
D. Paul Miller		32	$720.00	State

TO COUNTY SUPERINTENDENTS AND SCHOOL-DISTRICT CLERKS

This report is required by Section 268, School Laws 1937 (72-1008). In order to secure correct reports to the state department, as required of county superintendents, the State Superintendent makes the following suggestions and requests:

That the school-district clerk require, at the close of every school term, a full and correct report on Form No. 12-A of all the facts therein called for. (Section 277, School Laws of 1937 (72-1316).)

That the school-district clerk draw all orders, both on the county treasurer and the district treasurer, ... keeping stubs showing date, amount

Picture 20 - The school budget at Bunker Hill School, during my 3rd year of teaching in Canton, Kansas, 1940.

Several of the years while I was teaching, my sister, Ruth, and both brothers, Dennis and Emerson attended Hesston College, and lived in the basement of a private home. I often visited them on week-ends and was also involved in some social life with Hesston friends, both men and women.

Hesston College offered a spring term, a six-week session designed especially for the country school teachers on eight month schedules. I registered for and participated in three of these spring terms, thereby and earning six additional college credits each term. I must admit that at that time I did not realize what an advantage it would give me toward graduation in the future. Actually it enabled me to graduate from Goshen College in one year and a summer after my four years in CPS.

It was easy for me to enroll in these spring terms since my brothers and older sister were in school at Hesston, living in a basement apartment and allowed me to join them with very little additional expense.

Track Meet

Another drawing card for me at the time was that I was permitted to participate in the college track meet held each spring. I had participated in and had done quite well the first year I was there. Among other events I broke the school record in the 220 yard dash. As I recall, the record had been 29 seconds. I did it in 27 seconds. I guess that was not too "shabby" considering the circumstances. I was a country boy coming in off the farm, and with no coaching. At Hesston we were not permitted to wear shorts. It was against the school rules, apparently for modesty reasons. I did however roll up my pant legs to the knees and put rubber bands around them to hold them up. In addition, I had a pair of track shoes with spikes, which was a new innovation at Hesston. None of the other participants had spikes; in fact many of them

Picture 21 - Track meet at Hesston College (Hesston, KS), D. Paul on the inside lane, left side. 1937.

had never seen a pair of spikes before.

One year all three of us boys, Dennis, Emerson, and I participated. Our best events were the dashes, the 50, 100, and 220-yard dashes. It so happened that I owned two pair of spikes. Through some of my friends at Protection High, I had obtained a pair of spikes, and somehow had acquired a second pair. When we three boys participated the same year, I gave Dennis and Emerson each a pair of my spikes to wear, and I taped the bottom of my bare feet and toes with adhesive tape to keep them from blistering, and ran barefooted.

Interestingly, in the three dashes, Dennis, Emerson & I, each won first place in one of the races. The three of us won first, second, and third, in all three races with the exception that the judges disqualified Dennis for a third place finish in the 100, for interfering with an opponent next to him. We did not have marked lanes and ran on a dirt road however we were instructed to stay a certain distance from other racers. The judges said Dennis didn't do that. I won the first race, the 100, and Emerson won the 220 and Dennis the 50. I got along well barefooted in the 100. In the 50 I had worn some blisters and finished third, in the 220 I ran with blistered and sore feet, however finished a distant third again. I have a copy of the report of this meet which appeared in the *Hesston College Journal.*

My brother Dennis had also acquired an elementary teaching certificate and was teaching at a country school near Newton. In my third year of these short sessions, Dennis was also enrolled. He and I were on the college relay team where each of us ran a 220 lap. By this time we had only one good pair of track shoes. So in the relay I ran the first lap with the spikes, then quickly I gave them to Dennis. He put them on while our team mates ran the second and third laps, and Dennis took the last lap. And in that event we not only won the race but broke the college record.

In the meet where the three brothers ran, we were extremely pleased that our father and mother had come from Protection to see the meet. Paul Erb, one of the faculty members at the time said to Dad, "Your boys must have learned to run from the jack-rabbits in Comanche County." Dad and Mom both seemed to be excited seeing their boys run.

I'm including here an experience not really in context, but I'm unaware of a better place to put it. A couple of my friends in 2011 have baseballs signed by Joe DiMaggio, which they say if auctioned off would bring several thousand dollars. When I tell them my only "claim to fame" in the baseball world is my experience with Bobby Feller, they encourage me to record it, so here it is: Years ago when I was probably 19 or 20 years old, I, with some friends, attended a Cleveland Indian baseball game. I inquired of an official: where does Bobby Feller make his entrance into the stadium? He told me Feller's pattern. Following the official's instructions, I went down to the player's parking lot, and sure enough Feller came driving in, in his big car. As he got out of his car I approached him and while actually feeling his arm and muscle, I commented, "So this is the arm that throws those fast balls." He grinned and nodded and walked on into the stadium, and I went back and watched the game.

Follow-Up with Former Students

Just a few years ago, probably 1995 or '96, I made contact with Dorothea Regier, the daughter of C.P. Regier who I boarded with and helped with the milking, my first year teaching at Peabody.

She was my 4th and 5th grade student, 1937 and '38. She reminded me that when I was with their family, I was conditioning for the track meet at Hesston, and would have her and her sister time me running various distances in their farm yard. I had forgotten about this until she mentioned it.

Picture 22- D. Paul's Girl's Quartet at the Pleasant Valley one-room rural school in 1939 sang four-part harmony. The girls, from left to right, are Dorthea Regier (4th grade), Salina Stovall (6th grade), Darlene Regier (6th grade) and Margie Loepp (4th grade).

Dorothea sang in my girl's quartet which I had organized in my school at Peabody. She was a 4th grader. I had two 4th graders and two 6th graders in a girl's quartet which sang four-part music. In our visit she expressed appreciation for the fact that I had gotten her started in music and that because of her grade school singing, she has sang in choirs most of her life.

Picture 23 - D. Paul in front of his school, Peabody, KS, 1939.

This reminds me of another experience with one of my grade school students. I had a little 4th grade boy in Bunker Hill School, at Canton, Wilbur Koehn, who was an ideal little pupil, a bright boy and a good artist. Wilbur was from a Holdeman Mennonite family. In 2002, he called me. He and his wife were visiting relatives in Ohio and traveling to their home in Kansas. While they were in Ohio, he and his cousin whom he was visiting had gotten my name, address telephone number through the internet. He called me, identified himself asking if I was the D. Paul Miller who long ago taught grade school at Canton, Kansas, and wondered if they could stop in and say hello as they were traveling through. It was a unique opportunity for me and I was happy to welcome their stop. They came and we visited couple hours. Today he is an organic farmer, on 1500 acres in western Kansas, selling much of his produce abroad. After visiting they wanted to drive on that day. He was very complimentary and appreciative of his grade school teacher, and we were both happy to be able to reconnect.

The very next year, 2003, another former student called me from Florida. It was Lawrence Regier who was a first grader in my first year of teaching. I had him in grades one and two. He was an eager little bright boy, with a classmate, Dicky Baughman, both of whom were good learners who could read from their pre-primers by Thanksgiving time. I felt that these little fellows were the best evidence I ever had that I was actually teaching. They were unable to read when they started school and before long were actually reading.

Lawrence indicated in his call that they were visiting a relative in Chicago, and would like to stop in to say hello. We invited them to stay overnight with us, a Saturday evening, they went to church with us the next morning and I introduced him to the congregation during our introduction time. In that introduction I explained the background which went back 60 years. Again this was an interesting contact which I was happy to make, but we realized some incompatibility in our religious and political philosophies. He was sporting a big American flag on the side of his car along with Bush/Cheney stickers. He was affiliated with a conservative religious group quite evangelical and was somewhat bent on setting me straight in my personal theology. Unfortunately, the fellow I had known as my bright little first grader years ago had not even graduated from high-school. He had taken one year at Hesston Academy, then got a job, and never had more schooling. That helps explain his conservative views.

For some reason, I get more positive feedback from my grade school students having taught only four years, than I do from my 32 years of college teaching. I have to wonder why. Is this because older kids (college age) just don't respond to their college teachers, perhaps because they have so many different teachers, while grade school students have only one teacher for an entire year, or is it because I was a better teacher at grade school level? Having spent the major part of my professional life teaching in college, did I miss my calling? Even though I'll never know the answer to that question, in general I do feel good about my college teaching experience, and hope I did have some positive influence on some young college students, even if I don't hear too much from them after they get out of school.

Protection Revisited

April 14, 15, & 16, 2001, the three kids, Brenda, Rich & Don, along with Mac, Marianne & Stanley Miller, Anne & I, all met at Protection to visit "dad's old stomping grounds." After returning home I wrote a letter to each of my living siblings describing in some detail our experiences in Protection. That visit can best be described by simply inserting a copy of the letter at this point. It follows:

Dear Ruth, Dennis and Ethel,

We returned home yesterday about 3:00 pm from our Protection excursion. As I look back on it, the whole thing was a highly successful venture. For me, and I think all three kids as well, it was sort of an emotional experience that was important for us to have. Brenda, Mac, Anne and I were visiting with Lillie (Hopkins) Christopher, a former classmate, looking over our class pictures, getting caught up on former classmates, etc., when Rich and Don appeared at her door. In a small town it wasn't hard for them to find our two vehicles parked in front of Lillie's place. With all of our family at Lillie's place we had a hilarious time. She seemed to really enjoy meeting my family. Then our three kids, Mac, also Marianne (Krahn) Miller, her husband Stanley, Anne and I, ate at the restaurant, and were all checked into the Protection Motel by Thursday evening, and were ready for the big day tomorrow.

As you can imagine, the whole town was aware that a Miller family had invaded Protection. An article had appeared in the paper that day that we were coming. I think I have copies of that paper for each of you.

Here is the "blow by blow" account of the excursion. We left home on Wednesday. We drove our pick-up, it had more leg room and I figured the 4-W drive would come in handy at Protection, and it did. On our trip from home we had rain and some wind all across the state of Missouri. The wind kept increasing and in Kansas it was so windy—60 and 70 mph winds—we could hardly travel. Some big trucks had blown off the road and were upset. We did make it arriving in Hillsboro at Anne's sister Erna's place about 5:00 pm. We had left home at 5:30 am. The next morning we drove to N. Newton. Stopped at Graber's Nursery, bought a native Sugar Maple tree (more on that later), then visited our friends Emerson and LaWanda Wiens, good friends who had moved from Normal to Newton less than a year ago. We had lunch with them, and then took off for Protection about 1:00 pm. Weather was perfect. It was all such a contrast from the day before.

At Protection, on Friday, after breakfast, we drove south in two 4-W drive vehicles, eight of us, our four kids, Marianne, Stanley, Anne and I. Stopped briefly and talked about the old Murray School, where Dad did his first teaching, then to the old Church grounds and cemetery. I had the commemorative plate with the history, plus your description, Ethel, in your story. We looked at the graves of many of our older relatives, and then drove south to our old place. Spent quite a bit of time checking out the rooms of the old house (again with your diagram,

Ethel), the old privy, etc. Drove thru the Enos Miller place -- Stan's brother Steve lives there now -- then south to the slab.

The kids were fascinated with the slab and the stories I could tell about it and Bluff Creek. We then moved on to the site of Cimarron School and Putch Town. Next around the section to the old home place which Larry and Diane Petty now own, back to Billie's place, the old Cimarron School building and on down to the creek, and to the Big Tree, which for some reason I was not very much aware of until I read about it in BJ's Bluff Creek Stories. We went back to town for lunch, then to Ralph Sanders who showed us many of his own personal things and also told many stories. He took us to the place where our home stood on the "eighty." Then to the Cimarron River bridge where I'll bet you folks didn't know or at least didn't remember that Dad had me drive our 4-horse team moving dirt to build the road when they were building the bridge back in the '30s on the WPA project. That project with our horse "Short" on the four-horse team was not a pleasant experience.

We got back into town about 4:00, rested and cleaned up, ate supper, then to the "come and go" party at the Church Fellowship Hall. Had a surprisingly large number of people, Mennonite and non-Mennonite, probably 40 to 50 people.

We had planned for a "tree-planting-ceremony" ahead of time. I had talked to the pastor, Raymond Unruh, inquiring as to whether or not he would welcome a nice tree. He was very enthusiastic about it, and agreed to participate in the ceremony at 9:00 o'clock Saturday morning. We had invited anyone interested to join us. Besides our group, Mary Willems, and Alta (Beyler) Remple, and the pastor, were there. I made a few comments. We were doing this in honor of our parents who served as pastor of the church for 22 years as well as honoring their family, those not here as well as those attending today. Brenda made a few comments about her response to our experiences, then the pastor spoke briefly, read a scripture about "planting a tree by the rivers of water that bringeth forth fruit in its season," then said a prayer. It was a touching ceremony. The tree is planted to the front of the church ground, near the road, just north of the north entrance. It was a tree probably 6 or 7 feet tall and nice shape. The nursery people told us it was a native sugar maple. Leaves will turn either yellow or scarlet in the fall.

Brenda and Mac left for home immediately after the ceremony. We did a little checking at the park and at Orlin Loucks' Auto Shop and museum, checked out of the motel and headed for the airport in Wichita Don and Rich had flown in. Rich got out that afternoon. Don's ticket didn't allow him out 'til Sunday but he had the rented car, and we got a leg on into Missouri yet Sat and arrived home Sunday. Now it's back to the routine, but we are glad to be home and have a (according the kid's comments) really awesome experience completed.

We were so thankful that the weather was perfect Thursday, Friday and also Saturday, particularly after the wind the day before. It was cool, but had sunshine.

Thought the three of you could all relate to our adventures, thus the detail.

Love and Best Wishes, D. Paul

All in all, those who participated in this visit seemed to feel it was a constructive and worthwhile experience. Our family had previously been to Anne's home and the community where she grew up, many times, but had never been to my childhood home community.

Picture 24 - Pictures of our family's house and the outhouse on our home place taken in 2001.

It was especially interesting for me to return and simply realize the extreme changes that had taken place. Our home place, though dilapidated, was still recognizable; the "slab" over Bluff Creek, a mile south of our home was still much the same. The church five miles south of town was torn down, but the cemetery is still much the same.

Picture 25 - Pictures of "the slab" along with D Paul standing in front of Cimarron School house that he attended in 1927-1931. These pictures were taken in 2001.

We saw the bridge I helped to build with a four-horse team pulling a "slip," in the WPA (Works Progress Administration), a relief program provided by the government in the late 1930s to provide employment for the poverty-stricken). We spent quite a bit of time with Ralph Sanders, who was farming the land where the home, where I was born, once stood. The experience left me with a feeling of satisfaction for having returned to my old "stomping grounds" with Anne and the three kids.

II - Beyond Protection

D.D. Millers Move to Berlin

In the late 1930s and early '40s, dad and mom would occasionally talk about leaving Protection. I've often wondered why, but for some reason dad seemed to feel that his mission at Protection was pretty well completed.

Insofar as he included his children in the discussions, I recall him considering quite seriously moving to Oregon or maybe Idaho. Also, strong on his list was Holmes County, Ohio. He would often comment that he was trying to follow the "leading of the Lord." Eventually, this took him to Ohio. I think the decision of where to go depended largely on the strength of the invitation from the various congregations. Anyway, Berlin and Millersburg churches won out and he decided to move to Berlin.

During the summer they moved, I was in the Hesston area helping Ralph Vogt harvest so was not at home and did not personally accompany them on the move. Emerson & Dennis often described the move, pulling the trailer with garden tools, furniture, and the like, tied onto the trailer pulled with our 1937 Ford without brakes. Before his death, Emerson related the time he was driving, at the edge of a city, going down a hill, a man was walking across the road and he knew he couldn't stop so he stuck his head out the window and hollered at the man who must have realized his plight and scurried out of the way.

Dad had bought a 65-acre wooded property that had a very small house, a nice barn, and a natural spring that never went dry and drained into a small lake below the house. This place was located about a mile south of Berlin. I appeared on the scene shortly after the family had moved and I remember how we worked to fix our lane and build a cattle-guard where our lane entered the road so we could drive in and out without getting out to open the gate. One of my strongest memories was how profusely we sweated in the Ohio humidity. We were used to arid Kansas.

This 65-acre property with a small old house was home for us for several years. Even though we had done a lot of work on the lane it was still difficult at times getting in and out, particularly when it rained. That and the inadequacy of the small house were factors leading to another move. Dad's history, which was read at the D.D. Miller reunion, November 23, 1962, indicates that Dad "purchased the 65-acres of wooded hills for $1,450, and later sold it for $3,250." He thought he had done real well on the deal and at the time it did seem so. The folks bought and moved into a large house on Main Street in Berlin. When the folks sold that house it was turned into a quilt shop.

In October, 2000, I returned to Berlin for a CPS reunion, looked up the 65 acre woods dad at one time owned, talked to people about the value of real estate property, and different people said one wouldn't be able to buy that property today because the owner wouldn't consider selling, but if it were sold it'd probably be in the millions. This increased value is due to the intense tourist developments that have taken place in Berlin in the past few decades.

Marriage, Family, and the Empty Nest

In this section I'll leave my parental family and deal with the family Anne and I are more directly responsible for. We were married August 14, 1947. Anne was born and raised in Beatrice, Nebraska. I was born and raised in Protection, Kansas. She was General Conference Mennonite, went to Bethel College. I was

Old Mennonite and went to Goshen College. Many people have wondered and inquired about how we ever got together. It happened in Delaware. She was asked by MCC to work with CPS camps, teaching music in the summer, 1945. The Farnhurst Unit was one she was scheduled to visit. Being the director of the Unit, I had to be responsible to see that she was met at the bus, taken to meals, and provided lodging. Details of this are described in more detail in "My CPS Story."

During my senior year at Goshen, I visited Anne and her family in Beatrice, Nebraska. It was during this visit that we became engaged. In that visit I was particularly impressed with her extended family which was together to celebrate Christmas. Her entire extended family including her mother, four sisters, two brothers, and five in-laws, were extremely friendly to me, and easy to visit with. (Her father had been killed in a farm accident earlier.) The family had a wholesome and congenial relationship. It seemed like a "safe and even desirable" family to get involved with. Also, I was convinced that one married not only a wife, but also the wife's relationships.

It was during this visit that we discussed the matter of marriage. We were both old enough that we considered matters beyond sheer romantic appeal. Interestingly, when I made a serious proposal, she did not have an immediate answer. She said she would let me know tomorrow. This was really not a surprise to me. I presumed, and correctly, so, that she wanted to discuss this serious move with her family. Furthermore, I was not particularly surprised when she gave me an affirmative answer. And from that point, our discussions centered pretty much around plans for our future. I then returned to Goshen College to finish my bachelor's degree.

Goshen College

After returning from my Houston adventure where, as described earlier, I was assigned by MCC to console some cattle attendants who were becoming disgruntled because their departure was delayed for some unknown reason, I spent six weeks at home in Berlin, Ohio, working at the Pottery factory at Fredericksburg, then went to Goshen to finish my college work. I registered for their summer session and Carl Kreider, who was dean at the time, worked out a schedule which allowed me to graduate at the end of the year, spring of 1947. My brother, Dennis and I had similar programs and graduated in the same class.

During the school year, I got the job of working with Roman Gingerich in the recreation department. I was considered the Assistant Athletic Director. This was considered one of the better student's jobs so far as the nature of the job, and pay were concerned; also the job was very attractive to me personally. It was work I could enjoy. I do not recall the wages, but I was instructed to keep track of my time, have Roman sign the time sheet, then turn it in to the business office to be applied to my college bill. I got my spending money by doing "black-market" barbering. I say black-market because I did not have a barber's license and the town barbers did not like the college boys taking away their business by cutting hair on campus.

I ran a pretty tight schedule in my barbering. I cut hair on Wednesday evening and Saturday morning. I carried my appointment book with me during the day, took down name of fellows asking for a haircut, and schedule a customer every fifteen minutes. I had permission to set-up in the old and not-being-used chemistry lab where they had hot and cold running water. I used the hot water to make the lather to shave the neck and around the ears of my customers. Because I wasn't licensed I could not charge but we had the understanding that I'd get a fifty-cent donation for each job. I had adequate spending money from barbering, and at the end of the school year, I had enough work- time completed that it paid for all of my college bills and interestingly, the college owed and actually paid me forty-two dollars at the end of the year for extra time I had spent in my work. So I left Goshen College with a degree and debt-free, and a little money in my pocket.

It was during summer school and the following academic year in college, that my relationship with Anne became increasingly serious. Interaction was mostly by letter-writing. She did, however, stop to visit me on her way home from one of her choir schools in Minnesota and was present near the end of the summer session. During that visit I played and won the summer-school inter-mural tennis tournament championship, with a Mr. Cressman, who was the college librarian that summer. I visited her in Nebraska during Christmas vacation, and she visited me at Goshen one more time during exam week at the end of my last semester. I felt that her visit at that time did reduce my study time, and probably affected my grade in Harold Bender's Church History course, but I did finish with respectable grades.

On my Christmas visit to Beatrice, Nebraska, I traveled to Lincoln by bus where Anne picked me up and took me to her home. Naturally I was a bit nervous about what I was getting into, however, as just described; I was very favorably impressed with her family

Before leaving my Goshen experiences, I want to relate another incident, along an entirely different line but which for me is somewhat noteworthy. I have the honor, or perhaps I should say dis-honor, of being the first person to play tennis on the Goshen College campus, in shorts. They had an old sign at the tennis courts indicating the rules to observe: tennis shoes only, time limit if others are waiting, no shorts, etc. Having played a lot of tennis in CPS, in shorts, it was difficult for me to believe that such a policy could be current at that time. And I was aware that all the basketball games were played in shorts, so without giving it much thought I played tennis in shorts.

One day I received a notice from President Ernest Miller indicating he'd like to see me in his office at a specified time. When I arrived for the appointment, also present were Glenn Miller the chemistry professor who was faculty athletic advisor, Roman Gingerich, the athletic director and my boss, along with the President.

The discussion went immediately to the issue of me playing tennis on the campus in shorts which was against the rules. The discussion was good natured and I felt that no one was particularly critical or even surprised that I had played in shorts. I mentioned that basketball games were played in shorts. The answer to that was that those games are played inside where the public doesn't see it. And they did insist that it was against the rules and they felt it their duty to enforce it. I assured them that I would abide by the rule if that was their wish. One of President Miller's final remarks was, "Paul, when we can get our church leaders like your father to accept it, we won't stop you from playing in shorts." (At that time my father was a church representative on the Goshen College Board.)

This incident reflects the conservative nature of the Mennonite Church at the time, and observing developments that followed, I noticed that one of the many changes that occurred in Mennonite communities, including Goshen College campus, shortly thereafter, was shorts in public worn by both men and women. Shorts on the tennis court were soon common dress.

Hillsboro and Graduate School

Anne and I planned to get married in the summer following graduation. Hillsboro High School, where she was teaching music had a Social Science position opening and hired me to fill that. I worked on the farm for Louie Penner, Anne's sister Gertrude's husband, during the summer. We were married August 14, 1947, took a honeymoon to Minnesota, then visited my folks in Ohio before returning to Hillsboro, Kansas where we were both scheduled to teach.

The first semester of teaching after four years in CPS, was rough for me. Coming out of CPS, I figured that if you'd treat kids fair, they'd return the favor. I found that wasn't true and I had discipline problems, particularly with my large American History class of mostly senior boys. One of the shenanigans one of the boys pulled was to jump out the window as soon as the bell rang for the noon break. The class was from 11:00 to 12:00 am. I didn't see it but the principal called my attention to it later. In another instance, someone threw a piece of chalk at me while I was writing on the board. It didn't hit me but hit the board. I survived the semester and learned a lot from the experience. The second semester was better. I had a different group of kids; I clamped down on them from the beginning, and had a better semester.

Brenda was born during my second year at Hillsboro. Between the two years at Hillsboro, I attended summer school doing graduate work at the University of Nebraska. We lived with Anne's mother on the farm near Beatrice, and I car-pooled with two men from Beatrice who also attended the University.

After being released from CPS, I was able to establish home residency in three different states. One was Kansas, where I had lived most of my boyhood life, another, Ohio, where my folks lived at the time I was discharged. It was more difficult to establish residency in Nebraska, but I succeeded after I worked my case through the appeal board.

I liked the Sociology Department at the University of Nebraska, and it was close to Anne's home, so I resigned my teaching job at Hillsboro High School after two years and we ventured out, neither Anne nor I with a job, with very little money, and little Brenda less than a year old. Life was not simple. Also I did not have GI benefits like most of my colleagues who had just come out of military service.

We had saved enough money from our teaching in Hillsboro, to get started in graduate school. After a semester of graduate work, I got a student teaching job teaching the introductory course in the Sociology Department. I also had a job assisting my major professor, Paul Meadows, reading test papers, and substituting for him occasionally. We lived in a basement apartment in Lincoln where I was janitor, stoking the furnace, emptying garbage pails, shoveling snow, washing windows and so forth, for most of our rent. When I was in school, Anne had to stoke the furnace to keep the apartment building warm. Also, Anne got a job with Walt's Music Store teaching piano lessons. When we visited Anne's folks in Beatrice on week-ends, they were good at giving us meat, eggs, and milk from the farm. The relatives all realized our stringent financial circumstances and were always sympathetic and helpful.

I received my Master's Degree at semester time, 1950. After that I taught off-campus classes for teachers, driving as far as Broken Bow and St. Paul, one hundred fifty miles from Lincoln, using a University car. I would sometimes schedule two classes, on a week-end, teaching one Friday evening and the other Saturday morning, driving home after the class on Saturday.

In addition to Anne's teaching piano, and my part-time teaching at the university, I took on a salesman's job selling *Baby Tendas* in my "spare time," and also dabbled with selling Progress Tailor custom-made suits. The Baby Tenda is an item to replace the high-chair for young children. The Baby Tenda sales were enough to contribute some to our income. The suit-selling didn't amount to much. Most of the suits I sold were to relatives and sold at cost.

My thesis topic for my Master's degree was "Amish Acculturation." My field work was centered in the Amish of Yoder, Kansas. My Uncle Alf, my father's brother, was living in the Yoder community at that time, he knew most of the Amish families in the community, and was helpful in making contacts for me.

Little Dicky appeared on the scene in March, 1950. It was soon after Dicky was born, and after I had completed my master's degree that Joyce Hertzler, chairman of the sociology department at the University, approached me one day with a letter from Emporia State Teachers College, asking if the university had a graduate student who might be interested in teaching on a one-year assignment to replace a man on a sabbatical. Here they offered $4,400 for the year. In our financial straits at the time, this sounded like a windfall we couldn't refuse.

I accepted that position for the following year, 1950-51, and we moved to Emporia, Kansas, where I experienced my first year of full-time sociology teaching. It was at Emporia where we met

Dixon and Ole Smith who became life-long friends whom we have visited and interacted with through the years, even to the present time. One of the summers I was at Boulder, we met the Dixon Smith family and most of their family and ours climbed Long's Peak together.

We returned to Lincoln after my year at Emporia State College, and bought a small home on Sherman Street, with a basement apartment which made most of the payments on the house. My Ph.D. degree was confirmed in 1953. My dissertation was, *Community Adjustment: Jansen, Nebraska.* I made many trips from Lincoln to the Jansen community to do that study. Henry Hirschlers lived in the Jansen community. Occasionally, I would stay overnight with them and work the Jansen community from that base.

When I met with my committee to defend my dissertation, I was interested in the fact that the committee members did very little with the subject matter of the dissertation itself. Most of their questions related to my personal life. They were interested in the experiences of a Mennonite farm-boy, from a conservative religious background, getting a higher degree, and developing some of the philosophical and religious views I expressed. They seemed satisfied, and the degree was confirmed with no qualifications.

When I came out of the room of the meeting, Anne was there with Brenda and Dicky to greet and congratulate me. Don was born in July 26, 1953. Anne had just been released from the hospital after Don's birth and came directly to the University from the hospital. The hospital did the first baby-sitting for Don.

Frequently, when reviewing my graduate work experiences I say, five important events took place in our family in 1953. One, Don was born; two, I received my PhD; three, I got my first permanent college teaching job at the State Teacher's College, Wayne, Nebraska; four, we sold our home on Sherman Street in Lincoln; and five, we bought a new Willys car.

College Teaching

Picture 26 -Anne with the three kids at the lake, 1954.

I was ready to get on a regular income. One of the professors in the Education Department of the University, with whom I had a research grant, was personally acquainted with Dr. Rice the president at Wayne State College, Wayne, Nebraska He assured me that if I wanted the Wayne job, he could secure it for me. I went to Wayne for the interview and everything worked out favorably. We accepted the job, moved to Wayne and into a college house just across the street from the campus. I taught at the college for three years. I began with a contract for $4,400 for two semesters, with the option of summer school for an additional $600, a total of $5,000 for the year. After living in graduate school poverty for four years, this seemed like a fantastic salary.

Picture 27 - The three kids on a ferry during a camping trip, 1954.

The only form of recreation in the Wayne community outside of the college activities was a country club and golf course. We joined the club and got Brenda and Dicky little golf clubs, I had my own which were purchased from Dr. Reinhardt, one of my college professors, and Brenda, Dicky and I spent quite a bit of time chasing our balls around the course. Donny was still too small to join us.

In those days teaching opportunities would show up quite frequently. We didn't view Wayne, Nebraska as our permanent home so it was only natural that we would look at various job opportunities that came up. We had an opportunity to take a position at Mankato State College, in Minnesota It was an advancement in salary and Minnesota seemed like a good place for family activities, so after due consideration we took the position.

The first year in Minnesota we bought a boat and our family got a good start on water-skiing. Our first boat was a red Herter's open boat with a 25 hp Johnson motor I had bought from my Uncle Frank Garber, who lived in Alpha, about 50 miles south of

Picture 28 - D. Paul & Anne, along with their three children, from right to left, Brenda, Dicky (Rich) and Donny (Don) in Wayne, NE, c.a. 1955.

Mankato. Our kids all learned to ski almost as soon as they could walk, actually around age six or seven. We did a lot of skiing, camping, fishing and other outdoor activities and were happy with our move to Mankato.

Our first residence was a rented a farm house on a busy highway a few miles east of Mankato. We had a barn and other out buildings. We bought two Shetland ponies, Flicka and

Picture 29 - Baking cookies together in the kitchen in Wayne, NE, c.a. 1955. left to right, Brenda, Dicky, Anne and Don.

White Sox. Flicka was good with small children and our kids rode her a great deal. White Sox was a young, about half grown pony with three white legs from the knee to the hoof, thus the name White Sox. Other activities on the farm included raising chickens, having a bunny rabbit, flooding our yard for ice skating, and simply enjoying the fresh out-of-door country living.

I rode my bicycle to school when the weather permitted, and the kids, Brenda and Dicky took the bus to school. The highway was very busy, cycling was dangerous, and the kids didn't respond well to riding the school bus, so we decided we'd be better off living in town closer to our schools. We purchased a modest home, 131 Electa Blvd., in town, very near a good grade school and less than a mile from the college. This arrangement worked out better for our family and we lived at this location until we left Minnesota

It was while we were in Minnesota that Tommy was born with Downs Syndrome. For me that was probably the biggest emotional blow in my life. We experienced not only emotional trauma but spent a lot of time contemplating the direction we should take in dealing with him in his condition.

We researched every conceivable study on Downs Syndrome we could get our hands on. My parents accompanied us to Mayo's Clinic in Rochester to get a diagnosis and a second opinion. We made telephone calls to a group in Florida that was studying and publishing articles on Downs Syndrome. We received telephone calls from friends and relatives. Some thought we should keep him at home, others suggested we listen to professionals we were working with, along with and our minister of the Methodist church where we attended, and use our own judgment.

All in all we felt the greatest push was to institutionalize. Our minister where we attended church recommended it, our doctor recommended it and so did most of our relatives. So that is the direction we took. Our relationship with him since moving to Illinois has been distant. We get periodic reports from his supervisors; we have visited him on several occasions. All three of our kids have visited him in recent years. We find that he is completely non-verbal. His behavior and communication is almost completely by way of gestures and habit. He is currently living in what appears to be a nice private home with several other patients, and under the care of a supervisor. He performs some simple tasks in a working arrangement that has been set up for him.

In the early going we paid a monthly fee for his support for a number of years. Eventually the State supported him and when he was eighteen years of age he was supported completely by Social Security and the State of Minnesota. We feel that he is getting the best treatment possible and that his case, however unfortunate, is something we have tried to deal with in the best way we know how.

While living in Minnesota we attended the Methodist Church. Occasionally we traveled to Mountain Lake, about 60 miles away to attend the Mennonite Church there. It was too far to do this with any degree of regularity. At that time, Anne

Picture 30 - Richard & Don barefoot skiing together behind our boat on Lake Decatur (Decatur, IL) in 1972.

in particular was concerned about raising our kids Mennonite. At that time this was not very important to me. I was having some "religion adjustment" problems which are described in some detail in my "Spiritual Journey" chapter.

I became somewhat disenchanted with my teaching load at the college. We were on the quarter system teaching a sixteen hour load each quarter with large classes, meeting four days a week for four quarters in the school year. I felt that we would scarcely get acquainted with our students, the quarter would end, a whole new set of students would come in, and we'd start all over again. So we kept alert to new opportunities. The Illinois

Wesleyan University opportunity opened up. It was a position as Chairman of the Department, semester calendar, and a nine-hour teaching load, attractive in every way except salary.

Picture 32 - Donny, Dicky and Brenda, left to right, taking a break while hiking down Barr Trail; Pike's Peak, 1959.

At the time I had a contract at Mankato as Associate Professor, for $8,000 with $2,000 additional for summer teaching. The IWU position was two semesters, a salary of $7000 and no summer teaching. To take this position would be a definite financial sacrifice. The Wesleyan President, Lloyd Bertholf, sweetened the offer by offering me the rank of full Professor. It was a difficult decision, but we decided to accept it. A week later, reconsidering and thinking about the financial sacrifice, along with the hectic process of moving the family, with the kids all in grade school, we called President Bertholf and told him we decided to change our mind.

Picture 31 - Hiking up and down Pike's Peak in 1959 are Brenda (11), Donny (Don) (8) and Dicky (Rich (10) (left to right), picture on the Barr Trail.

It was at this point that Bertholf put some pressure on us. He told me he thought my credentials just fitted their needs and they really would like me to come, furthermore, he could go one step farther. Ordinarily, the college pays five percent and the faculty member pays five percent of the salary, into the retirement program. He said if I'd come, the college could put the total amount, ten percent, into the retirement program. Apparently, that was enough to tip the scale, anyway we again accepted Wesleyan's offer and made the move.

It's a move I have never regretted. Normal had an active Mennonite Church, and job-satisfaction for me was an important factor. In addition, at the time we were considering the move, we did not realize the possibilities of summer teaching that existed. My summer teaching became a bright spot in our Wesleyan move. We have had summer opportunities which cannot be evaluated in terms of dollars and cents. Our stint at Illinois Wesleyan ran from 1960 to my retirement in 1982. I will describe the summer teaching experiences below.

Summer Teaching Jobs

Since I was not employed in summer teaching at Wesleyan, I applied for summer teaching at various places in the United States and Canada I would go to the library, get the "Blue Book," which listed universities all over the United States and Canada I would prepare a vita including several courses I was prepared to teach, and asking for a summer only assignment. I'd send out approximately one hundred applications every summer. Almost without fail, I'd get offers from two or three different places, and would then make a decision based on the offer plus what we judged would be the most beneficial and enjoyable location for our family to spend the summer.

In 1961, our first summer in Illinois, I was offered a visiting professor job at Syracuse University, New York. Our entire family went to Syracuse, pulling our boat with all our water-skiing equipment. We enjoyed the Finger Lake region and in addition to the teaching, spent quite a bit of time boating on Lake Skaneateles. In 1962, I had a National Science Foundation Grant to attend the Anthropology Institute in Boulder, Colorado. Here I got acquainted with some of the Sociology staff at the University of Colorado and in 1965, was invited to return as a visiting professor at the University.

In these two years at Boulder, our family specialized in Rock Climbing, hiking Long's Peak, and other out-of-doors activities. One of our major achievements was climbing the 3rd Flat Iron and rappelling off the back, a drop of 125 feet, with all three of our kids. Although we realize after the fact, that we did not use the best safety measures, we did survive.

In the summer 1964, the year between our two Boulder jaunts, I was visiting professor at the University of Rhode Island, Kingston, Rhode Island. I got this opportunity through one of the participants at the Anthropology Institute who was chairman of the Sociology Department at the University of Rhode Island. Here again we pulled our boat and did a lot of boating on the ocean along with water skiing and using the boat to find and dig steamers. On one occasion we had about fifteen crabs in our bath tub, a surprise for Anne when she came home. The kids and I boating on the ocean had gotten them from some lobster fishermen. We talked to them; they were ready to throw the crabs back into the ocean, so we took them home.

Picture 33 - Richard, Brenda, Anne, Paul and Don (left to right) on board the Gripsholm in 1967.

In 1968, we had just returned from our full-year sabbatical in Europe and chose to return home and remain at home that summer. I applied for and received the opportunity to teach at Illinois State University. This was not a particularly eventful summer although the family was ready to be at home. Our year's sabbatical is a separate story which I'll describe later.

The summer of 1969, I taught at the University of Alberta, Edmonton, Canada. The kids were now becoming adults and weren't always anxious to spend eight or ten weeks with Dad teaching, also, they had various responsibilities with summer jobs, summer school, and the like, so Anne stayed home to supervise the family activities while I traveled to Edmonton in my little Renault. I stayed in a dorm reserved for faculty and staff. In this environment it was easy to meet and get acquainted with lots of people.

Besides my teaching, I spent weekends and July 4, traveling and exploring the country. For practical reasons I considered my major objective was to find a bear trap. To have a major objective of that nature often allowed me to get into places and approach people who, without the objective, would have been difficult. In times past many people did trap bears in this area I located two traps that were available for purchase, paid eighteen dollars for each and brought them home. My best one was purchased from a Mrs. Goodswimmer, who lived on an Indian Reservation. The other trap had only one mainspring. A shop in Edmonton put a second spring on it, so it looked more like a bear trap, however I never did particularly like it so sold it on our clock auction, July, 1977. It brought one hundred, seventy-five dollars. In our division of things when we downsized before moving into the Mennonite Residential Community, the good trap became part of Rich's "loot."

Another memorable occasion at Edmonton was that in a dormitory lobby filled with people, we saw the landing on the moon in 1969. When my summer session was completed, Anne flew to Edmonton and we drove home together. On the way home we stopped to visit my cousin Jerry Miller in Montana. He and I had been in Hesston College together, and he was a close friend. We hadn't seen each other for thirty years. Jerry is the person most responsible for motivating and teaching me to pitch horseshoe and play checkers.

In 1970, I spent the summer in Flagstaff, Arizona Anne was with me the first part of the summer, then she went home to help Brenda prepare for her wedding. Don had been working at Hirschlers during the summer, had purchased a motorcycle and rode it out to Flagstaff, and spent a week or so with me before we returned home. While there he disassembled the motorcycle and we put it in the back of the Pontiac to bring home at the close of my teaching session.

Highlights of the summer in Flagstaff were my hikes down and up the Grand Canyon. I did that three Saturdays in a row. It seemed we always had guests who wanted to take this hike, so I served as their guide and did the hike, always down and back up the same day, down the Kaibab Trail and up the Bright Angel Trail.

Another experience in the Flagstaff area was the high dive Don made. There was a swimming hole with a high cliff, forty feet above which people with enough nerve dived off. Don made the dive and I got a good picture of him in the air. It is in my slide collection which Rich is working with at present, having hundreds of slides put in the computer so we can all view and/or copy them.

Picture 34 - Don diving off a forty-foot cliff near Flagstaff, AZ, 1970.

The summers of 1971, '72, & '73, were spent in Normal doing research on a "Creativity Study." This was supported by a National Science Foundation grant. I have a 206 page manuscript resulting from this study. The study included interviews with seventeen artists in Denmark, who had been awarded the *Staatens Kunstfond* award, the state's major art award. These interviews were made while in Copenhagen on my year-abroad sabbatical. A general summary conclusion drawn from this study is that "creativity is conflict resolution."

For three summers in a row, 1974, '75, '76, I taught at Johnson State College, Vermont. The first summer, Anne was with me and we became good friends with a family with two small girls. The man taught music and the wife had a course on "women's rights." It was during this stint in Vermont that Rich, Jan, and grandson Brian, then about seven months old, visited us in on their return from Zaire, Africa. I remember carrying Brian in a back-pack when we were going through the line at the cafeteria.

A common recreation here was to hike the Long's Trail, which extended from Canada to the Appalachian Trail in Virginia Long's Trail was less than a mile of Johnson. I also hiked Mt. Mansfield a number of times, the highest mountain in Vermont. I was well enough acquainted with the hike from experiences the first two years that the last year there, I served as guide for a group of students taking the hike.

My last summer job was at Eastern Illinois University, 1979, where they gave me the title Distinguished Visiting Faculty Member. I conducted a workshop on Amish Life and Trades. In this session I used pretty much the same format I used in the course Amish Society, which I taught at Illinois Wesleyan after my sabbatical, living with the Old Order Amish family in Arthur, Illinois. Incidentally, the course, Amish Society was probably the most successful course I taught at IWU, at least from the standpoint of student interest and appreciation.

Trips Abroad

Cattle Boat Attendant: Germany

All told, to date, I have taken six trips abroad during my lifetime. The first was to Germany, March, 1946, as a cattle-attendant on the Gainesville Victory, to Germany with a shipload of 500 bred heifers, destination Austria, as part of the relief program after World War ll. My brother, Dennis, and I both took this trip after being released from CPS. We shipped out from Newport News, Virginia, and unloaded in Bremen, Germany. Two or three heifers died on the trip and were thrown overboard. Nine or ten calves were born so we ended up with more live animals than we started with.

Impression 1: One of the heifers that died just two days before we arrived was not thrown overboard, but unloaded at the dock in Bremen. It was on the ground for only couple hours until it had completely disappeared, little by little, with starving people cutting off hunks of meat and even taking the bones to eat, in a meat-hungry world after WW II, 1946.

Impression 2: Mass destruction from the bombing, homes, business places, churches, almost everything flattened from the bombing.

Impression 3: People, no matter who you talked to, and no matter what topics you wanted to discuss, would always come back to "we are hungry, we need food, clothing and cigarettes."

Impression 4: For Americans, service men or other guests, transportation and telegrams home, were free. My brother, Dennis, along with another member of our group, and I, took a train to Hamburg while in Germany with no charge. You just board the train fight for a seat or crowd in. Trains and buses always over-crowded with refugees, people on the move, and even hanging on the outside of the car.

The ocean was relatively smooth going over. Coming back empty it was rough. Our empty ship with the living quarters for the idle cattle attendants in the back of the ship, right above the propeller, caused a lot of sea sickness. My brother, Dennis, was in his bunk, seasick most of the return trip. I was not particularly affected by the rough sea, and it was on this trip that I with several other beginners learned to play bridge. Four of the men were experienced bridge players and had a bridge table going a big part of most days. They were patient in teaching a few of us beginners the rules of the game.

European Sabbatical

Trip Two: Our European trip was on a sabbatical from Illinois Wesleyan University, for the school year 1967-68. We went with the entire family of five. I had two options for the sabbatical, half year with full pay or full year with half pay. We decided that we'd involve the entire family and take the full year. My banker told me to enjoy the year and he would keep money in my checking account, of course all to be repaid after we returned. Even though we had a number of rather serious let-downs, we did have a good year and a fifteen thousand dollar debt to work on upon our return.

At that time it was possible to book passage on ships. Our family liked the idea so we decided to take that route both going over and coming home. We booked passage on the Swedish ship, the Gripsholm going from New York to Copenhagen, Denmark. On the return we booked passage on the Dutch ship, the Rotterdam, from Amsterdam to New York. Our family in general enjoyed the ship-travel both ways, particularly since it wasn't long after our return until bookings on ships for regular passengers were discontinued.

My sabbatical program was to participate in a so-called World Culture course offered by "The College of Copenhagen." I had received some attractive blurbs on this program and had several correspondence exchanges with the director regarding his program and their physical facilities. I also discussed this with the president of IWU, Lloyd Bertholf, and we decided that it should be a constructive program for a sociologist on sabbatical. We were informed by the director that they would be able to accommodate our family with living quarters and they would have a kitchen to share.

We ordered a new VW camper from the dealer here in Bloomington, to be picked up in Copenhagen for our use in Europe during our stay there.

We made arrangements for Brenda who was to be a college freshman, to attend Schiller College in Frankfurt. Rich was a high-school senior and Don, a high-school freshmen. In our original plans they were scheduled to attend the International High School in Copenhagen. I was registered to join the 10-week trip through the communist countries by VW bus during the summer with the College of Copenhagen, Brenda & Rich (Don wasn't old enough) joined a volunteer youth group building a fire trail in the mountains of Lugano, Switzerland, while Anne and Don were to volunteer at the Bienenberg, a Mennonite school/restaurant combination near Bern, Switzerland. With all these plans and arrangements we figured we had our bases pretty well covered.

The trip on the Gripsholm was great. The captain told us at the captain's dinner that this was the smoothest sea he had traveled in his 32 years of sailing. Anne, who is usually bothered with sea-sickness, nor any of us, got sea-sick. I won the shuffle-board tournament and received a nice little Swedish glass trophy. On arrival, our camper was in Copenhagen and we picked that up on schedule; So far so good.

We ran into our first serious problem when we arrived at the College of Copenhagen. We found that the College of Copenhagen was no college at all. A man by the name of Bertlestein had a big house with many rooms, located in the city of Copenhagen, had invited approximately 25 to 30 people to participate in his program, each paid a "hefty" fee, and his program was that, after the trip through Russia, they would spend the winter visiting tourist sights, museums, cathedrals, departments of the Danish government, and the like, then spend time in informal discussion groups during the year which he referred to as seminars. There were no trained personnel or specialists except the director and he seemed to us to be sort of a simpleton.

In addition there was no possibility for any kind of family life; kitchen use was a "cat-and-dog" "come-and-go" competition with all the other participants. We realized early that this program was not for our family. We did have our summer plans well laid out and we followed those OK. I went with the group on the Russian tour. Anne, Brenda, and Rich had driver's licenses, so they, along with Don, took the camper and headed for their respective assignments in Switzerland while I headed out on the Russian trip. United States and Russia were in a real cold-war political relationship at the time and I was very anxious for the communist countries experience. So far, all was working out but we had little notion of what was to emerge after the summer. We all agreed that it would not be at the College of Copenhagen.

My summer was fabulous, informational and enjoyable. We were a group of, I think, 28 people in four VW busses. We went by ferry to Oslo, then drove to Stockholm and Helsinki, spending a day or two in each capital city, then on to the Russian border. Here we picked up one of our Russian guides, Kuelli, a nice looking and friendly and really lovely lady who spoke good English. She was a communist who was supposedly my political enemy. I was riding in the bus in which she rode to Leningrad, and could visit very personally with her. The relationship from the beginning was very positive. From my very first contacts I loved the Russian people.

In Leningrad we picked up our three other guides so we had a guide for each bus. They were Zena another lady, Gene and another fellow whose name escapes me. We had two young men and two ladies all four of whom spoke very good English.

Ours was an exceptionally good trip, ten weeks from beginning to end. We spent time along the way observing the country side, stopping for interesting sights, traveling to Novgorod, Moscow, Kiev, and on south to Odessa on the Black Sea. At most lodging stops, it was common for us to have meetings with young people, industrial groups, and other Russian citizens, where we'd have good discussions, questions and answers from both sides of the communist/capitalist issue.

We left Russia and our guides at the Romanian border. It was a sad parting after having spent three weeks of rather intimate relationships with them. We toured Romania, Hungary, Czechoslovakia, Poland, and on into East Germany. From Budapest I called Anne at the Bienenberg. We arranged by phone to meet at the Mennonite fellowship in West Berlin and there I would leave the tour group and our family would venture out into our uncharted world.

Anne and the kids had, what appeared to them at the time to be, a rather harrowing experiences driving from Austria north into communist East Germany to West Berlin. Having had no previous experience with communist politics, and after being warned by the embassy officials that they were traveling at their own risk as private tourists, they had to give up their passports at the check-point, change license plates on the camper, and then just the sheer fact of mother and the kids driving hundreds of miles through the communist East Germany was in itself a challenging experience for Anne and the kids.

We met as planned in West Germany, stayed overnight and the next morning started driving to, we-didn't-know-where. The next few days were an emotionally stressful time for all five of us. The plan for Brenda at Schiller College was the only one that stood. She was to report there in a few days.

While in Berlin we checked on the possibility of Anne teaching at the John F. Kennedy School in West Berlin. The year before, in Boulder, Colorado we became acquainted with a German professor who was teaching at the University of Colorado, and who was a board member of the John F. Kennedy School. We learned from him that there was to be an opening when a pregnant teacher would go on leave, but that was probably not for couple months.

Our home in Normal was leased and occupied with a one-year contract. Our situation was sufficiently serious that had our home in Normal been available we might very well have returned home. We considered that as a serious option. Our trunks with all our one-year supply of clothing we brought from home were in Copenhagen. As we drove out of West Berlin we had verbal conflicts, we argued, we wept. I literally cried under the emotional strain.

We decided to drive to the Bienenberg where Anne and Don had spent the summer. There we began calling various places about the possibility of getting Rich and Don into a high school. After several hours of calling we found that Institute Montana near Zug had openings for both boys. The freshman opening for Don had just occurred that morning. The father of one of their incoming freshmen had been killed in an airplane accident and the son had withdrawn from school. We asked when school began. They said "tomorrow." We said, "We'll be there." And we were.

So we got the boys settled at Institute Montana with a scanty supply of clothing. (Our trunks were still in Copenhagen.) We got Brenda settled in Schiller College in Frankfurt, also with a limited supply of clothing. It was now September when Anne and I took off for Copenhagen in our camper to retrieve our trunks. With the kids settled we figured we could live in our camper. We arrived in Copenhagen, loaded our trunks in the camper, took supplies of clothing and the like to the kids at their respective schools, then Anne and I had to decide, what next. We would go someplace for the winter. We decided the location must meet two requirements: one, a university city, and two, where they speak the German language. We decided on Vienna, Austria

We drove to Vienna, lived in our camper until October 23rd. After much searching and difficulty finding an apartment, because we didn't want to sign a lease, we found a small apartment in the Vienna Woods, poorly equipped but adequate. We had to open up the sofa for our bed and sleep near the gas heater which emitted fumes. We were located a ten-minute walk to the bus and a 45 minute ride into the city. I enrolled in two classes at the University, Anne and I quite often attended the *Stats Oper* where we could get *Stehplatz* tickets for seven schillings (27 cents). We attended the opera a couple times a week.

We spent Christmas vacation with the kids. Our nephew Stephen, my brother Emerson's son, was also attending Schiller College. He traveled with our family for about a week through Germany, France and Spain. The Schiller College experience for Brenda was not what she and we wished it to be. There were things going on there that she and we did not like, so we arranged for her to return home and go to Bluffton College for the second semester. We got the boys back to Institute Montana then we returned to Vienna to our apartment.

We had almost forgotten about the pregnant woman at the JFK School in West Berlin who might need a substitute, when we awoke one morning with a telegram under our door. The telegram stated that a vacancy did in fact exist and if Anne was still interested she could begin teaching at a specified date, early in January.

It was a welcomed opportunity. We closed out with our landlord in Vienna and headed north the next day to West Berlin. There they had a nice furnished apartment available to us. We moved in, Anne began her teaching in the bi-lingual JFK School. Now it was necessary for me to find something constructive to do in Berlin.

That, however, was not difficult. A year earlier while at Wesleyan, I had contacted a professor at Humboldt University in East Berlin regarding a sabbatical proposal, but that project did not materialize at the time. The professor at Humboldt had accepted my proposal but some other hitch occurred that prevented the sabbatical from materializing. I seized this opportunity and went to East Berlin, renewed my contact personally, and found that this Humboldt University professor, along with other university personnel, were very accommodating and even seemed anxious for me to do research in their library.

My project was to compare criminal records in East Germany, West Germany, Poland, and the United States. They at Humboldt University made their stacks and archives open to me, so I began almost daily visits to Humboldt University, in East Germany, going through the common crime records of the specified countries. The seven common crimes which I checked and which I think are universally recognized were arson, homicide, rape, aggravated assault, robbery, larceny and burglary. With the help of the Humboldt criminologist I was able to chart detailed records of each crime in each of the specified countries.

Interestingly both the East and West Germanys used the same law books. Each considered itself the official Germany so both used the same law books that were used by the unified Germany before the war.

It soon became obvious why they at Humboldt were so eager to cooperate with me in my project. East Germany had significantly lower crime rates than the other three countries.

Poland was next lowest, then West Germany and finally, the U.S. The records ran so high for the U.S. that they could not be charted on the scale I used for the others.

It is important to note also that these records exclude political crimes which were high in both East Germany and Poland. They were higher in the communist countries because so many people attempted to escape, were caught and imprisoned. But these crimes were not included among the common crimes I checked in my proposal.

As spring approached we began thinking in terms of returning to our home in Normal. We pulled Rich and Don out of their school at Easter time. We took a rather extended trip into Great Britain and Ireland. It was on this trip that we became acquainted with Jack and Betty Milner in York, who gave us the lamp we have hanging in our living room.

We returned to West Berlin, Anne continued and seemed to enjoy her professional contacts and teaching at JFK. Dad and the boys soon left for Amsterdam in the camper loaded with most of our baggage to make preparation for our return home on the Rotterdam. Before leaving we purchased a new Pontiac through the PX which Anne had access to by virtue of her teaching at JFK. It was to be picked at a dealer in New Jersey.

In Amsterdam the boys and I lived in a small rented apartment. We booked passage for the camper, our baggage and the four of us to travel on a date after Anne's school closed. Anne came by train to Amsterdam, and we were all on our way home, again by ship, at the scheduled time.

After leaving Amsterdam, the Rotterdam docked in England overnight. Anne wrote and mailed a number of cards to friends while we were docked in the English Channel. We left the next day and before long encountered a severe storm. The sea was very rough. At the captain's dinner the captain reported that this was the roughest sea he had encountered in seven years. Anne got desperately sea sick. She missed most of the meals on the entire voyage, even the captain's dinner. The sea was so rough that it delayed our arrival and we docked in New York a day later than originally scheduled.

In New York, Betsy and Jim Lehman were there to meet us, Jim took us to the dealer to get our Pontiac, we stayed with Lehmans overnight and then sent Rich and Don home in the camper loaded to the hilt with all our baggage. The boys wanted to get home for Rich's graduation. Anne and I drove to Washington, D.C. for a short visit with Dennis and Jean Ann, and then we too headed for Normal.

Our home on Wilmette Drive had been vacated by our renters on schedule. I had made arrangements to teach at ISU during that summer, 1968, and we were all glad to settle in at home after our long year on sabbatical. With all the ups and downs, we had our trying times but it was a year we will always remember.

Russia: January Short Term

Trips three and four were with students during IWU's January Short Term, as part of my teaching assignment. These were possible because I had good connections which were made during my sabbatical, a year earlier. The trips included visits to London, Vienna, Budapest, Kiev, Leningrad and Moscow. We had guides and pre-planned programs in all our stops. One of the more memorable experiences in Russia was a 30-hour train ride from Kiev to Leningrad. Our Russian experiences came during the early 1970's when the communist politics placed definite limitations on our activities. Most of our contacts were places I had visited before, but they were new and, I think, educational for the students.

Senegal, Africa

Trip number five: The trip to Senegal in itself became an adventure. It was during Christmas vacation, 1980, to visit Rich, Jan and there, boys in Africa. Rich was on an assignment under the auspices of USAID and we decided to visit them while they were still on assignment.

Flight arrangements were for us to fly Bloomington to O'Hare, to JFK New York, to Dakar, Senegal, all quite direct with very little airport delays. However a labor strike in Chicago in extremely cold weather caused a major delay in departing Chicago. Consequently we were late at JFK, missed our trans-Atlantic flight to Dakar and the airline issued taxi fare, hotel accommodations in the city and breakfast fare. We were assigned to a run-down hotel with a broken window, insufficient blankets, and poor heating. Our night in this hotel was not comfortable. We tried to call Jan and Rich in Africa but mainly because of the language barrier (only French speaking operator on late night duty) could not make contact.

The up-side is that because of the delay in reaching New York and missing our scheduled flight to Dakar, we were given first-class flight accommodations, the only seats available at the time, for the New York to Dakar flight. Flying first-class was a new experience for us. We had individual reclining seats that made into comfortable beds. We had choice of several options of first-class meals, the stewardess hung up our coats on hangers; we were allowed to board last and depart first.

Rich and Jan did not get any warning of our delay and late arrival, but Jan said irregularities were not uncommon in Africa and that she had planned to meet every flight until we arrived. She and the boys met us at the airport a day later than originally planned. It was good to have finally arrived.

Rich and Jan had very fine living quarters in a nice section of the city. While there, however, we saw many signs of abject poverty and unsanitary conditions. In the early mornings one could see people coming out of their shambled houses emptying their latrines into an open drainage ditch. Jan and Rich had a native watchman on duty, night and day. It was considered a good investment to hire the native watchman otherwise they would be vulnerable to vandalism and theft.

During this adventure we took a three-day trip to the joining country to the north, Mauritania, during migration season for birds. Here we saw millions (more or less) of birds, more birds than I've ever seen in a given area in my life. Also, in a different part of our trip we saw nomads who were living in tents and it was normal for them to be on the move constantly during their entire lifetime.

All in all it was a new experience for us to visit Africa; it was informational, and also good for us to make contact with Rich and his family while on their assignment in Africa

Sabbatical with the Amish

Illinois Wesleyan granted me a sabbatical for the semester 1978-79. My proposal was to study the Amish society. I had been making various contacts in the Arthur, Illinois Amish community searching for an Amish home that would be willing to have me move in and live with them for a period. My proposal was that I would be able and willing to work for my room and board. In my search, I had located several families who said they would consider it but each time the final answer was that it just doesn't suit. One family had suggested I live in their "doughty" house which was empty at the time. They had several children including couple girls 10 or 12 years of age. Although the man didn't tell me, I heard from other sources that he had misgivings about the influence a stranger would have on his children. And he thought it might not be safe for his older girls.

Another man was setting up a new woodworking shop and said he would like me to work with him in the shop, and that he would be willing to pay motel bill at Atwood, a small town nearby, if I'd come in and work every day. This would defeat my objective since I wanted the experience of living with a family. He wasn't willing for me to move in with his family, he said his wife was uncomfortable around strange men.

One of the selling points I used in approaching the Amish people about living with a family was the fact that my father was a Mennonite Bishop. Even with this selling point, however, up to this point it never quite achieved the objective.

Someone suggested Freeman Beachy, who owned and operated a large woodworking shop. I went to see him. He seemed interested but was not willing to make a decision immediately. He said give me a few days, I'd like to consult my family and the workers in the shop. This was on Wednesday. He said I should come back on Friday and he'd have an answer. I came back and asked him if he had made up his mind. His comment was, "We're going to try it." I could have shouted for joy because I had been working on this for, actually over a year. However, I remained calm and asked him when I could start. He said, "Monday." I said what time to you go to work. He said, "7:00 o'clock in the morning." I said, "I'll be there." So I started my life with the Beachy family. They had two adopted children, Ernie a 4th grader, and Julie, a 2nd grader. My first assignment was to count out 100 nails for a customer buying nails. Then I was put to work gluing plastic strips on the edge of shelving boards.

That evening when the kids got home from school, Julie, the second grader, came out to the shop to visit with me. She was a talkative little girl and apparently felt very free to talk. One of her comments I remember was, "The first time I saw you I thought you were English." The Amish people refer to non-Amish people as *English*. She had seen Anne and me at an Amish church service several weeks earlier at bishop, Chris Otto's, home. Julie knew we were visitors there, but now that I had come to live with them, in her mind I was no longer English, but Amish.

Ernie had given up his bedroom for me to sleep in. He took serious interest in showing me how to light the kerosene lamp and how to blow it out. Strike the match on the bottom of the drawer, he said, so it doesn't mark the furniture. Then to extinguish it, don't just blow into the globe, rather hold your hand on the opposite side and blow against your hand. Also, Ernie gave me his wooden foot-ruler he thought I could use. I still have the ruler in my shop today.

Freeman Beachy, the owner and operator of the shop was very considerate of me. He wanted me to have the experience of working in every department in the shop, sawing, gluing, sanding, mil-work with his brother-in-law living at a different location, and the like. The first week or so, my major job was to help with the construction of the *Schlacht Haus*. This was the building to house the meat-processing business which they were starting up. It was located just east of the wood-working shop. I was on the roof helping with the shingling in February when the snow was flying. We also insulated the interior rooms for the freezer and refrigeration.

We had it completed and everything was ready to open shop except the freezing and refrigeration equipment which had been ordered earlier from a company in Milwaukee had not arrived. For some reason that was being held up. They learned that the hold-up was intentional on the part of the sellers. When the equipment was ordered the Amish men instructed the company to include everything that was needed right down to, but not including the electric motors. The company was refusing to ship the equipment because they were not convinced that it could be operated without electricity and they were concerned about their warranties.

So Freeman, his brother-in-law Lester Miller who was to be the manager of the meat-processing business, called the company and made an appointment to go to Milwaukee to talk personally to the people selling the equipment. They requested an appointment with the chief engineer so they could explain to someone who would understand how they plan to operate the equipment. After it was explained to the engineer, he told the Amish men that this was one of the most ingenious hook-ups he had ever heard of, and shortly after the appointment, the equipment was sent, it was then installed Amish style, and the *Schlacht Haus* was soon in operation.

Freeman asked me early if we could run some errands with my car. At that time we had the gold two-seated, four-door Pontiac. He wanted to go to Hindsboro, about twenty miles away, to get some measurements for a kitchen cabinet they were making in the shop. I drove him to that place and from then on my taxi service never stopped. I'd take someone to a telephone, a grocery store, Freemen and Bertha with another Amish couple to

Decatur to shop; I took one of their employees home who had gotten sick on the job. And as it turned out, there was not a single day, except the day I had lost my car keys that we didn't use the car to run errands of some sort for some Amish people. The advantage to me, in addition to the service to the Amish, was that it always gave me a break from work. Sometimes this was a very welcome break. Also it gave me contacts with various Amish people.

One day when someone requested the use of the car, I could not find my keys. We did not run the errand that day, and the next day I found my keys on the ground besides a snow-drift. I had dropped them in the snow and when the snow melted enough to expose the keys we were back in business.

Part of the agreement when I came to work was that I would be permitted to take time off occasionally to make some contacts for my research. I didn't use the word "research." That would have confused the issue. It was difficult enough for me, a college professor, to come into the family and community who do not, as part of their religious belief, go to school beyond the 8th grade. The Beachys did know that I wanted to get acquainted with the various bishops and others in the Amish community. So occasionally I did take off a half day to make such contacts. Also, on one occasion Freeman invited me to quit my work and attend a funeral with him.

At that time, the spring semester of 1979, there were thirteen church districts or congregations in the Arthur Amish community, each headed by a bishop, a pastor and a deacon. I met and got quite well acquainted with all thirteen bishops and many of the pastors, as well as other members. From each of the bishops or from someone the bishops delegated, I obtained the information needed to complete the directory for my book titled The Illinois Amish (D. Paul Miller). In addition to the directory, the book included a history of the Amish settlement, Amish economic activity, a description of the schools and Amish education, along with maps and a directory of every Amish person living in the community at that time. *The Illinois Amish* was published by Pequea Publishers, Gordonville, Pennsylvania, in 1980.

The sabbatical experience living with the Amish family was enriching. At Wesleyan, I became "the authority" on Amish. I offered a course, *Amish Society*, which became a popular course. The course always included a field trip visiting an Amish school, getting into an Amish home, visiting several shops (harness, buggy, wood-working, the *Schlacht Haus*, and on one occasion, a ride in an Amish buggy. Even thirty years later, we, Anne and I, maintain contact with the Beachys and a few other Amish friends in the Arthur community.

Clock Repair

While I was teaching in Mankato, one of my students would often come to my office to just visit. On one occasion he expressed real enthusiasm for antiques. He was a collector and introduced me to the little book "Treasures in Truck and Trash." As I recall, the book was out of print at the time, and I made special effort and finally located a copy at a used book store. This incident, the book, along with the enthusiasm of the student, got me interested collecting antiques. Soon, I began specializing in clocks.

I had a number of clocks, some needing repair, so I began taking some of them apart, not really knowing what I was doing. It was about this time that we moved to Illinois. Here I had the opportunity to buy out a clock and watch repair man who was retiring and going out of business. I purchased his jeweler's bench, several lathes, staking sets, watches and watch parts, and other miscellaneous equipment. I had tools and equipment, some appeared to be valuable, but I didn't really know what to do with them. I contacted Fred Schroeder, a jeweler and watch-maker at Sorg's Jewelry Store, here in Bloomington. He said he'd be interested in seeing them, and came to our home to see what I was talking about.

In our conversation, Fred, who has since become a very good friend, told me of a Clock Repair Class to begin at Parkland College in Champaign. He and another local jeweler, Werner Theobald, who was a German craftsman, were driving to Champaign for the classes, and invited me to join them. Theobald was teaching the jewelry class and Fred was enrolled in his class. In this program a clock repair class was offered, meeting for a three-hour session on the same evenings. I enrolled in the class and car-pooled with them.

In my billing books which I used to describe my work and in turn give each customer a copy, the earliest listing is 1975. I had done some earlier work for a few people before I began to take it serious enough to list the work and give each customer a bill.

To give you some idea of the extent to which I got into repairing clocks, I have been using the billing books which have fifty pages, each with a carbon. For each job I'd have the date, customer's name, address and telephone number, indicate the work done, the amount charged, give the customer the original, and keep the carbon copies. I am currently, (June, 2010) in Book 20, which with 50 customers per book, translates into approximately one thousand repair jobs. Since we have downsized, and moved into the Mennonite Residential Community, (June, 2010) I have taken in jobs totaling more than four thousand, three hundred dollars.

In the class at Parkland College, they had all the tools needed for repair work. They had tools similar to those I had at home but I didn't know how to use mine. It was truly an educational experience for me. Each participant was required to bring a clock to tear apart, repair and put in functioning order. It was no problem for me to find a clock that needed repair. I had quite a few. Some of the students in the class had to obtain a clock from a friend because they didn't have one.

Our assignment was to take the clock completely apart, take all the gears out, and unwind the mainsprings, clean everything, repair what was needed, and reassemble it. In addition we were taught how to replace a broken tooth in a gear, how to unwind and replace a mainspring, along with the many functions of the lathe and anything else that would ever need to be done to a clock.

I was so motivated with the class that I enrolled for the second class, "Clock Repair ll." In this class we were required to bring either a clock with both chime and strike, one with three mainsprings, or a cuckoo clock. For that clock I brought a cuckoo clock and worked it over. Fred Schroeder and Werner Theobald saw the work I was doing and Fred asked me if I would be interested in doing some work for Sorg's, the jewelry store where he was working. I took a job he had on hand at the time, and that was the beginning of my "clock repair career."

Fred was more of a watch maker or jeweler, and not so much interested in clocks. The repairman can make more money repairing and cleaning watches than clocks. For watch repairs they remove the movement from the case, put ten to fifteen movements in the ultra-sonic cleaner, run them through in fifteen minutes, remove them and put them back into the case and have them ready for the customer. Watch repair is more mass production. With clock repair, it is much more individual hand-work. It takes longer for each job and the charge for a clock repair is probably much the same as for one watch. So jewelers are often willing, sometimes anxious to farm out clock repair work and specialize on watches.

For a few years I had jewelers from Lincoln and Gibson City bringing me clocks, sometimes ten or twelve clocks in their van, and anxious to have them completed in a few weeks. This was in addition to three or four jewelry stores here in Bloomington-Normal who had me repair their clocks. It got to be more than I was comfortable with and I tried to tell people I'm trying to retire from clock repair.

Since moving into the Mennonite Residential Community, my clock-work has been reduced significantly, although I still do house calls, and take work from individuals who bring them in. When our new residence was in the construction stage, I requested they petition off a section of the basement for a clock shop. This was done at an additional cost of six hundred dollars. As indicated earlier, I've kept record of the work I've done in the new shop and again I mention that the addition of a clock repair room to our duplex has been not only a good investment but a constructive activity for me as well. At this stage of life it is sometimes relaxing for me to go to the shop and work on a repair job, but I do not want to get involved to the point that I feel pressured to get the job done.

I have very good equipment, including a Swiss-made Bergeon bushing tool, a good spring winder, staking set, a lathe, a stand to hang weight clocks with long pendulums, a drill press, a jeweler's bench with the drawers filled with good equipment, various repair parts, and an almost endless array of good hand tools. My philosophy has always been, if you really need and will use a tool, buy it.

Clock repair has been an added dimension to my life, one that I had never really planned for or anticipated. It is very rewarding for me to see a clock in the process of being worked over, lay on my table in a thousand pieces (more or less), and later put back together and see it running. Clockwork provides opportunity for creative

Picture 35 – Replacing bushings in a clock with one of the grandkids, Normal, IL.

activity, and is thoroughly enjoyable if one keeps it in moderation and does not allow it to dictate.

Some years ago I acquired four clocks which were not in running condition, and offered to my four older grandchildren that if they would come and spend several days with me, we would take the clock apart, repair it, get it running, then they could have the clock. This offer was accepted by three of the grandchildren (Darrick, Chris, and Nara) relatively early. For Brian, we were not able to work out a time until just recently.

We did arrive at a satisfactory date for Brian. He came in, in early June, 2010. We worked on his clock, disassembled it completely, cleaned, repaired, re-assembled, lubricated, and adjusted it, got it running and he took it home with him to Atlanta, Georgia on June 14, 2010. His father, Rich, from Evanston, and his fiancée, Kristyn, were also here for several days, and we all had a good visit.

An interesting observation is that Brian, 35, was older when he did his clock-work and no doubt achieved more from the experience than the other grandchildren. Although I say each of the other three took the job seriously, were very much interested in what they were doing, and did excellent work. Also, society's technology had advanced to a higher level and he, Brian, took a series of photos of the clock in its various stages of repair. He did this with his digitized cell phone camera, and as a result, I have a good series of photos in my computer that I can view at leisure. Among other stages, (thirteen in all) the photos show the clock parts in their completely disassembled state, the bushing process, winding and unwinding the mainsprings, and the finished clock in the hands of its owner.

It was gratifying for me personally to have completed my offer for the fourth grandchild. I do not know whether or not I'll be able to continue my offer for Don and Sharon's two recently adopted twins, my granddaughters. If I am still functioning when they are old enough to value the experience, I would like to follow up on the offer.

Retirement and Downsizing

Anne retired at Thanksgiving time, 1981, and I retired at the end of the school year, May, 1982. Anne was having vision problems. Her ophthalmologist, Dr. Ringer of the Gailey Eye Clinic, diagnosed her condition as having an optic cyst in the retina of the right eye, a condition that could not be treated or remedied. There is no known cause, but some say it is related to stress, and since she was having some vision difficulty in her school work, she decided to quit teaching. With Dr. Ringer's recommendation, we went to the eye clinic at the University of Iowa for a second opinion. There they told us almost precisely the same thing Dr. Ringer had told us. No remedy. You have to accept and live with it.

I approached our dean, our good friend Wendell Hess, about some provisions the University might make if I'd retire at the end of the school year. This would be a year earlier than the regular University policy for retirement. The University recommends that you teach the year you turn 65 and then hang it up. Hess told me to write my letter indicating some reasonable terms and they'd consider it. I wrote the letter of resignation asking that they would (1) allow Anne to attend any classes tuition-free, and (2) have the university pay the medical premium for my wife. (It was University policy to pay the premium for the retiree, but not for the spouse.) Hess submitted my letter to President Eckley, and in a few days I had a reply that they had accepted my resignation with the terms I requested. So I quit teaching at the end of the school year in which Anne retired at Thanksgiving time.

Anne worked with the pottery teacher, Anna Holcomb, and enrolled in several pottery classes, making some nice pottery items. At the time I retired the premium for the Wesleyan health plan was $600 per year. In the years since, with the advancing health and medical costs, the premium has jumped to couple thousand dollars per year, so this arrangement has turned out to be a good move for us.

I think Anne and I both experienced a period of somewhat challenging readjustment. We had to realize and adjust to the fact that the institutions from which we retired were going to continue even after we left them. This was not always easy but gradually we accepted it and began to really enjoy the new freedom that was ours. We could go places and do things without having to get substitutes. We began to appreciate what has probably become the most enjoyable period of our lives. I think, however, that this degree of pleasure and enjoyment diminishes as we face the increasing limitations of aging. I say this at New Years' time, February, 2005, twenty-three years after we quit teaching.

Anne and I both began to realize that it would be wise for us to sooner or later make some major changes regarding downsizing, getting rid of many of our possessions collected over the years, and even changing our residence.

We had many quite valuable antiques and other items that we had accumulated. Our attic and basement, our cupboards, and house in general, were filled with "things" that sooner or later would have to be disposed of. I often thought of how much easier it would be for the kids if we would take responsibility for doing this while we were able to make some of the decisions ourselves.

An opening at the Mennonite Residential Community came up. Larry Reeser, the chairman of the MRC Board, approached us when we were at Builders Retreat at Camp Friendenswald. He said they had a unit that would just fit us. At the time we didn't give it much serious consideration, but on the other hand we sort of put the idea on the back burner. It was on the way home from Four Seasons on the following Monday morning after the Friedenswald week-end that Anne said, "Maybe we should look at that unit." I had been thinking the same thing but was reluctant to be the first one to express my thoughts. After Anne made the comment we discussed it openly and more seriously, and that week went to the MRC to look at the unit which at the time was under construction.

Several things about the unit made it appear very favorable. The unit had a basement in which we could have a recreation room, bedroom and clock shop plus adequate storage space. The main floor had two bedrooms and almost as much living and kitchen space as our Wilmette Drive residence. The garage was large, quite a bit larger than our present one, and another strong attraction was the view of the green area from our picture window. This area was reserved as a drain basin and would never be developed. This unit was the last one to be developed in the MRC, and I have often said since, "if all of the 29 units in the MRC were open and I had my choice, this would be my first pick." And this was the last one to be developed. We decided to take it, and by the following Sunday, Larry had the contract ready and we signed up. We put our Wilmette Drive place up for sale, it sold in two weeks, and soon our new residence was ready to be occupied, and we moved in, October 22, 1998, a move neither Anne nor I have ever regretted.

When we got ready to clear out of our house on Wilmette Drive, I invited three or four good friends, to help clear out our attic. Tim Waltner, being of short stature, and I were in the attic, handed things down to the other fellows, and they stacked things in the garage. When we got ready to physically move to the new residence, we had the Menno-Movers load and carry all the smaller things in their trucks and pick-ups. We hired professional movers to handle the freezer, refrigerator, washing machine, dryer, drill press and stand, and the heavy metal cabinet from the clock shop. Erma Stutzman offered to prepare a meal for the Menno-Movers. We moved in and spent our first night in our new home October 22, 1998.

After we had definitely planned to move, one of the major chores that needed to be done was the physical disposition of these "earthly goods," we wanted to keep in the family, the things we wanted to pass along to the kids. We were somewhat concerned that this be done, the items divided up among the three children, so that they would all be satisfied and through it all have peace and good feeling in the family. So I very carefully drew up a plan which I thought would be fair and would work. We had decided ahead of time that Brenda would get the reed-organ which had come from Anne's grandmother's home. We felt that Brenda should have it because she was the only one at the time who had a permanent home and a practical place to put it, beside she had expressed a definite interest in it. That would be her first choice then the boys could choose items of equal value to compensate.

The three kids came in on October 11, 1998. When it came time to get down to the business of dividing, they were not too enthusiastic about my plan. They told us to take a walk and they would handle the situation and assured us that they would all be satisfied. We left for an hour or so and when we returned things were going smoothly and they were having a good time. In the end, things were well divided and all three of them seemed satisfied.

I kept a notebook record of the items each of the kids took. A general listing is as follows: Brenda: organ, spinning wheel, Amish "schuckle," White Mountain ice-cream freezer, wine glasses made in occupied Japan, antique doctor's bleeding tool, railroad box-car lock and key, plus other miscellaneous items. Rich: the bear trap, two good antique guns, log with musket balls from Civil War, 10-piece chamber set, Acorn clock, marble-top parlor table, marble base Russian ink-well set, ivory carved Russian bears, broad axe, Russian glass Easter egg, plus other miscellaneous items. Don: the Round Oak wood-burning stove, walnut parlor table, two antique telephones (We had three but Rich didn't want one.), glass display case with some rare artifacts, Russian Easter egg with inscription "He is Risen," tuning fork, Budweiser beer wagon with metal Clydesdale horses, British taxi horn, plus other miscellaneous items.

In addition to the things for each of the kids mentioned above, I had several sheets of "moon-flight" U.S. postal stamps for each, each a porcelain clock plus a small ironclad clock, several coyote and skunk traps for each, each a Wiebe milk crate, each a jewelers lathe and a jeweler's staking set, and each one or two of my antique jack collection. A number of the things we are still using were assigned and it seems the kids all have things they appreciate and seem to be satisfied with. Also, Anne and I feel somewhat relaxed to have the things unloaded. In fact, it's a big burden off our minds.

As I write, February, 2005, we have lived in our new residence now for over six years, Anne still works at Crossroads couple times a month, practices her scales and some songs on the piano with enlarged music scores that Brenda had prepared for her to play at the Wiebe Reunion. I am involved in managing the woods at "Rocky Branch" and "Hedgewood," doing some clock repair work, and both of us go to Four Seasons five days a week for a 2-hour workout.

We both get "ribbed" occasionally for getting up so early to get to Four Seasons every morning by the time it opens at 5:00 am and to do this when retired. We justify this by explaining that we have tried different schedules since we retired from teaching. If we go after breakfast at 9:00 or 10:00 o'clock, it shoots half the day. The same can be said about working out in the afternoon. But if we go at 5:00 am, and finish at 7:00, get home and eat breakfast at 7:30, we're finished with our exercise and breakfast by 8:00 am and have the whole day ahead of us. We do usually lie down for a nap after lunch but can skip that if something important comes up. We've been on this schedule for years and both like it, but all the while we realize that someday we will have to give it up. But as they say, "you don't criticize a winner."

Up-Date, April, 2010: Anne's Death

Life is dynamic, change is inevitable, not only change, but major changes occur which require major adjustments. Several years ago Anne was gradually having more and more difficulty walking. We terminated our membership at Four Seasons because she could no longer negotiate the steps there. She used our treadmill at home which we moved into our living room, and, I began using Shirk center, IWU's fitness center.

Anne's condition became so painful that we went to the doctor to have things checked out. Dr. Kneezel ordered x-ray of her spine, January, 2007, and, according to the report, she had two fractured vertebra

Her pain was quite severe for about a month. However, it healed to the point that she no longer had pain, but it affected her walking. She could walk inside only by using the walker, and we could use the wheel-chair to go places, to church, around the oval, where we live, and even traveled to "Rocky Branch" several times with the wheel-chair in the car. She enjoyed stopping at the Amish surplus store near Arthur. I'd push the wheel chair and pull the grocery cart, and she was good at picking out the groceries she thought we needed. In the summer of 2008, we put the wheel-chair in the car and traveled to the Wiebe reunion in Michigan. For our rest-room stops, I'd simply wheel her into the men's room, announce, if men were around, that I'm bringing my wife in the wheel-chair. We would then go into the handicap stall and take care of our business.

I felt personally rewarded that I was physically able to be her care-giver. A major factor in my positive feeling was that she was always so free to express her appreciation for what we were doing for her. E. g., our schedule was shower twice a week, Tuesday and Saturday nights. Never, literally never, did she fail to say "Thank you for the good shower," or "I feel so good after a good shower, thank you." I always knew that such a comment would be forthcoming.

On Friday, January 29, she needed to go to the bathroom. She had difficulty getting up out of her lift-chair, but made it OK. I noticed that she was weak, she walked with knees bent more than usual, and I followed her with the wheel-chair. In the bathroom she said she couldn't walk, and with some difficulty I got her on the wheel-chair and back to her chair. She had difficulty talking; her mouth was full of saliva. It was obvious that her condition was not normal. I asked if I should call the doctor. She said, "No, I'll be all right." I realized she was not good, and called our parish nurse, Marge Nester. She came in just a few minutes, looked at Anne and said, *"She'll have to go to the hospital."* She then called 911, and soon the ambulance and fire-truck with eight men were in the room.

Her oxygen count was 62 percent. The men in charge were concerned that she might not make it to the emergency room. There they gave her oxygen and got her count into the 90s, and ordered that she stay in the hospital overnight. She was in the hospital four nights, and then transferred to the Meadows nursing home, where she spent three nights, and passed away at 1:42 am,

Friday, February 5, a few hours less than a week after her attack. The diagnosis was a severe heart attack.

Our three children all appeared on the scene as soon as they were notified of her illness, and could make travel arrangements. Brenda took a special interest in caring for her mother. She insisted on sleeping in the room with her on a reclining chair every night, both in the hospital and nursing home. Don was also with her most nights. Rich stayed until the last day or two in the nursing home then went back home to Evanston. He spent a lot of time on the computer notifying relatives of her condition. After her death, he spent time pulling up pictures for a slide show in our visitation and memorial services. He also had a good picture of Anne on a hike at "Rocky Branch" enlarged which was displayed at the front of the church in our memorial service.

At the nursing home, Anne went to the dining hall to eat every meal, to the very last. The kids and I ate with her most meals. Brenda very faithfully stayed every night. Her last day, Thursday, February 4, 2010, Don, Brenda and I were with her for her noon meal. We had to feed her. She was asking mostly for ice cream. I was feeding her the ice cream and she continued to ask for more ice cream, more strawberry ice cream, and ate a lot at noon. For supper, Brenda said she did not swallow any food. Don and Brenda were both with her after supper. I had gone home and returned after supper. Anne was in a coma when I returned, was not responding when we spoke to her. I left for home again at 9:30, Don came home later. I was asleep, Don had just gotten home when Brenda called and reported that Mother had passed away.

Don woke me, we both went back to Meadows, called the funeral home, they came and picked up the body, and we all got back to home around 4:00 am, and did get a few hours of sleep yet that night.

All the while she was in the hospital and nursing home; she said she did not have pain. She died peacefully and in her sleep without ever complaining of pain.

The other family members were notified. Rich continued to keep relatives notified, and working on his slide. Sharon and the girls came in, Mac, Darrick and Nara came, Jan, Chris's mother brought him. The extended family, all except Brian, was here for the visitation and memorial services. Brian had visited a few months earlier over Christmas.

We arranged with Tim Schrag, our minister, that we would have the visitation on Sunday afternoon, 2:00 to 4:00, and a memorial service Monday, 10:00 am, followed by lunch. They were well attended. Family members dispersed gradually to meet their plane schedules returning home, and it was necessary for all of us to begin the adjustment to life without Anne.

Life is different for me, a big void, but as time passes, I'm getting adjusted to a schedule being alone. I often wish she were here to give her input and help make decisions. I realize that she was a person in her own right, a very forceful influence, but always a reasonable and considerate person in helping to manage our household. I miss, but am learning to live without her companionship. I have no other choice. Friends and family advise that "You just have to keep moving forward."

III - Civilian Public Service

Introduction

The U.S. Government made provision for Conscientious Objectors to serve in alternative service during World War II, in the Selective Service and Training Act (Burk-Wadsworth Bill), 1940. This provision resulted from specific requests and a number of intense meetings of representatives of the Historic Peace Churches (Mennonite, Brethren and Friends) with military and congressional personnel.

I was given my 4E (conscientious objector) classification in Kansas where I was teaching elementary school in McPherson County at the time of registration. I had simply filled out the application and submitted it to the Post Office and received the draft card in the mail with 4-E classification. It was easy for me to receive the 4E classification since I was living in a Mennonite community and the draft board was familiar with the peace stand of the Mennonite Church. As I look back I feel that it might have been good for me had I been required to defend my position.

Some young men, particularly those not from one of the "historic peace churches," had real difficulty obtaining a 4-E classification; difficulty to the point that when they refused to report to the military, they were arrested and sent to prison. A few isolated cases reported cruel treatment and genuine hardship in prison. However, such cases were rare. More often, appeals resulted in the eventual granting the 4-E classification. It was not until I had been in camp a while that I began thinking more seriously about implications, where I was, the difficulty some others had had in receiving 4-E classification, and what this all means for me to be here in camp.

I was drafted into Civilian Public Service on January 14, 1942, and released from service January 24, 1946, for a total of four years and ten days. The induction took me out of school a few weeks before the end of the semester at Goshen College, in Indiana. It was necessary for me to finish some of my course work after arriving in camp. This was done and I was given full credit for all courses when I returned to Goshen College after CPS.

Although I was two years older than my brother Dennis, we were both of draft age, and by the luck of the draw his number came up before mine, so he was inducted a few weeks ahead of me. Dennis, my brother-in-law, Abe Willems and I were inducted into the base camp at Sideling Hill, Pennsylvania. Experiences at Sideling Hill will be discussed later. My brother, Emerson was two years younger than Dennis, and because of his age, was not required to register when Dennis and I did, but was inducted into Camp Luray, in Virginia, October 1, 1943.

Emerson transferred from Camp Luray, and Abe from Sideling Hill, to a hospital for mentally retarded children in Exeter, Rhode Island. Abe was married to my sister Ruth, and they had a small son at the time. Eventually, Ruth and their son, Arnie, joined Abe in Rhode Island.

Sideling Hill Camp

Dennis and I were both inducted into Sideling Hill Camp, Unit #20, Wells Tannery, Pennsylvania. I left Millersburg, Ohio, by Greyhound bus on my official induction date, January 14, 1942, and arrived at Sideling Hill Camp, on the Turnpike in Pennsylvania. Dennis had arrived in camp approximately two weeks ahead of me. The bus stopped along the Turnpike just before entering the Sideling Hill Tunnel, perhaps no more than two hundred yards from the camp office. This was another beginning, or perhaps better to say, a continuation of the good life described in the previous chapter, which I experienced when leaving home for the first time and attending Hesston College. It was new experience and personally enjoyable.

Picture 36 - D. Paul & Dennis (left to right) at Sidling Hill CPS camp at the mouth of the Sideling Hill tunnel on the Pennsylvania Turnpike, 1942.

This is not to discredit my home life growing up in Protection, but it was a real contrast to the life I had been living at home, and I liked it. Looking back from today's perspective, I feel that the reason I was so impressed with the good and enjoyable life, is that

Picture 37 - Working on the Midway project in CPS on the Pennsylvania turnpike, 1942.

up to eighteen years of age I had lived at home on the farm, isolated pretty much from the world except church and school, and in high school I had virtually no social activities or other interaction outside of classes and a limited number of musical events.

My father was very strict in what he allowed us children to participate in, in high school. Some of the limitations placed on us in high school were due to economic circumstances. It was during the depression (1931-35). We lived on the farm, eleven miles south of town, we drove to school in a Model A Ford, picked up passengers along the way to help defray transportation costs, and our car was always full of students from neighboring families, who wished to car-pool. Never in those days would anyone have considered making a special trip to attend an athletic event, or for a music lesson for one person. My father supervised his children and controlled our home life quite rigidly, at least up to the time I went away to college. I should add that being the oldest boy, I was perhaps subjected to limitations not experienced by my younger siblings; at least it seemed to me that when a restriction was lifted for me, my younger brothers could enjoy it as soon as I did.

At Sideling Hill I continued to feel free. I was on my own except under the rules of the camp, which to me still represented freedom. I had the feeling that the boys in camp tended to be either good boys or bad boys. Some smoked and swore, chased women and seemed to be constant complainers and trouble-makers for the camp. Others seemed by nature to be cooperative. I think I tended to polarize the fellows because of my strict upbringing in the home. Upon entering camp we were cautioned to be ever mindful and careful about public opinion. In general, the public simply did not like conscientious objectors. That was no problem for me. I was just happy to go to camp, meet new friends, and take advantage of the many opportunities I did not have in my earlier life at Protection.

So, as I look back, I feel it is a fair statement to say that my best friends were among what I considered to be the "good boys." For example, in camp perhaps my closest friend was Cleo Swope. He arrived in Sideling Hill after I had been there a while, and he was assigned to be the Camp's business manager. He had training in that field and was a mature individual a year older than me.

He had access to the camp's pickup for getting supplies and running official errands. He was assigned to bunk in our dorm, and had a bed next to mine. We seemed to hit it off well right from the start. I was often invited to go with him, particularly on weekend errands. We got started going to Springs, Pennsylvania, together and got acquainted with two girls who were first cousins, Louise and Alta Otto. Cleo and I spent quite a bit of time with these girls up to the time that I transferred to Farnhurst, Delaware.

Some of the fellows in camp would go to town in the evenings and weekends and get involved with the girls in the local bars. It was on some of these occasions that the local citizen would sometimes object to the "yellow-bellied COs" having a good time while their own boys were away fighting in the trenches and in some instances killed in action. I was told that on a few occasions town officials or citizens in the community came to camp and complained to the camp director about some of the activities of the CPS boys when they came to town.

Somehow Cleo met and arranged a date with Alta Otto from the Mennonite Church in Springs. He had spoken to her about his friend, Paul, and they decided that we, Cleo and I, should come together and I would have a date with her cousin, Louise.

Fortunately, we had sort of a built-in access to a ride to Springs on weekends. One of our crew foremen, on a government assignment, lived near Springs, PA. He was very cordial and having found out that we had interests in Springs, offered to take Cleo and me along to Springs any week-end we chose to go. And I might say that that became a somewhat frequent weekend venture for Cleo and me.

In those days we did not have good communication facilities in our camp circumstances. Use of the camp telephone for personal reasons was not permitted. So, Cleo planned to go and suggested I go along. We went unannounced, planning that I go out with Louise. However, when we arrived, we learned that Louise had a date with another fellow.

Naturally, I was disappointed, but Alta suggested she ask her neighbor girl for me to take out that night. Even though I had not met or even seen the neighbor girl, I agreed. After all what do you do? Cleo wanted to stay and spend the evening with Alta, and I was along and didn't have a way back to camp before Monday morning with the crew foreman. I met this new girl at church and we were all set up for a date Sunday night. She was not nearly as attractive as Louise but was an OK date.

As things worked out, we were at Alta's home, for Sunday dinner. In the afternoon Alta, her cousin Louise, Cleo and I played croquet. We had a fun time, talking, laughing, and just being lighthearted in general. After the croquet game Cleo and I went for a walk, and the girls went in the house. When we returned, Alta called Cleo to the side for a private conversation. She told him Louise had changed her mind. She would like to go out with me, and would be willing to break her date with this other fellow if I would break mine with the neighbor girl. This was kind of an embarrassing thing for us to do, but Louise was a very attractive person and I really wanted to pursue her friendship. So, we both broke our dates and were together that evening.

From that point on, we had quite a serious relationship, even to the point that I spent a week of my furlough working for Louise's father, in his brick factory. And I might add that that week intensified our relationship. But as the ball bounces, I was eventually transferred to Farnhurst. After that we carried on a light correspondence, for a while but eventually that stopped and I thought we forgot about each other.

Years later, 1946, after I was discharged from CPS, and had a summer job working in a pottery factory, Louise, with her father and mother stopped at my folk's home in Berlin, Ohio. At the time I was working and my mother was the only one at home. They asked about Paul. My mother was not aware of my former relationship with Louise, and told them I was working in the pottery factory and was planning to attend Goshen College later this summer and winter and graduate a year from now.

Apparently that was discouraging enough that they drove on without revealing to my mother anything about the relationship Louise and I had had while I was at Sideling Hill. My mother asked me why they would drive out of their way so far for nothing, and I had some explaining to do. On that occasion I did not see Louise or her parents, and the relationship just died a natural death. I must admit, however, that fond memories linger.

Work Crews at Sideling Hill

Most of the work at Sideling Hill Camp was in forestry service and soil conservation. The camp accommodated between 125 and 150 fellows. We had four work crews with twenty or so in each. Some of the fellows were assigned to camp duty: cooking, clean-up, laundry, janitorial, office, and the like, all of which were functions necessary to keep the camp operating.

I chose to join one of the crews so I could get away from camp. I was lucky. I was assigned to Shambaugh's crew. Mr. Shambaugh was recognized to be the most reasonable of the four government foremen. My friend, Daryl Frey, was assigned to Mr. English's crew. As I recall conversation with Daryl and others on English's crew, he was a driver. The boys on his crew complained constantly that they were kept on the go all day long. Mr. Shambaugh kept us reasonably busy but often he would encourage us to rest. Occasionally he would leave the crew alone, come back and see us loafing and just join us. Particularly in the winter-time, on cold days he'd have us build a fire and sit around and keep warm, at least he never told us to work harder. He often commented about how the CPS boys were getting a lot more work done than the CCC boys he had supervised earlier in FDR's work program. He'd tell us just keep warm.

Sometimes we'd talk to him about our lack of ambition or whether we might have a problem if we didn't get more work done. He said he figured that we were in camp because of our conscience. We were spending some of the prime days of our life and working for no wages and that we should not be driven, at least to any degree of discomfort.

The CCC Program had operated from these same barracks in the 1930s. Our CPS camp was re-constructed from the CCC Camp of the '30s to the CO Camp of the '40s. Mr. Shambaugh's evaluation is borne out from Col. Lewis F. Kosch's statement in a Senate Subcommittee Hearing, August 19, 1942, when he said,

"We have mature men who know how to do the work and how to handle tools, while in the CCC we just had boys who didn't know a shovel from an ax ..."

He, Shambaugh, often expressed appreciation for our cooperation, which he said didn't exist in the CCC Camp. The fellows on Mr. English's crew complained that they never had opportunity to even enjoy break time.

I was at Sideling Hill nine months, January to October, 1941. This period provided all kinds of climate and working conditions. We were in the heart of the Appalachian Mountains, out of doors every day, rain or shine, hot or cold. I was in good physical condition, slept well and ate heartily.

Every morning we'd report in, at the camp yard for work at 8:00 o'clock. We'd ride to work in the big army trucks provided by the government. We'd load our tools, axes, brush hooks, pruning or digging tools or whatever we'd be using, and then all climb into the back of the big truck on steps that could be pulled in and out from under the bed of the truck. In the truck we would sit on side benches, protected by canvass top and side covers, which could be tied shut in cold or rainy weather. Some of the campers who had truck drivers' licenses would drive the trucks. One or two of the driver's buddies would usually ride in the cab beside him. The rest of the crew would ride in the back, and we'd head for our project, sometimes up to 30 or 40 miles away. Our closest project was planting trees and bushes, (sorry to admit it, thousands of honeysuckle) on the slopes above Sideling Hill Tunnel next to camp. I say sorry because honeysuckle, a non-native and invasive plant, has become a serious problem in our parks and woodlands today, and which foresters and environmentalists are working hard to eradicate.

Each day the kitchen crew would pack lunches for us, and at noon each of us had his individual sack lunch. Lunch hour was always enjoyable. We'd sit under shade trees in the summer time or around the fire in the winter, chat, joke, kid each other or see who could tell the tallest yarns.

One episode I recall, perhaps I should call it a prank, was with Jake Herr, a Lancaster County camper who was accused by someone in our crew of having lice. He assured us that he didn't and became somewhat vehement about it. With our insistence, and his blatant denial, he finally offered to prove it. While some of the fellows were "egging him on," I ran to the truck to get my camera Jake pulled down his pants and was showing us his pubic hair with no lice when I snapped a picture of the procedure. I had the film developed by one of the photographers in camp. We questioned whether or not a commercial developer would develop the film in those days because they would consider it pornographic, and refuse. At any rate it came out a beauty, a prized photo.

We had a lot of fun with it in camp and I kept it in a protected place, but my picture was confiscated years later by Anna Wiebe, Anne's (my wife) brother's wife, when her girls Evelyn and Esther, then about ten and seven years old had snooped into my suitcase when we were living with Grandma Wiebe, Anne's mother, on the farm at Beatrice, Nebraska, when I was commuting to Lincoln for graduate school one summer. Apparently the girls showed their mother the picture they had found and she, Anna, my wife's sister-in-law, was not only shocked, but she destroyed the picture without saying anything to me. She later mentioned it to Anne, but by that time the picture was gone.

Now back to our work project in camp. We would work till quitting time and start back to camp so we'd arrive there at 5:00 pm. This general program continued day after day, week after week and month after month. Off duty activities were pretty much what the campers made it. In the summer time we had an intense softball program going. In the winter time we did some cross-country skiing, hiking, and occasionally go to town to do miscellaneous shopping.

Picture 38 – The Miller boys 'horsing around' smoking cigars on the porch in 1942 and again c.a. 1990; from left to right, are Emerson, Paul and Dennis Miller, along with their brother-in-law, Abe Willems.

Extra-Curricular Activities

I bought my first pair of cross-country skis while at Sideling Hill Camp. It was a pair of wooden skis with no bindings. They were made available by the camp office to the campers for seven dollars, fifty cents a pair. This was supposedly a good deal so I bought a pair. Bindings were not available at the time I bought the skis, and for the few times I went cross-country skiing while in camp, I simply borrowed skis from other campers. I kept that original pair of skis with my earthly possessions all the way to Normal, Illinois, from 1942 to the 1960s, and never used them. Even here in Normal, they were stored in the attic for several years. Eventually, I got them down and put them on a garage for, I think, one or two dollars.

In summer time softball was our main extracurricular activity. We had four dorms in our camp and each dorm had a team. Games were scheduled so that each played the same number of games with each of the other teams. I was in Dorm 1 which had just half as many fellows as each of the other three dorms. The chapel occupied one-half of our barrack. However, by some coincidence, we had good softball players in our half dorm. A full barrack housed approximately forty campers. Ours had space for approximately twenty beds and twenty fellows.

Probably most significant for the ball team was the fact that we had an Amish boy, Alvin Schrock, who was a good pitcher. When he came in he boasted that in all the games he had ever pitched at home, he had never lost a game. In camp he was beaten occasionally, but he was still the best pitcher in camp. We had a snappy infield: Quinton Martin, at second base, Willie Beachy, an Amish boy, at short stop, and Paul Miller at third base. During the summer I was in camp, 1942, we played two rounds of probably twenty or so games per round, and as I recall, Dorm 1 won both rounds. We played practically every evening of the week, and sometimes on Saturday. The camp administration and some of the more conservative fellows frowned at playing on Sunday. It was during this summer in Sideling Hill Camp, that I improved my ball playing skills noticeably. This interest was carried over into our still more serious ball playing at Delaware State Hospital, and the following year at Goshen College.

CPS campers were given furloughs for vacations at the same rate as the enlisted military men, thirty days per year. We would use this time in a variety of ways. It was common for some of the fellows with homes in the same area to plan their furloughs together, then someone with a car or van would take a load home for their furlough vacation.

One of the more important activities not mentioned above was men's chorus. We did quite a lot of singing. On one occasion while I was in Sideling Hill, the members of the men's chorus planned their furloughs together and took a tour through Pennsylvania and Ohio giving musical programs at the various Mennonite churches in the areas.

In addition to the chorus, we had a quartet composed of my brother Dennis, my brother-in-law Abe Willems, Orie Yoder and me. Orie was first tenor, Abe second tenor, Dennis bass and I was baritone. We all got along well together, harmonized well, worked hard, and practiced a lot. We were a scheduled part of the program and rendered several numbers on each of the programs where the chorus appeared. Our quartet was broken up when Orie Yoder enlisted in the army. Later, Dennis and I transferred to Delaware State Hospital, and Abe went to Exeter, Rhode Island so that was the end of that quartet except for memories, and occasional reminiscing with Dennis and Abe when our families got together. I met and had breakfast with Orie once in Smithville, Ohio when we were visiting our son Rich and his wife several decades later. Although he was a good first tenor as a young fellow in camp, he had given up singing altogether.

With a group of one hundred to one hundred fifty fellows together for an extended period of time in an isolated spot in an abnormal environment such as a CPS camp, one will inevitably find spontaneous and creative ways to break the monotony. Some of these such as the music and softball programs described above are constructive and socially acceptable.

Others tend to be on the marginal side, pranks and tricks, and sometimes at the expense of the other person. One event in which I participated causes me to chuckle even forty years after the fact. One of the fellows in our dorm, Dorm 1, had heard while working on the project during the day that one of the fellows from Dorm III had some kind of dislike for one of our Dorm I residents and was planning to upset his bed while he was asleep tonight. The plan was that this fellow was to come in after lights were out and everyone supposedly asleep, upset this fellow's bed and hightail it out the other end of the dorm.

The arrangement of beds in our dorm was such that my bed was on the east-side of the isle running down the middle of the dorm, and the last bed on the south end of the dorm, next to the chapel. The fellow who was to be upset was across the aisle from me and second from the end next to the chapel. None of us liked the idea of anyone from an outside dorm intruding, furthermore, we had enough of the "dorm spirit," that we tended to stick together and defend each other much like a family. Naturally, we had internal spats, disagreements, and conflicts in a normal fashion, but let an outside intruder pick on one of our number and we were together to defend him.

Consequently, when we heard the plan, we prepared to meet the challenge head on. We placed a dummy in the bed to be upset. The regular occupant was moved temporarily to another bed in our dorm which at the time was unoccupied. Our plan was to let the outsider come in, upset the bed, then I was to pounce on him since I was in the end bed next to the chapel, then the others would come to my aid. If we caught him, we were to take him to the shower, which was a hundred yards down a path in a separate building, force him to take off his clothes and give him a good cold shower.

We were all set, none of us was asleep. Sure enough, half an hour after the lights were out and all was quiet, the north door of our dorm opened and in walked Howard Yoder, a big guy, six feet, two inches, weighing 190 pounds. He had a very pronounced walk pretending not to be hiding anything. After all occasionally some of our own dorm mates, having been out to the toilet, would come in and return to bed without trying to hide anything. Howard walked the length of the dorm, came to his target bed, grabbed it, tipped it upside down and ran for the chapel door. I sprang out of bed in pursuit. He got half way through the chapel before I caught up with him. I grabbed him around his shoulders from the back, wrestled him to the floor, and held him for a while. My dorm mates, I think all twenty of them, were "Johnny on the spot," right there behind me.

We gave Howard our orders. They were such that he didn't question them or any of us. He marched to the shower. We were on all sides of him so there was no way he could escape. He stripped without resistance and we turned on the shower forcing him to stay in the shower till he was cooled off, then told him to leave his clothes off and go back to his dorm. We ushered him to his dorm door, and left him there, returning to our dorm dying with laughter. The next day the whole camp found out about it. The circumstances were such that without question, it discouraged others from intruding in other dorms, at least with unfriendly intent.

My nine months in Sideling Hill was a pleasant experience for me and had a positive influence on my life. Some of the fellows were always bitching and complaining; others were constant trouble-makers. It was hard for me to understand this. I was still experiencing the early years of my liberation period and was enjoying it.

Dorm Captain

Sometime before this Howard Yoder incident, I had been selected dorm captain. Each dorm had a captain who was to represent the dorm at staff meetings, and report personnel problems when they arose, and also was responsible for carrying out discipline should it be necessary. For instance, the captain was to see that the lights were turned off at the stipulated time, report AWOLs should they occur, and deal with things which needed to be reported to the administration. It was a system whereby the camp administration could keep in touch at the grass roots.

Periodically, we had dorm council meetings to discuss personnel problems, gripes, and the like. The captain was to be re-elected periodically. I think every three or four months. I accepted the first election somewhat as a mandate or responsibility everyone should be willing to assume. The second time around I thought it was time for a change. Some of the fellows talked to me about continuing for a second time around. At first I refused. I couldn't understand why they wouldn't want Cleo Swope. He was a camper and had been appointed as the camp's business manager. He was a neat, handsome fellow whom everybody liked.

When we were anticipating the election, I campaigned for Cleo, and encouraged my dorm mates to vote for him. When the election was held, again I was really surprised and actually somewhat perplexed. I was elected again, and by a large majority. In a way I was disappointed. After all it was a responsibility that wasn't always easy, and too, I knew that Cleo would have been a good and sort of a natural choice since he, as business manager, was working closely with the director and other administrative personnel. On the other hand, I must admit that to be elected a second time was rewarding. It represented good rapport with my peers. Also, personally, it contributed to my personal liberation process which I was experiencing.

Recalling my boyhood background, I was a bashful, country boy, from a conservative Mennonite family. I went barefooted all summer long, even after I was in high school, and wore bibbed overalls and went barefooted to our country church on Sunday evening. For some reason I had a pronounced inferiority complex. My younger brother, Dennis, was taller and bigger than I was, and I thought he was better liked by the girls and everyone else, than I was. I didn't really get over this inferiority feeling completely until I had been through my four years of CPS, and was in Goshen College. It was a slow process. My camp experiences and later Goshen College helped me to gain some real confidence. As I look back on this election experience at Sideling Hill, I consider it a sort of a beginning of "coming out of my shell."

I can still remember vividly, even after six decades, one of my experiences in handling discipline problems as dorm captain. Not only do I remember it but also the other party most directly involved remembers it as well. Lights in the dorms were to go out at 10:00 o'clock. After a reasonable time (never clearly defined) everyone was to be quiet. Usually, when things were noisy, I'd simply shout, "All right, you guys, shut up," or some similar comment. That'd do the trick.

One evening that didn't work. Several fellows were talking and one in particular was talking loud. I had given them the signal to be quiet, and had done so several times, and still they continued talking and laughing. I was getting irritated and wasn't sure just what I could do. The noise was coming from about half way down our dorm. There were probably four or five beds between me and the noise makers. One of them, John Martin, was sitting up in bed and laughing in his loud boisterous manner. I picked up one of my work shoes and threw it at him. It hit him between the shoulders. At first he didn't know what had hit him. He began to catch on when he saw the shoe; then he heard me shout again, "I told you guys to shut up."

From that point, things were desperately quiet, and no more problems, at least for that night. To this day, when I see John at reunions he will invariably recall the day I threw my shoe at him and then follow with his loud boisterous laugh. The other fellows in my dorm commended me on different occasions for the way I stopped the noise. They knew they were all allowed to have a good time, and they also knew that sometimes a good time can be overdone. I think my unwritten policy was that when it's at the expense of someone else, then it's time to stop. Most of us had to go to work the next day so we needed sleep.

Another one of my experiences that made a negative impression on me and one that I vividly recall even after decades, was, Merlo Zimmerman pulling Sammy Stoltzfus' whiskers as we were riding to work in the back of our truck. Naturally, riding twenty to thirty miles to work in the back of a big truck, sitting on the benches along the sides and front of the bed, day after day, became monotonous. And, naturally, energetic young men will find something to do to break the monotony.

Sammy was an Amishman with a long beard. He was somewhat mentally handicapped. The report was that he would never have passed the physical examination of the army, but for conscientious objectors the physicals were not so important, and also it was quite obvious that COs were never given mental tests with their physicals. So he was in camp and the tendency on the part of many of the boys was to use Sammy as part of their entertainment.

Sammy seemed to enjoy the attention until they started picking on him physically. Merlo had the habit of pulling Sammy's whiskers. He'd nip them a little. Sammy would ignore it. Merlo would pick again, and again. Eventually Sammy would fight back. He'd hit Merlo when he'd reach for his whiskers. This would continue until Sammy would get so mad, he'd stand up in the truck, all the while it was rolling down the turnpike at near speed limit, and sometimes Sammy would actually start fighting.

The tussling and fighting would go on until at times it appeared that there was danger of someone falling out the back of the truck. After so much of this, I started coming to Sammy's rescue. Several times I really laid into Merlo when he'd start picking on Sammy. It seemed to help some, but as I look back on the scene, it appears that Sammy was the victim of the fun-making for as long as I was in Sideling Hill Camp.

Merlo Zimmerman was transferred to, the parachuting fire-fighting unit in Montana, and I was told that through the efforts of the camp administration, Sammy was eventually given a physical and mental examination and from that obtained his release from service. Obviously, Merlo pulling Sammy's whiskers came to a halt, but probably not until after the transfer and release of these fellows and after I had transferred out of Sideling Hill.

Life in CPS was always somewhat unsettling. To us when considering registering, having been reared in the Mennonite family and church community, CPS seemed to be the natural way to go. Some boys did go to prison when not given CO classification, and some Mennonites enlisted in the army even though it was contrary to the church policy. Occasionally some of our CPS boys would become frustrated and dissatisfied with camp life and enlist then transfer to the military.

For those of us who chose CPS, and did not want to participate in the military, we knew our only viable option was to stay in CPS service, but even so, we would sometimes become disgruntled and feel that we were wasting time. We were wasting time at a stage in life that should be the most productive years of our life. As I looks back on it half a century later, the time in CPS was in no sense a waste of time. Rather, it was a genuine enriching experience.

Because of our feeling at the time many of us kept abreast of the various opportunities, and were looking for other projects to which we might transfer and which might perhaps be more meaningful for us. After serving for a few months in a base camp, and upon recommendation of the director, it became possible for campers to transfer to units with more specialized lines of work.

Among various projects approved by the National Service Board for Religious Objectors, were mental hospital service, agricultural experimental stations, dairy farmers, smoke jumpers, coast and geodetic survey, public health in Puerto Rico, training schools, dairy herd testing, guinea pig starvation project at the University of Minnesota, and the like.

After having been in camp for several months and with the negative aspects rising to the fore with increasing frequency, some of us began to look rather seriously for something different. Realizing how important it was to have a group of compatible fellows with similar interests and values we began looking not only at the nature of the units that opened up, but also at the campers who would consider volunteering.

In such a situation we learned that Delaware State Hospital was requesting a unit of twenty-five boys. Those interested tended to discuss among themselves and to advertise it among others who were thought to be potentially compatible members of the group. The interest became more intense when Dr. Tarumianz, Superintendent at Delaware State Hospital, came to our camp and had a meeting for all the boys who thought they might be interested in transferring to his hospital.

I can recall vividly when my friend Daryl Frey sat down and discussed seriously with my brother and me, and a number of others who were interested, the pros and cons of transferring to this unit at this time. The more we considered it the more attractive it seemed to become. We finally had a number of campers who were ready to commit themselves to transfer to Delaware State Hospital. We had a group of nineteen men from Sideling Hill Camp. Then the additional four to make up the twenty-five, came from the Howard CPS Camp, Howard, Pennsylvania, which was a side camp of Sideling Hill.

Formal applications were submitted to the camp office for the nineteen. The paper work was put in process and we had only to wait for the official "go" from The National Service Board for Religious Objectors, Washington, D.C.. That office gave approval, and they in turn, notified the superintendent at Delaware State Hospital of our arrival date.

The twenty five were selected and plans were completed. We were ready to make the move. Of the original group, five were married. The wives were welcomed employees at the hospital. Two of the wives, Ruth Hess and Esther Beck, went ahead of the campers, and were on the grounds and had received their job assignments before the fellows arrived.

Assistant Director Assigned

Our camp director at Sideling Hill at the time was Sanford G. Shetler of Johnstown, Pennsylvania. Soon after the members of our unit were picked and we were awaiting the official transfers notice, Shetler approached me and asked if I'd be willing to serve as the leader and official representative or spokesman for the group in the transfer process. That would mean to carry the official papers, answer any official questions that might arise regarding a group of military-age men traveling together like this during the war. Then it would be necessary for this person to make official contact with the administrative personnel at the hospital when the group arrived.

When approached with this opportunity, my first reaction was "why me?" Surely someone else in the group would be better qualified than me. I was reluctant and expressed that sentiment to Shetler at the time. He said, "Think about it and let me know in a day or two."

Today as I attempt to analyze my reactions and attitude in situations such as this, the best explanation I can come up with is that in our home, we were conditioned with the attitude of *demut* (humility). Rather than to jump at such an opportunity, and to push myself to the front, I seemed to have the tendency to fall back, and let someone else do it.

To a large extent I think I have overcome this tendency, perhaps even too much. Nonetheless, I knew I must make a decision for Shetler. While I was thinking about it, some of the fellows who were in our assigned group approached me and encouraged me to accept the assignment. Again, to reflect the strong influence Daryl Frey had on my life, he came to me and talked very pointedly, "Paul, by all means do it. If you don't he's going to appoint so and so," a fellow in our group we didn't particularly like. I was so strongly encouraged by a number of the fellows in the group, that I told Shetler I would accept the assignment.

This was a more important decision than I ever imagined at the time, and was one I have never regretted. In fact, I often think of how different my life might have been had I not accepted this assignment. When this decision was made, I, and I think Sanford Shetler as well, had the notion that this assignment was to extend only during the period of transfer from camp to the Delaware State Hospital, just a few days, and then I would go back to regular camper status.

That, however, was not the case. The superintendent of the hospital delegated to me the assignment of being director of the unit at the hospital, right from the beginning. My official title was to be Assistant Director of the CPS Unit #58. The Superintendent himself, Dr. M.A Tarumianz, a strong-willed, patriarchal, Jewish doctor, let it be known that he was the official director. I was to be his assistant. My assignment involved half-time administrative duties from the beginning, and when the unit was expanded to thirty-five the following spring, I was given full time for my administrative duties.

I do not recall the details of how the original nineteen from Sideling Hill made the trip to Farnhurst, Delaware. Some of the boys had furloughs built up and took their days off before reporting to the hospital on the specified date of arrival. The fellows who lived in Lancaster, or other points between Sideling Hill and Delaware, drove their own cars at their own expense, and reported on the designated arrival date. As I recall, we had a week-end and a day to report. We were to check in on October 14, 1942.

The Farnhurst Story

Let's regress a bit and consider how I got started in writing up the CPS Story. At the 1989 Farnhurst reunion held on the Bluffton College campus, I gave a talk on some of the background events of our unit. I had done considerable research and tried to pull together material which would be of interest to particularly the men and women who had spent time at Farnhurst. It was surprising to me that I ended up with a seventy page, single spaced computer printed manuscript. After presenting the material, a number of the fellows asked me for a copy of the material I had presented. I had done the original thing for myself and had included a great deal of material on my personal and early life not really related to Farnhurst. So I promised them I'd have something ready for the Farnhurst group at our next reunion. This meant doing some serious editing and organizing of my material.

The nature of my duties as assistant director of the Unit provided materials that would be useful in my report. I had served as assistant director of the Farnhurst CPS Unit #58, during my entire Farnhurst stint. I was appointed leader for the transfer from Sideling Hill, October, 1942, served as the assistant director, and remained with the unit until my discharge in January, 1946. My duties as director included keeping records of work days, furloughs of the group and sending monthly reports to the National Service Board for Religious Objectors (NSBRO) in Washington, D.C.

I also had unofficial records of and information about the group, records of our anniversary meetings held on or near October 14, each year. I dug up material on our committees and the constitution of our Unit Council. I had a detailed account of the performances of the Crusaders Quartet; I kept a rather detailed record and scrapbook on our softball team, games played, and scores, team standing in the league, batting averages, news clippings, and the like.

In addition to these materials which I had kept in my files, I had a copy of the book *Congress Looks at the Conscientious Objector,* which was published in 1943. It gives a rather detailed account of all the governmental meetings and transactions which transpired between various governmental agencies, church leaders, and other groups interested in the conscientious objectors, prior to, and during the war years. The more pertinent parts of this will be included in Appendix III, page 351.

I attempted to glean out the parts that I thought would be of most interest to the people in our Farnhurst Unit and make this available to those interested, and deliver my book at the 50th anniversary reunion to be held, August, 1992. I accepted all of this as a challenge and went to work.

In preparing the story it was difficult for me to know just where to draw the line, what to include and what to leave out. Obviously, some of the experiences I relate, for example, on the work crew at Sideling Hill, will have more interest to those of our group who were also on the same work crew, and would possibly be of little interest to others. And I apologized to all those who might have to wade through the non-pertinent materials. In the following pages I will summarize the information I pulled together.

I was in the Sideling Hill Camp nine months. It was from Sideling Hill and the Sideling Hill side-camp of Howard that the original twenty-five fellows in the Farnhurst unit came. Others in our unit were transferred from other CPS units at later dates and consequently would not be as directly related to the Sideling Hill story. Also, I am aware that the unit continued for approximately eight months after I was discharged, and my report does not include events that transpired after my discharge. In fact, I am not acquainted with and have never met some of the men who came in the later months to replace those being discharged. Since this is My Story, I limited it to my experiences and observations.

That material was put together in a spiral bound book and distributed at the 1992 Farnhurst reunion.

Our Arrival and Introduction to Hospital Work

When we arrived at Farnhurst everything was well planned at the hospital. They were ready to receive us. It was a rainy afternoon. People in the store were looking out of the window at us and people on the sidewalks would gaze curiously. We learned later that Dr. Tarumianz had told the employees that COs were different. They would look different, they dressed different, and they would do different things and be different from other people. It was surprising to some to discover that the COs were being just as human as they.

First we were instructed to move into Kent Hall, our living quarters, and then we were to report to the auditorium for the orientation they had planned for us with Miss Kahl in charge. Three or four psychiatric doctors, who served the various wards, gave us lectures which, at that time, were virtually meaningless to us. Here we were, a bunch of conservative COs, mostly farmers and many with only eighth grade education trying to make sense of these lectures which were all spoken in broken English. The psychiatrists were all foreign Jewish psychiatrists and used technical words utterly foreign to us. We learned later that most of the ward doctors really could not communicate well, and were probably not qualified to serve outside in private practice. After this ordeal of listening to the doctor's lecture, we were then to receive our assignments from Dr. Tarumianz, and be prepared to report to work the next day.

As mentioned above, everyone reported on the assigned arrival date. I met Dr. Trumianz personally and submitted the legal papers to him. Our first instructions were to move into our living quarters. Our dorm, Kent Hall, was a long one-story building with an L-shaped wing on each end and made up mostly of small individual rooms. Just inside the entrance door at the center of the long building was the reception room where the housemother, Mrs. Scope, spent most of her on-duty hours. To the left as one enters was the section for the single men. To the right was the section with larger rooms for married couples.

We were fortunate to have one building where all the CPS men and couples could live in close proximity. We were not aware at the time but later realized now how important those common living quarters were. They provided the opportunity for close interaction within the group, and a strong sense of community spirit. I am convinced today that it was this factor perhaps more than any other which causes our group to feel bonded and to respond so favorably to continuing reunions, and keeping a circular letter going for the next sixty years.

As I edit this, February, 2005, the report now is that we had our final reunion in Richland, Ohio, October, 2004. Eleven former campers and 10 wives were present, the youngest 78, and several in poor health. It had become obvious to us at our reunion 2002, that we would soon reach a "dead end," but decided to try it again. At this last reunion, after discussing the matter seriously, we decided the time had come. It was our final reunion. Also, the circle-letter started by several wives in the early 1950s was continued until after it had been lost and re-started for the third time and finally discontinued April, 2009. The reunions and circle letter will be discussed in more detail later.

Now, let's go back to our 1942 story. In our orientation, we met Miss Mose who was in charge of the work schedules for attendants. She had to keep account of days off, getting substitutes for days off, sickness, and the like. She was sort of a "queer." In a way a little retarded, at least unconventional and difficult to reason with, but still very precise in performing her duties. She was the type of person who, would have had a hard time keeping a job in the outside world, but could manage okay in the mental hospital setting. When we speak about her to each other, or even mention her name years later, it usually brings understanding smiles or comments.

I recall how she made it clear and emphasized that whenever Dr. Tarumianz, the superintendent, enters the room we were to all stand at attention and remain standing until we were told to be seated. We were instructed further, to do this whenever any of our superiors entered the room.

To describe Miss Mose's personality more fully, it might be helpful to include one of the remarks I made in my third anniversary celebration speech, October 13, 1945. I copy this quote from the notes of my speech, "Miss Mose, you've been keeping the work schedule, arranging time, etc., for the CPS men for three years. The fellows say that sometimes you try to get hardboiled and strict with them, but there's not one of them, not a single one who wouldn't defend you to their last breath. We can't say that about everybody. Tell us why. Is it your personality? How do you do it? What is your secret?" I do not recall her response; however she took it in a humorous vein and considered it a compliment as it was meant to be.

The orientation also included an explanation of how the various buildings contained various kinds of patients. Patients were assigned to the various wards depending on their conditions. They had men's wards, women's wards, white wards and colored wards, reception wards, violent wards, observation ward, and so on. Attendants were assigned to work twelve-hour shifts.

Little did any of us realize when appointments were being made, how important that bit of information was. We did not know that some jobs had considerably shorter and more desirable working hours, and that there was a big difference in some of the jobs. And here we had some choices but at the time did not realize how important those choices were until we got into the daily routine of our assignments.

In the lectures we were told that these people in the hospital were not insane, but were ill, mentally ill, and that we were treating them for their illness. After approximately two hours of these talks and listening to a lot of general information about how they served the meals, took care of our laundry, and other incidentals, the Big Chief, Dr. Tarumianz, walked in. And you should have seen the response of the obedient COs. We all rose to our feet immediately. He appeared to be pleased, told us to be seated and then got right down to business at hand, to make specific assignments for each of the twenty-five fellows assigned to his hospital. It did not take us long to learn that Tarumianz was the boss. He was, in a very real sense, the chief of his hospital.

He did not know any of our names, but his plan was to allow choices in the order of the amount of education each had. In time it became obvious to us that he was very status conscious. He first asked how many of us were college graduates. Two raised their hands, Daryl Frey and Eugene Bassinger. He then told these two they could choose first from the various jobs available. Daryl chose to work in the recreation department. Eugene Bassinger couldn't make up his mind, after all what did he have to base his decision on? Consequently, his decision was postponed. Dr.Tarumianz moved on and next got to those who had two years of college. This included my brother, Dennis, and I. We both chose to go to the recreation department with Daryl Frey. He then went to those with one year of college, then to those who graduated from high school. Lester Charles went to the bookkeeping office, I'm not sure of his educational level, but he got a good job with good hours mainly because he had been working in the office and doing bookkeeping at Sideling Hill Camp and requested an office position here. Dr. Tarumianz then went down the levels by years of high school, and finally to those who had only a grade school education. Those remaining were assigned as attendants to the various wards. I felt that the hospital administration, in general, attempted to take advantage of the various skills, and to some extent, take into account the interests and desires of the fellows.

Eugene Bassinger, who as a college graduate, had first choice but had not yet made up his mind, was assigned to the Observation Ward. It was a small separate building some distance from the complex of buildings which housed the other wards. We found out later that this was the ward for patients with money, those who did not want to be placed with the rank and file of mental patients. Eventually, all the fellows received their assignments and were told to report the next day. A new world was awaiting all of us. And we were eager to get started.

During the time of our service at the hospital we had fellows in many different roles, laundrymen, office clerks, truck drivers, cooks, switch board operators, laboratory and x-ray technicians, recreation supervisors, hydro-therapist, superintendent's private chauffeur, barber and ground supervisor. Some of these latter positions were not open at the time of the original assignments but were assigned later as the needs arose. It didn't take long for us to realize that a few of us were, inadvertently lucky so far as the particular job assignments were concerned. All of the attendants worked a grueling twelve hour shift. The others had eight-hour shifts, and some of those were rather loose eight-hour jobs.

To clarify, the three of us in the recreation department had responsibilities of taking patients on walks around the grounds, supervising ball games for patients who were capable of this level of activity, working on the grounds raking leaves, or on rainy days go to the gym or art shop and supervise whatever activities were available for patients.

Meals were served to the patients on the wards at 11:00 am, so we had to have all patients back on the wards by meal time. Our duties were consequently finished as soon as we got the patients back to the ward. The evening meal for patients was served at four o'clock. So again, our duties were usually finished for the day around four o'clock.

Our office for the recreation personnel was the art shop, actually a large space in the basement of one of the main buildings where tables and chairs were set up for crafts, painting, drawing and the like. We would meet here to plan the activities of the day and receive orders in case the main office or ground supervisors had jobs for us to do.

When Dennis, Daryl, and I began our work two other people were also working in the department, George and Grace. I do not know their last names were but both had been former patients. Grace was responsible for the art work. She worked mostly with women. George worked with Dennis, Daryl and me taking patients for walks, supervising ground crews, and the like. Even though both had formerly been patients, they were both reasonable, very easy to work with and performed their jobs well as regular employees. We soon learned that not all ex-patients who were discharged and put on the payroll were as well qualified and easy to be around as the two we were working with. In some cases, and particularly with alcoholics, the ex-patient was certainly not as dependable as George and Grace.

You can see why I described our jobs in the recreation department as loosely structured and why we felt fortunate to have these assignments. We were very much on our honor. We had a wide variety of activities, and the hours were as ideal as one could ask. I feel that we assumed responsibility for our work and did perhaps more than was asked of us even though our tasks were of such a nature that they could often be sacrificed for other responsibilities which at a particular time might be considered by the hospital administration to be more important.

Several months after we were on duty someone was needed in the laundry, to drive the truck to pick up and deliver laundry, so they pulled Dennis out of the recreation department and put him on the laundry truck in a permanent position. He liked this job and remained in this position for the remainder of his time at the hospital. I worked in the recreation department only in the forenoon and spent the afternoon in the office.

My office was an old but adequate big room on the ground floor of one of the main buildings. It was in a good location in the sense that it was located in the flow of traffic between our lodging house and dining hall where we ate. It was readily available for any of our group who wanted to see me for any reason. Frey was shifted to the out-of-door maintenance department and recreation department in combination. After a year or so, our group was expanded to thirty-five, and I was assigned full time to administrative duties.

As alluded to earlier, my administrative duties included keeping daily records of all members of our unit, the number working, those on sick leave, scheduling furlough or leave assignments and the like. These records had to be sent to the National Service Board for Religious Objectors in Washington, D.C.. I was responsible to receive and answer all correspondence directed to our Unit. It was also my duty to receive guests and arrange for their meals, and lodging. When complaints or personnel problems arose, it was my responsibility to work these out and/or convey the problem to Dr. Tarumianz. When matters were to be discussed with Dr. Tarumianz, my time with him was almost always between four and four-thirty in the afternoon.

It was usually a somewhat tense ordeal to deal with Tarumianz. He was dictatorial and demanding. He had a way of putting across the message that he was boss. It was usually hopeless to try to get him to reconsider or change his mind on an issue when he had once made a decision. There were occasions where he would have obviously been better off to listen to the opinions of others but he ran a tight ship, carried out his wishes, and in spite of it was well respected, not only on the hospital grounds but in the State Legislature, and also by the general public. He almost always treated the CPS boys with favor. In general, I am not aware that any of the fellows or their wives working at the hospital, ever definitely opposed him or expressed hostility toward him personally. On the contrary, Dr. Tarumianz always demanded respect.

As I look back on the relationship he had with members of our unit, I have to appreciate his tolerance and what I feel was his genuine appreciation for us as honest and dependable workers. For example, he had the wife of one of our boys, Ruth Hess, at the front office, working at the telephone switch-board. She was the receptionist, the first person visitors and guests would contact when they visited the hospital.

The thing that made this more intriguing was that she was a member of the Brethren in Christ church, a nice appearing woman, wore plain clothes, with an attractive white prayer head covering. She was distinguished by her dress, always neat, but it was different from anything they were used to here at the hospital. Her husband, Raymond Hess, was assigned by Dr. Tarumianz to be his personal chauffeur. The hospital owned two state cars, both Pontiacs. I think we usually considered the Hess' jobs to be the most prestigious since they were working in the main office, close to the people at the top.

Regarding wages in CPS, in base camp, Sideling Hill, as well as all base camps, draftees received nothing in actual pay. We were provided room, board and laundry, also medical attention that could be administered in camp. Usually, each camp had a nurse. At Sideling Hill, we were fortunate to have a medical doctor and a nurse, Dr. Merle Schwartz and his wife Dorothy were assigned to our camp at Sideling Hill for a period of time. He was a medical missionary, she a nurse. The reason for the availability of this type of medical personnel is a story I'll relate later.

The legislators and military personnel in the U.S. Government insisted on no wages for conscientious objectors. They considered this to be a test of good faith on the part of the boys choosing to register as COs. Also, the top brass in government considered it easier to deal with the public on the CO issue if they were not receiving wages from the government. The legislators and Selective Service personnel in charge, felt that it was best that COs be required to sacrifice for their faith and that this would help avoid potential public criticism that might otherwise occur.

Occasionally friends from home, parents, or in some cases individual churches would send small money gifts to the boys from their own congregation. But no monies whatsoever came from government agencies for the work performed. The three historical peace churches, Mennonite, Brethren, and Friends, supplied funds to carry on the operation of the camps for their boys of draft age. I think the administrators in camp who were not drafted received a modest wage, but no wages were provided the drafted fellows.

When we transferred to Delaware State Hospital, Selective Service permitted the hospital to pay us five dollars a month plus the necessary uniforms. This was in addition to room, board, laundry, and medical expenses, including dental work. Later our allowance was increased to ten dollars per month, but we were to supply our own uniform. This applied largely to the attendants who were to wear white coats on the wards. As it turned out, the people who issued supplies, particularly coats and shoes, were very liberal with the CPS fellows and provided these things without pay, even though the official hospital policy was that attendants pay for their uniforms after the ten dollar increase. Our allowance was finally increased to fifteen dollars. I recall the time that I bought a new hat, a Stetson at Wanamaker's in Philadelphia I paid fifteen dollars, one month's wages. It was a good hat. I wore it for many years and at this writing have it stored in the original box in our basement.

Merle & Dorothy Schwartz

Now to catch loose ends on the story of Merle and Dorothy Schwartz, the medical doctor and nurse who served at Sideling Hill Camp. It was unusual to have a medical doctor and registered nurse in the same camp, but they were at Sideling Hill for a period of four months, while I was stationed there in 1942. They were available because of a misfortune that had befallen them on their way to the Congo, in Africa. They had been assigned to go to Africa as medical missionaries. Because of the German blockades around Africa at the time, they were headed for Cape Town in South Africa and from there were to go by rail north to the Congo. In the Atlantic Ocean while still four days from Cape Town, their boat was torpedoed by the Germans and sunk. They were rescued on lifeboats, picked up by the same boat that sank them, and taken to France.

People of several different nationalities were on the ship. Most of them were from countries engaged in war with the Germans co were taken as prisoners of war. The Schwartzs were not detained as prisoners of war because the United States was not formally engaged in the war at that time. From France they were then allowed to return home, and since no one was permitted to go to Africa by any means, at that time, and they wanted to be in work closely allied with the peace movement, they took the assignment at Sideling Hill Camp while waiting for their permanent assignment.

Experiences with Patients

Our regular face-to-face contact with the patients allowed us to get personally acquainted with certain ones. The one patient I learned to know well and really developed an appreciation for was Martin L (LL). He was a distinguished artist. He had studied art in Italy and Spain in his early years. He was diagnosed as schizophrenia with a split personality. He would hear voices that no one else heard. You could be carrying on a conversation with him, he would be talking and responding in a very normal and rational fashion, and all of a sudden he would turn his head and speak to "someone" in sort of a half-whisper, half-audible voice. I sometimes asked him who he was talking to, he would respond, "They" said so and so, or "they" did this or that. It was always "they" doing something to him or for him, and he never could identify or define "they."

Other than that peculiarity, he conversed very intelligently. He was philosophical and usually rational in his abstract thinking and discourse. He spent most of his time in the art shop painting. One could always depend on LL being in his corner with his easel, oil paints and brush, working on some oil painting project. Since I worked in the recreation department, and our "office" or place we met before and after our work was the art shop, I got well acquainted with him and spent many hours interacting with him in various ways. We could discuss religion, politics, the war, morality, or practically any subject one might bring up and he would contribute intelligently.

One project that was a big one for him as well as for me was to paint my portrait with me posing hours on end. Incidentally, posing is one of the most difficult things one can imagine, sitting quiet, not talking and doing nothing but just sitting in the position he wanted me to sit for hours at a time. An hour or two at one sitting was about all I could take. He informed me that that is about as long as anyone wanted to sit in one sitting. All told, I sat approximately forty hours before he was satisfied with the portrait. I still have that portrait wrapped up and stored in the attic.

He also did a portrait for my brother Dennis, as well as others. For some reason he did not take nearly as much time to finish Dennis' as he did mine and we agreed that the finished portrait of Dennis was more realistic than mine. Even LL agreed and said that Dennis's was easier to paint. When I asked him to explain the difference, he commented that since we had spent so much time together he knew so much more detail about me and it was that fact that complicated his painting. The detail he knew was obtained from our many hours we spent in conversation through the three and a half years we were at the hospital. I spent more time just sitting and visiting with him than Dennis had.

Martin LL was an idealist. He was extremely conscientious, and ethical. He would never wrong anyone, he would always want to pay his due whether the other party wanted pay or not. He was the type of person I tried to keep in contact with even after we left the hospital. On one of my return visits probably ten years or more after we were discharged, I learned that he had died and was given a good burial by his relatives.

Another project LL did at my request was to design the CPS pin which was produced and sold to quite a large number of draftees during the war years. The pin was three-fourths of an inch across, diagonally. The design was a diamond shape with two hands gripping the top two sides, a round map of the world in the center, overlaying a cross with both the vertical and horizontal bars of equal length. The word "Civilian" was written above the world in the top left hand quadrant.

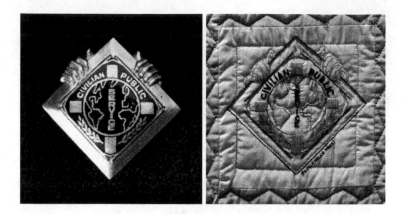

Picture 39 - Original CPS pin and the pin copied in a block of the CPS quilt.

The word "Public" was written across the top of the right hand quadrant, and the word "Service" was in a vertical position up and down across the world. The business aspects of transferring this design to gold and gold-plated pins was handled by one of our fellow-campers, Art Wolgumuth, who had business experience before being drafted. The pin sold two dollars, fifty cents for the gold plated, and four-fifty for the 10k solid gold. I bought two pins. I gave one to Anne (who later became my wife) when she visited our camp to help with our music program. I have both pins in my possession today. The significance of Anne's visit to our camp in 1945 will be detailed later.

Some of the other patients who received employee status and with whom we became quite well acquainted were usually the alcoholics who came into the hospital to be "dried out." They would then continue to work for the hospital and be OK in this favorable environment. When released, it usually would not be long until they returned dead drunk. One such person was Lawson but I do not recall his first name. He was an attractive person to be around. He was intelligent, personable and enjoyed discussing ideas and issues. He became a particularly close personal friend of Daryl Frey. He was friendly and well acquainted with all of the COs. He was hired by the hospital and worked with us in the recreation department for, couple years. In fact, he was still around when we were discharged, but during our stay, he never went back to drinking.

Years later when Anne and I visited the Freys in Barrington, Illinois, I inquired of Daryl whether he ever had any contact with Lawson. He said he found out that Lawson was located in Chicago, and invited him to his home in Barrington. Daryl said he met him at the train station, and when they met Lawson was drunk. Daryl brought him home, housed him overnight and fed him, he was still in such bad shape yet the next day that he, Daryl, took him to the doctor, who gave him some drugs for his condition, they then put him on the train and sent him home. Daryl has never had any contact with him since. This is a sad ending to a story which I always hoped would end on a positive note. All of us who knew Lawson as a sane and sober man shared this sympathy for him.

Point J. was another alcoholic who spent quite a bit of time at the hospital, part of the time on the payroll and part of the time as a patient. He was a good tennis player and according to his story had played some professional tennis. He was tall and handsome, and friendly. He was more reserved than Lawson. He did not live in Kent Hall with the COs and never really became too friendly with the CPS fellows. During our years at the hospital, Point was in and out several times. He would go out into society and try to make it on his own, but it never worked more than a few weeks or perhaps a few months if he was lucky, till he returned to be dried out again. We CPS men soon learned that it is not easy for a serious alcoholic to be rescued.

Leslie G. was another somewhat similar case. He had been a car salesman, he would go on a binge, wouldn't be able to handle it, and come back to the hospital for help. He was employed in the clothing distribution department at the hospital and had his living quarters in the singles section of Kent Hall with the CPS fellows. He was always jovial, and a big talker, but had difficulty coping with his alcohol problem.

Another patient of an entirely different nature was Cotton S. He was an extreme case on D-Ward, the violent ward, for rough, tough, hopeless patients. He was a little man, always dirty, rough looking, chewed tobacco, usually had tobacco juice running down the sides of his mouth, and was about the roughest talker I've ever heard.

John Martin, (the fellow I threw the shoe at in Dorm I at Sideling Hill) was the attendant in charge of the violent ward, and he did a bang-up job with these difficult D-Ward patients. John had a sense of humor, an essential quality for that job, a loud voice, and was a responsible attendant. I'll not repeat the words Cotton S. could use, but he could string together the roughest combination of cuss words you would ever hear anyone utter, along with his words, he was a comical old man who everybody knew and liked to tease. It wouldn't take much to get him going but looking back on some of the cases we worked with, even though it was obvious, it seemed almost unbelievable to me at the time, that human beings could degrade to that level.

The patient story would not be complete with describing Sammy H. Sammy was from a wealthy home. He was a young man probably twenty-five to twenty-eight years of age. He had a beautiful baritone singing voice. That, however, was about all Sammy had going for him. His folks could not, at least did not, tolerate him at home, and so they contributed money to the hospital which in turn was paid to Sammy in what he believed to be wages. He then thought he was an employee of the hospital. He spent most of his time in the recreation department. He would follow us around as we took groups of patients for walks, worked on the grounds, and the like, and all the time thought he was helping us. I think Daryl Frey got the brunt of supervising Sammy.

On one occasion, Daryl was assigned the job of burying one of the patients who had died, in Potter's Field, the hospital's cemetery. This patient had no relatives interested in claiming the body, so the hospital assumed the responsibility of burial. At the burial, Daryl had Sammy sing, "The Lord's Prayer," in respect for, even the forgotten dead. Sammy could be very serious and did a fine job in this role. He was sort of a nuisance, always coming up close to a person and wanting attention. But it appears that perhaps the main function of CPS boys in the mental hospitals was to attend to people who were failures in society, and often had no one else who cared. Sammy is one person who received a lot of attention from the CPS boys.

Price was another young man, again of an entirely different nature. He was a black boy who had been taught to assume a subservient role in a white world. He was energetic and always willing to run errands. He was good help for Dennis and Marion Albrecht on the laundry truck. Because of his good nature and willingness to work, he became the official bat-boy for our softball team. We took him along to most of our games. He was helpful in carrying equipment, and simply doing any tasks that needed to be done. He is prominent, center, front row, on the picture of our softball team. He felt rewarded for having the opportunity to serve in the roll of our official bat-boy, and he contributed sufficiently and deserved every bit of the attention given him. He was appreciated by every member on the team.

Social Activities

Our group of fellows and wives in the CPS Unit at Delaware State Hospital seemed to be extremely active. The activity seemed to be a good balance between organized and informal spontaneous activity. I had the feeling that we as a group had a lot of fun, lots of jokes, and pranks, along with informal bull sessions, dating, parties, and the like, along with performing our work duties responsibly.

A somewhat humorous prank I recall was some of our fellows teasing or at least testing the patience of Mrs. Schofield, our matron at Kent Hall. You might recall from my earlier description of our residence hall that we had a reception room in the center and long halls running both to the right and to the left. Each hall extended probably sixty or seventy feet in opposite directions. Mrs. Schofield's assignment as matron was to sit in her office in the reception room area particularly in the evenings with people off work, to supervise and enforce good behavior. Her job was also to answer the telephone. We had only one phone for the entire Hall, no phones in our individual rooms, so all phone calls were made from the matron's office.

One of the pranks was for one of the fellows to be at the far end of each of the long halls off of the reception room. Then from one end, they would roll a basketball down the hall through the reception room where Mrs. Schofield was sitting and on down the opposite long hall. The long halls turned into an L-shape at the far end, so by the time Mrs. Schofield could get up and look down either hall, no one was in sight. They were hiding around the bend. She'd get settled and here it'd come again. When she wouldn't pay enough attention to them or when they'd feel a little more rambunctious, they'd get two basketballs, start them at the same time from opposite ends, and the point was to have them meet in the middle, and bounce in the reception room where Mrs. Schofield was sitting. Mrs. Schofield was heavy and moved slowly, so it was difficult to impossible for her to trace down the culprit. From the speech I made at our third anniversary celebration, one of the recollections I made was, "Mrs. Schofield told Norman Norman Keller just the other day, 'I think you've come a long way since you've been here." Also, knowing my brother, Dennis with his mischievous tendencies, I think he was in on his share of these pranks.

Another comment in my celebration speech identifies another prankster, "Harvey, in the past three years there have been frequent rumors of you being sent back to camp. Some time ago our Hospital Press came out with the headlines, 'Harvey Mumaw Survives Again.' Harvey, could you please explain to us how?"

In my scrapbook, I have a Notice signed by M.A Tarumianz, M.D., Superintendent, stating "According to the orders received from Gen. Lewis B. Hershey, Director of Selective Service .... All members of the camp must be on the grounds not later than 11 pm"

Another note, also over Dr. Tarumianz's signature states,

"So there will be no misinterpretation of the house rules governing Kent Hall, you are requested to observe the following: All radios to be shut off by 10:30 pm. It should not be necessary to write rules governing the behavior of gentlemen living under one roof who should understand the requirements of their neighbors relative to hours of sleep required. Acrobatic stunts, wrestling, and loud talking together with an excessive volume on the radio over that necessary for a particular room, are conditions which should not have to be written to people who feel they have an ordinary respect for their home."

These notes were apparently instigated by complaints that came from Kent Hall and reached the top office. I do not know whether or not it came from Mrs. Schofield, our Kent Hall matron, or some of the non-draftee residents in the hall (We always seemed to have a few employees in our living quarters who were not members of the CPS Unit, and sometimes were not particularly friendly.), or whether perhaps some of our own group might have gotten disgusted with some of the horsing around, loud talk, radios, or tussling and reported it. Anyway, the message got to the top and orders were conveyed to us through the assistant director, yours truly.

On the more conventional and socially acceptable side of our informal social activity, quite a number of our fellows were employed by Francis Harvey, a member of the Wilmington Friend's Fellowship, and who was manager of the Wilmington Kresge Store. He was usually short of help, particularly male help, and hired about as many as were willing to work on Saturdays, and evenings. He usually hired the CPS fellows as floor managers or to work in the stock room.

At the second anniversary celebration, one of the highlights mentioned was "Kresge's Christmas basket present to CPS Unit in Kent Hall." At the third year celebration one of the comments made was, "Francis, last year at our anniversary celebration, one of the highlights was 'Kresge's present Christmas basket ...'. We missed that this year. We'd like to know what we might do to get back into the rating.'"

One of the events that became a memorable occasion for the members of our group was the gift-giving by Dr. Tarumianz at Christmas time. He made this an important ritual. At a previously announced time he would have all of his employees come to his office to receive a gift from him personally. The gifts would be some small item such as a necktie, a billfold, a piece of jewelry, or a box of candy. To us, the gift was not as important as the ritual associated with it. It was important to us that we were called to his office. Each would shake hands with the superintendent personally, at which time he would say something personally, and extend best wishes. We usually went in as a group, but each waited his/her turn to receive the gift along with his personal word.

Another delightful social contact was Catherine B. Swift, an older but a sweet and friendly Quaker lady who frequently had groups of CPS men over to her house for meals, picnics, and occasionally canoe parties on the Brandywine River. She had a daughter, Jo, who always contributed to the parties and also she would invite friends outside the CPS fellows. These were contacts which, in some instances, worked into lasting relationships. Daryl Frey became interested in one of Mrs. Swift's friends, Blanche Anderson, and after his discharge, they were married. My wife, Anne, and I have maintained contact and exchange occasional overnight visits with the Freys even to date of this writing, fifty years later.

Even with all the drudgery, monotony, and patience-testing hardships associated with our CPS service, the fellows would unfailingly come through with a good sense of humor. Here's another comment appearing in my third anniversary celebration talk dated October 13, 1945, which reflects this humor:

"Six months ago Olen King and John Martin said that when the war is over, they and their gang were going to put broom sticks on their shoulders and march around Dr. T's house seven times, then blow their trumpets and shout, 'Who's keeping us here now?'"

Then the following comment in my speech notes was, "As far as I know none of them but Diener and Gerber have really done the marching." (Ed Diener and Carl Gerber were two of the older men who were to receive their discharge papers shortly.) Diener received his official discharge on October 20, 1945, and Gerber,

November 3, 1945. This was the beginning of the break-up of the Farnhurst CPS Unit.

Formal Committees

Our CPS Unit had three internal structures that were organized with the intent of giving more formal structure to our activities. These were the Religious Life Committee, the Recreation Committee, and the Unit Council. From my collection of materials, I have written records on two of these groups, the Religious Life Committee, and the Unit Council. From my memory, I have a fairly good notion of the activities of the Recreation Committee, although I do not have this in my records.

For the Religious Life Committee, I have A Statement of Organization and Policy. It indicates the members, the objectives and duties of the committee. Members were: Robert Jaberg, chairman; Roselle Holdeman, secretary; Leland Gerber, treasurer, and Roy Bucher, contact man. The following paragraphs were taken from the statement.

The above Committee met on January 6, 1944, and developed a policy that future services to be held in the chapel every Sunday evening. All services are to begin at 7:45 pm.

Table 1: Religious Committee Statement of Organization & Policy

1 - The Committee appoints a Leader for each meeting.
2 - The Leader is responsible for the scripture reading and prayer.
3 - He is also in charge of the procedure of the meeting.
4 - The Committee appoints a chorister for one month who works with the organist.
5 - The Committee appoints the organist.
6 - The Committee appoints two ushers. They are responsible for the distribution of song books and also for collecting them after each service. It is also their duty to open doors and see that heating and lighting is provided in the chapel.

This statement indicates that the group was interested in and serious about the religious activities. I can recall that some of the feelings reflected from time to time by certain members of the group were that athletic and recreational activities were emphasized at the expense of the religious activities. The organization of this committee was to help keep these in balance.

Another significant feature of this committee was that Roy Bucher was appointed as a "contact man." A contact man was considered necessary because of the friction existing between the married couples and the singles. I'll explain this more later, in connection with the constitution of the Unit Council.

The Recreation Committee was organized because some members in the unit felt that it would be good to have somewhat regular parties among the members of our group. Supposedly this would unify the group and also make some of the more questionable activities outside the unit less attractive. The committee did function, and I think it served a useful purpose. We had parties, occasionally with organized games. Guests were invited, particularly some of the nurses who might at a particular time be special friends of some members of our group. Also, occasionally guests from the home communities of some of the fellows would visit and attend the parties. I think the parties contributed to group unity, and I think further, that the fellows, wives and guests all enjoyed these get-togethers.

The Recreation Committee was also responsible for organizing and planning the Anniversary Celebrations held each year on or at about the anniversary date, October 14. A big part of the recreational activity of our unit that was not the responsibility of this committee was the softball, and basketball games, along with the tennis, horseshoe, and ping pong tournaments. These activities had a different kind of interest and were more self-propelling. The unit director, yours truly, handled the major share of the softball activities, contacting team managers, setting game dates, hiring umpires, and the like. The captain of the basketball team handled the scheduling of their games. I personally, had very little to do with the basketball program.

It appeared to me that some of the members of our group felt that too many of our fellows were involved too much with "outside stuff," going to movies, dating outsiders, spending time in town, and the like. Also, one could almost inevitably sense the development of two separate factions in our group, "the married couples" and "the singles." Each of these groups tended to have its interests which would, somewhat naturally, be different from those of the other. I was among the singles, and was accused on different occasions of favoring the singles at the expense of the married couples. Naturally, the married couples were more limited in the scope of their activities since dating and making new friends, going to outside parties, and the like were really not for them.

Various people particularly from the married couples worked to establish a Unit Council designed to remedy some of this discord. It was eventually drawn up, I think, by members from the Social and Recreation Committees. The Preamble to the Constitution suggests the desired unity and harmony did not exist and the Council was designed to promote this. Since the constitution reflects some of the qualities or characteristics of our group and also some definite concerns of particularly the married couples, I will include it in its entirety in Appendix II at end of the book.

This concludes the provisions of the Unit Council. As I look back on it years after the fact, I am impressed with the professional nature of its composition. This Constitution has a number of implications reflecting some dissention alluded to earlier, e.g.:

(1) The preamble would "promote unity, harmony, and a spirit of Christian fellowship...."
(2) Under duties, "the council will serve in an advisory capacity in all matters pertaining to the welfare of the unit... "
(3) And the poignant part is, "It will be the business of the unit director to carry out the advice of the council...."

As I recall, the Council functioned for some time, but with no particularly significant impact. Life in the unit went on as usual. Interest in the Council waned. The thing that really affected the problem most, if indeed a problem did exist and furthermore, if it was actually affected, was the fact that several of the singles got married in the later stages of their service. It was these marriages that really affected a solution to the problem, the marriage of several committed singles. Some singles were not married, and in spirit, members of both groups.

Probably the one most influential was the marriage of Roy Bucher. He had been a devoted and committed single for the whole time. He had been appointed "contact man" for the Religious Life Committee, and then all of a sudden, his marriage put him on the "other side." But he refused to be put. And he consciously made the point, and he made it emphatically and repeatedly, that he is a member of the singles although married. That is to say that he is still going to relate and communicate with his single friends just like he had before he was married even though now he is formally one of the married couples. This was a good position to take and increasingly it was the attitude accepted by the entire group.

In addition, one needs to put this problem along with its solution in proper perspective. It was happening at a time when discharges were either pending or actually occurring. At this stage of our service people had too many other things to think about besides the silly issue of singles vs. married.

Admittedly, softball was important to me and had a high priority in the CPS program at Delaware State Hospital. Since our CPS days, I have probably spoken more about our softball activities than any other single aspect of the CPS program in Delaware. I do not necessarily say that this is as it should be, but merely telling it as I see it. It was because of my special interest in the softball program that I kept a great deal of material, team records, newspaper clippings, batting averages, team standings, and the like and preserved them in a special scrapbook. It is from this information that I gather most of the following account of our athletic activities.

Athletic Activity

An important chapter in the story of the CPS Unit at Delaware State Hospital is the athletic activity. The softball program was the most active. In addition to softball, we had a good basketball team which played other teams in the area. Also, we ran intramural tournaments among ourselves in tennis, horseshoe, and table tennis. Fortunately, I kept scrapbooks in which I have pictures, bulletin board announcements, and clippings from the Wilmington papers, Journal Every Evening, and the Wilmington Star.

One scrapbook contains mainly cultural activities such as some of the musical programs our draftees participated in as well as programs they attended. The one alluded to here contains some of the tournament brackets played in tennis, horseshoe and table tennis. A third notebook contains information on our quartet programs, our repertoire, and a complete itinerary of programs and appearances our quartet made between April, 1943, and January, 1946. These in turn will be described in the following pages. All of these materials that I had on hand, along with two porcelain trophies which I won personally (horseshoe & tennis) have been donated to the Goshen Archives.

One of my reports submitted to the MCC office was titled, "Analysis of Activities of CPS Unit #58, Farnhurst, Delaware." This report contained activities in four areas, Religious, Recreational, Educational, and Social. Under Religious were four sections, church services, prayer meetings, male chorus, and Crusaders male quartet. The Educational and Social included the library in reception room of Kent Hall, a class on pacifism in charge of Daryl Frey, and some of the parties that had been staged in the past. The Recreation report was softball. It would, I think, be of interest, particularly to the participants and fans to quote this section of the report in full. It is of interest to note, particularly in relation to the previous discussion of the singles/married controversy, that this report is dated September, 1944, and the Constitution of the Unit Council described above had the same date, September, 1944. The quote is as follows:

"We have a softball team rated Class A in the State of Delaware. We played several outside teams and were defeated only by the last year and this year's state champions, the Wilmington Arrows. We lost to the Arrows in an extra-inning game, 6 to 4. The runner-up in the state tournament this year, the Edge Moor Coast Guard took a sound drubbing at the hands of our boys, 8 to 0. In this game our pitcher allowed only two hits behind very strong defense by his team-mates. We are anticipating entering a league next season. Our group was divided into two teams at the beginning of the season. With these two teams plus our single vs. married games we had some very interesting, exciting and well attended ball games this summer" (1944).

Our first summer in Delaware, 1943, was mostly getting settled in, and feeling our way. Our first official softball games did not come until the summer of 1944. We had organized among ourselves and played a schedule of perhaps a dozen or fifteen games along with a few games with outside teams in 1944, and it was not until then that we realized the extent of our talent. Considering the games we played with some of the better outside teams, we realized that we could rate well with teams in the main league in Wilmington.

Wilmington and vicinity had two leagues, the Sports League, and the Recreation League. The Sports League had the better teams, mostly commercial, service and institution teams. The Recreation League was sponsored by the local YMCA, and had lesser talent in teams representing neighborhoods, parks, schools and the YMCA. We had played some of the teams in the Sports League in the summer, 1944, and felt comfortable at that level of competition, so we joined that league and played the entire season, 1945.

The Sports League was comprised of the following teams: Red Comb Arrows, New York Oyster Bar, Delaware State Hospital, Ramblers, Coast Guard, Chamber Works, Electric Hose, DuPont Experiment, and General Chemical. The regular season included twenty-two games. In addition we had a four team playoff at the end of the season, plus we played some non-league games, along with a number of intramural games during the summer. The final league standing as published in the Wilmington papers is as follows:

Table 2: Sports League Softball Standings, 1945

	W	L	PCT	GB
Red Comb Arrow	18	4	818	
NY Oyster Bar	16	5	761	1 ½
State Hospital	16	6	727	2
Chamber Works	13	10	565	5 ½
Ramblers	10	10	500	
Coast Guard	6	8	428	
Electric Hose	3	12	225	

Two of the teams, DuPont, and General Chemical, had dropped out during the summer. Some of the teams had some problem of finding enough men to field a team because so many were in the military. Also, we were aware that even though this league was considered the major league of the area at that time, it no doubt was not as strong as it would have been had not so many of the young men been away in the service. The Arrows represented the state of Delaware in the regional tournament. I have no account or memory of how they fared in that tournament but in speaking to their manager and coach, Mr. Heckman, he informed me that their pitcher, "Cookie" Lucas, threw as hard as any pitcher in the country, but that his problem was control. In some of the games he played with us, it was not uncommon for Cookie to get behind in the count and have to lob in a few pitches to avoid a walk. This would give the batter a better chance of hitting.

The team chose me to be the manager/captain. It was my responsibility to submit the starting lineup, make substitutions, arrange practice sessions, schedule outside games, make contacts and represent the team in the league meetings, arrange for umpires, submit our playing roster, work out our signal systems, and the like. I always felt that Daryl Frey was more knowledgeable than I was and I had him call signals and coach first base. I coached third base and called signals when Frey was batting or running. Our signals included steal, bunt, and hit-and-run.

Based on the league standing and our overall win-loss record, our team was considered to be the third best in the state. Even though our record was not quite as good we felt were equal to or perhaps even better than the NY Oyster Bar team, which was second in our league. The Arrows were definitely better than we were, however, we did win one league game from them during the summer.

During the 1945 season we played a total of 44 games. Twenty-two were league games, two play-off games, ten were with teams from the outside, and ten were between two teams organized from among our own fellows. The latter we called Team I, and Team II. Of the thirty-four games our CPS Unit played with outside teams in the summer of 1945, we won 24 and lost 10. A detailed record was made of our "at bats," "hits," and "batting averages." The players with their numbers are listed below:

Picture 40 - D. Paul playing 3rd base on the CPS softball team at Sidling Hill, PA, 1942.

One of the better games outside the league was played with the CPS Unit at Norristown State Hospital. Delaware State Hospital won that one 2 to 0. A ball team does a lot to develop a team spirit and close relationship among its members. Also, we had a good following of fans, particularly for our home games.

Table 3 - Softball Team Batting Averages in 1945.

Name	AB	H	Pct
Hershberger	3	1	.333
R. Miller	19	6	.317
D. Miller	109	34	.312
Siemens	74	23	.311
Albrecht	93	27	.290
H. Mumaw	125	34	.288
Frey	80	23	.288
Steiner	112	31	.277
Vogt	47	13	.277
P. Miller	112	29	.259
W. Mumaw	97	27	.258
Jaberg	31	8	.258
R. Hostetler	68	16	.235
King	81	18	.226
Martin, Jr.	102	23	.225
Hartzler	18	4	.222
Myer	9	2	.222
W. Yoder	9	2	.222
Charles	16	3	.188
G. Yoder	51	9	.177
I. Nussbaum	6	1	.166
M. Hostetler	65	10	.154
Holderman	14	2	.143
Smoker	14	2	.143
Martin	7	1	.143
Hess	64	8	.125
Graber	2	0	.000
Bucher	2	0	.000
Esh	3	0	.000
Bixler	16	0	.000

Of particular importance to me was the relationship between my brother, Dennis, and me. My position was third base, Dennis played in left field. Dennis was an excellent fielder as well as good hitter. Of the regular players, he had the best batting average at 309. I always felt that my play was backed up well with Dennis in left field behind me. To give you some notion of the caliber of his play, I quote from *The Rambler*, a publication put out by the hospital, Vol. 2, No. 1, August, 1945, "Dennis Miller turned in the play of the year. With bases loaded and one away, he took a fly in left field and whipped home a perfect throw to cut off what would have been the tying run. DSH won the game 6 to 5."

One of the more sensational experiences of our softball team was a game played with the New Castle Army Air Base. This game was reported in *The Reporter*, a periodical published by the National Service Board for Religious Objectors, under the caption CPS Lore. It runs as follows, and is a direct quote from the December 1, 1945, issue:

Another in The Reporter's series of famous and infamous CO stories and legends:

It was last year that assignees at the Farnhurst, Delaware State Hospital were softball-mad. Farnhurst men will never forget that year. Earlier in the summer the CPS team had won a sensational and bitterly fought battle from the three-times state champions, the Wilmington Arrows. One man even got a broken leg in that game, in a mix-up at second base.

On August 14--a Tuesday it was--the CPS men were playing the New Castle Army Air Base, at the base. Things weren't looking so good. The game was nearly over and assignees were trailing three to five. Well sir, at about that point there was an announcement over the public address system: 'Japan surrenders unconditionally!'

The place was bedlam. Service men and spectators jumped and shouted and hooted and ran about the field yelling, 'We're civilians again.' Things quieted down after a bit and play was resumed. But it wasn't quite the same. It took the end of the war to do it, but the COs took five runs in the seventh and the final score was COs eight, Air Base five."

With this story we conclude the account of the softball experiences at Delaware State. The basketball story does not contain as much detail. I do not have data on the basketball team as I did on softball. I have a picture labeled "Delaware State Hospital Basketball Team –1946". It includes twelve fellows, standing back row, Walter Mumaw, John Vogt, Marion Albrecht, John Martin, Jr., Harvey Mumaw and Merle Hostetler. Front row, kneeling, Richard Steiner, a new fellow whose name I do not know, Dennis Miller, Milo Bixler, Paul Miller, Daryl Frey. It was difficult to get as much interest established in basketball as we did in softball. I attribute this mainly to fact that softball was played in the warm weather and people would more naturally be outside and it was more convenient to attend the softball games in the summer than basketball in the winter. Also, we were not in a basket-ball league and the program was not organized as well as the softball program. Games were not as regular, consequently, it was more difficult to get team spirit worked up and very few spectators became regular followers of the team.

Most of the basketball games played were with commercial and church teams in the city of Wilmington. The games that aroused the greatest team spirit were with the Norristown, Pennsylvania CPS team. I have the bulletin board notice of the second game with Norristown. It indicates that Norristown had won the first game from Farnhurst, 31 to 24, and that that was the only defeat in six games to date. Part of the notice says "Stop Ramseyer and Gunden!" It was played in the Friends' Gym, Alapocas, on January 14, 1946. Before filing this bulletin board notice away for my scrapbook, I made the note that we had won this second game 39 to 26. The low scores are indicative of the level of play.

Regarding the drawings for the bulletin board notices, Dick Steiner, who played shortstop on the softball team, and was our left-handed batter, and a good hitter and also good at drag bunting, did the drawings. They were comical action pictures, artistically done, and attracted a lot of attention.

I have in my scrapbook the elimination tournament sheets that were posted for the tennis, horseshoe and ping pong tournaments. I won both the tennis and horseshoe tournaments and was runner-up in the ping pong tournament in the summer of 1944. The entries for each of these are Tennis: Marion Albrecht, Wayne Yoder, Daryl Frey, John Martin, Paul Miller, Gail Yoder, Walter Mumaw, John Vogt, Wm. Keller, Harvey Mumaw, John Siemens, Dennis Miller, Normal Keller, Roy Bucher, Aquilla Smoker, and Robert Jaberg. Paul Miller defeated John Siemens in the finals, 6-1, 6-4 and 6-1, for the championship and received a nice porcelain trophy on which Bill Keller had painted the appropriate inscription. Daryl Frey defeated Norman Keller for third place.

The entries in the horseshoe tournament were Paul Miller, Dennis Miller, Gail Yoder, Walter Mumaw, John Siemens, Merle Mishler, Daryl Frey, John Martin, Edward Diener, Ralph Hartzler, Willard Herschberger, Robert Jaberg, and Marion Albrecht. Paul Miller defeated Merle Mishler in the finals for the championship and received another hand-painted trophy for winning this tournament. Mishler defeated Frey for third place.

The ping pong tournament entries were John Siemens, Leland Gerber, Dennis Miller, Aquilla Smoker, Paul Miller, Richard Steiner, Robert Jaberg, Walter Mumaw, Marion Albrecht, Gail Yoder, John Vogt, Roy Bucher, Ralph Hartzler, Merle Hostetler, and Alvin Bixler. John Siemens won this tournament, Paul Miller was runner-up, and Alvin Bixler won third place. John Siemens received the trophy for winning this tournament.

As I recall the tournament situation for the summer, 1945, we had just finished an exciting softball season in August, we posted a tennis tournament, some of the games were played but the tournament was never finished. I had been defeated by, John Vogt, but it seemed that no one pushed to get the matches completed to the end of the play-offs. Another important factor that played into the picture at this time is that the discharges were eminent, and it seems the tennis tournament had a low priority. Horseshoe and ping pong tournaments were never staged in 1945.

This concludes the chapter on our athletic adventures. By way of a concluding response after sixty years, it appeared that we may have given an undue amount of attention to athletic activities, and perhaps not enough to the larger social issues. For example, Daryl mentioned to me in a recent visit that we could and should have done more to pressure the hospital to desegregate their wards. All Negroes were segregated and placed in one ward for all the black men, and one for black women. The whites were classified by diagnosis and condition and distributed among five or six different wards depending on their diagnoses and conditions.

Admitting that more interest could have been shown for social concerns, I must also recognize the merits of an active athletic program. In a situation of this type, it is easy to rationalize our actions. These young men were taken from their families and home communities, in some cases married men separated from their wives, and others separated from families, girlfriends, and acquaintances, and the added fact that they did not volunteer to do this but were drafted. Also considering that they worked at difficult assignments, and without pay, with all of this, it became important for them to have attractive diversions. They were in situations which could have been very demoralizing. In spite of this, I felt that the morale in our unit was extraordinarily high. And, I am convinced that the diverse activities, with athletics being an important part, were responsible for the fellows being able to enjoy their service, and years later, look back on it with a great deal of satisfaction.

It was really not a period of our lives wasted, but rather a period generally considered to have been well spent. Sure, with our present knowledge and experience, we realize we might have attempted to exert pressure to bring about some badly needed social change in policy relating to racial prejudice in Delaware, but I feel that Mennonites at that time were not conditioned and trained to do this as much as they are at the present time.

Reunions

The high morale of the group is also reflected in the fact that even after forty-five years, this group still meets regularly for biannual reunions. Ralph Hartzler has assumed responsibility for starting the reunions, keeping record of mailing lists, publishing the newsletter, sending out invitations, and the like. He has indicated in a recent letter to me, dated March 30, 1989, that a total of seventy-five men served at one time or another in CPS Unit #58 and that he has sixty-five families on his mailing list. Although the Unit number never exceeded forty-five at one time, those not on the mailing list are either deceased or not responding. He indicates further that twenty-one Farnhurst Alumni Reunions have been held, starting 1947 at Kidron, Ohio, then again at Kidron in 1949, then at Messiah College and alternating with Bluffton College, except in 1973 at Tiskilwa, Illinois, at Menno Haven Campground. Shortly after the discharges were processed and the unit closed, October, 1946, someone was making plans for the first reunion. I have a copy of the *Farnhurst Times* which reports "the Second Annual Reunion Held at Camp Kidron, August 20 & 21." Ninety-four people, including wives and children attended this reunion.

I attribute credit for planning and carrying out the reunions for these many years to three couples in particular, Ralph and Virginia Hartzler, who sent announcements and kept records; Raymond and Ruth Hess who are instrumental in planning when the reunions were in Pennsylvania, in addition to Leland and Winnie Gerber for the reunions at the Bluffton College Campus in Ohio. Hats off to these individuals for their tireless effort and loyalty in maintaining the continuity of the Farnhurst CPS Unit #58.

It is perhaps appropriate, though not an optimistic note to mention here that those participating in CPS reunions are journeying down a dead-end street. The long-range future of this group is zero. Our posterity not only has no interest in maintaining the group after the older generation passes on, nor do they qualify for membership. Nonetheless, the continuation of the group for this length of time has been of real value to the participating individuals, and also, I feel that the record we leave will make its mark on the church and CPS history.

I personally extend hearty congratulations to the people who have been instrumental in encouraging and planning the reunions, and furthermore it is also important to note that it could not continue were it not for the faithful people who respond with their attendance and enthusiasm. Ralph informs me that two couples have attended all twenty-one reunions to date: he and Ginnie and Leon and Esther Myer. Hubers have missed only two, Ray Millers and Clarence Nussbaums have missed three, while Harvey Mumaw, Aquilla Smoker and Ezra Stalter have attended seventeen, missing only four. Sixteen of the seventy-five draftees have never been able to attend. I hope the interest continues as long as we can continue to move about.

(An update from February, 2005.) The 29th and final reunion of the Farnhurst Unit #58, was held in Richland, Ohio, October 5-7, 2004. Eleven CPSers were present. The youngest was 78, and several present were in poor health. Ten spouses also attended this reunion. After some serious discussion the group decided it was time to face reality and call it quits while regular reunions were still in process. Consequently, we do not plan to have another biannual reunion of the Farnhurst Unit. A circle letter for all Farnhurst members who wished to be included, and which had been "circling" for 59 years, but which was lost somewhere in the rounds, was started again at the close of this reunion. We are hoping to maintain some contact in this manner... if it gets around.)

Regarding the states of origin, thirty one men came from Ohio, twenty from Pennsylvania, eight from Kansas and sixteen from eleven other states. This accounts for seventy-five men for whom we have record. These seventy-five men put in one hundred, forty-four 'man-years' of service.

Thirty-nine wives participated in making a CPS quilt. It was planned at the 1979 reunion, finished and auctioned off at the 1981 reunion. Thirty-nine contributed patches, and several of the women finished the quilt, and it was auctioned off at the following reunion. The high bidder was John Martin, Sr., who outbid John Martin, Jr. It sold for $350.

The update here is that John Martin, the successful bidder on the quilt, died June, 2009. His wife, Margaret, realizing that the quilt was a unique item, asked what she should do with the quilt. I told her that if she was willing to part with it and would send it to me I would see that it would get to the Goshen Archives where they already have a Farnhurst collection.

I received the quilt a month or so after John Martin's death. John Gundy was photographing it in the church where Tim Schrag, our minister, saw it and requested that we delay sending it to the Archives until he could use it in a church service. We wanted pictures to send with a letter to surviving members of our Unit explaining what was happening to the quilt. All our CPS members involved with the quilt were happy to allow the church to use it. So it was held and used in the church service on Memorial Day, May 30, 2010. Our associate pastor, Jane Roeschley, interviewed me in the church service in what was called "ministry moment." We discussed CPS and the quilt briefly then the whole service, including the sermon was focused on CPS. The quilt along with two other items, circle-letter material, and material of the Mountain Anthems Choir, organized by Menno Beachy, one of our CPS men, were delivered to the Goshen Archives June 3, 2010.

Cultural Activities

Another important aspect of the diverse extra-curricular activities in our CPS Unit is the exposure to the many cultural events available in the metropolitan east. The hundreds of rural, conservative Mennonite youths would have never experienced these opportunities had they not gone to camps. For instance, I was not really aware of the meaning of classical music until I was exposed to it through the opportunities to attend symphonies, grand operas, recitals, and the like while in camp. I learned a great deal by talking about these things with the more knowledgeable campers or other employees contacted during my service years. This exposure also motivated me to do a lot of reading and listening to records of classical music.

The wife of one of the doctors in the hospital, Irene Freyhan, was a good soprano singer, and voice teacher. She was in the process of becoming established in the Wilmington Music School, and offered to give me voice lessons free of charge. I worked with her for probably two years while at Farnhurst. She eventually became one of the established staff members at the Wilmington Music School and at that time suggested that I study with another teacher. It was an educational experience for me to be exposed in this manner to a professional singer.

It was Mrs. Freyhan who introduced me to grand opera. She helped me to get tickets to see Giuseppe Verdi's Aida, told me to get the score at the library so I'd know the story, and discussed grand opera in a general way with me. As I recall, several of my fellow campers went with me to this rendition of Aida. According to the program I still have in my scrapbook, we sat in the Parquet Circle in the Academy of Music Hall, in Philadelphia. The date was March 7, 1944, at 8:00 o'clock.

Wilmington, Delaware was about a thirty-minute train ride to Philadelphia It was quite common for a group of two or three to half a dozen or ten fellows, sometimes with wives, to board the train in Wilmington, for a ride to Philadelphia for a concert. This was an unusual experience for me and I was so enthusiastic about the new exposure, that I kept most of my programs as souvenirs. Today I find these in my scrap book. Other programs include *Il Barbiere Di Siviglia* by Rossini, done by the Philadelphia Sa Scala Opera Company, Bizet's *Carmen*, several concerts by the Philadelphia Orchestra under the direction of Eugene Ormandy, a program by the Columbia Grand Opera Quartet, a recital by Ezio Pinza, basso at the Academy of Music, a series of summer concerts at the Robin Hood Dell, starring Gladys Swarthout, Marion Anderson, Jasha Heifetz, Paul Robeson. I attended these along with a number of other concerts in Philadelphia, also some in New York and in Wilmington.

On the local scene, the Wilmington Symphony Orchestra performed concerts, The Wilmington Society of Fine Arts and the Wilmington Music School sponsored concerts of various sorts. Being located at Farnhurst, we had opportunities like I had never experienced before. On at least two occasions I recall we made trips to New York City for programs. On one occasion, I saw the play, "Deep are the Roots," a very moving play depicting racial problems.

In my sheltered life heretofore, I never realized the extent of racial prejudice with associated problems until I saw this play. I should have made the connection at that time and felt the need to attack the prejudice problem in the hospital where we were working, but for some reason, this never entered my mind. I don't recall ever really thinking about the fact that it might be possible for us to influence the removal of, or at least call the problem to the attention of the hospital administration, and perhaps even bring about a reduction in the amount of racial discrimination in Delaware.

Along with the exposure to the classical music, we attended several major league baseball games, including the All Star Game in Shibe Park, July 13, 1943. I saw the Navy vs. Penn football game, ticket price was $2.28. Several of us went to see the Chicago Bears play the Philadelphia Eagles football team one evening.

Ray Schlichting, the budget director from MCC, who came periodically to audit our books, was visiting us on the day of the football game. He came unannounced so I told him of our plans to go to Philadelphia that evening and requested we complete the auditing in the forenoon. I recall his comment as we were going over the books, "Let's get our work done so we can go to the football game tonight". Then he added, "I never have a chance to get to anything like this at the Akron office." I was surprised but pleased to hear him make this comment. I always felt we had to be good around the MCC people, and for some reason, at that time, I had the feeling that attending a professional football game would not be viewed in the best favor. I guess I considered it somewhat on the fringe, something which I might enjoy but which our church leaders would not encourage.

Another important aspect of our camp life was participation in musical activity in the community. Fred Wyatt was an outstanding choir director at the Methodist Church in Wilmington. I sang in his choir regularly on Sunday mornings for several years. He also conducted the community choir called The Capella Club. In the spring of 1944, The Capella Club sang the *Brahms Requiem*, and in the spring, 1945, *The Requiem* by Mozart. My name is listed among the basses in both of these renditions. His choirs, including his church choir, were selected by try-outs.

At that time I was taking voice lessons with Mrs. Freyhan, was doing quite a bit of singing, and was always able to make Wyatt's choirs. For the tryout, believe it or not, I sang a section of *The Trumpet Shall Sound* from *The Messiah*.

At Christmas time we sang Handel's *The Messiah*. Several of the boys from our unit usually participated in that. I had helped sing the complete works while at Goshen prior to going to camp, so was fairly familiar with it. Then I sang in three renditions, Christmas, 1943, '44, and '45, of *The Messiah* while in Delaware. Even to this day, I thoroughly enjoy singing in *The Messiah*. I feel I am quite familiar with most of it, and, naturally, this makes it all the more enjoyable to sing.

Farnhurst Chorus and Quartet

The Delaware CPS Unit had an active men's chorus comprised of 26 members. We had printed programs and seemed to always receive good coverage in the Wilmington daily newspaper, *The Journal-Every Evening*. I have several clippings from the paper in my scrap book. One is captioned, "Chorus to be Heard in Concert Saturday." Another says "State Hospital Group to Present Concert." The article then appears as follows: "'The Capella male chorus' of the Civilian Public Service Unit at the Delaware State Hospital will present a concert Saturday at 8 pm in the Delaware Avenue-Bethany Baptist Church. The director of the chorus, composed of young men of various denominations, is Gail Yoder. The personnel consists of: First tenors, Roy Bucher, Leland Gerber, Lyle Myers, Wayne Yoder; second tenors, Lester Charles, Merle Hostetler, John Siemens, Walter Mumaw, Aquilla Smoker; first bass, Menno Holderman, D. Paul Miller, Robert Jaberg, John Vogt, Irvin Nussbaum, Richard Steiner, Willard Graber; second bass, Daryl Frey, Raymond Hess, Ralph Hartzler, Ray Hostetler, Willard Hershberger, Dennis Miller, John Martin, John P. Martin, Jr., Harvey Mumaw."

Another article from my clippings has the following paragraph in a news item describing the service of the Delaware Avenue-

Bethany Baptist Church. "A feature of the service was a concert by a male quartet composed of Mennonites registered as conscientious objectors, who are serving in Civilian Public Service Unit 58, Delaware State Hospital, Farnhurst. Two sets of brothers, Wayne and Gail Yoder and Paul and Dennis Miller, comprised the quartet which sang *a capella*."

Our unit had its own church service in the chapel at Delaware State Hospital held regularly every Sunday evening. As one might correctly assume from the articles above, our fellows were most active with the Baptist church. I sang in the choir in the Methodist church regularly for a period, and several others of our Unit also sang in *the Messiah* at the Methodist Church.

I was asked to be soloist at the Episcopal Church. After Mrs. Freyhan joined the staff of the Wilmington School of Music, she suggested that I study with another teacher, I forget her name, at the Wilmington Music School. After working with her for about a year, she told me that the Episcopal Church needed a soloist and recommended that I try it. They had come to her for her suggestions and apparently had confidence in her. She thought I was capable of handling the assignment and that I needed this kind of experience. The job was to pay ten dollars a month, for four Sundays. At that time this was an attractive opportunity, but

Picture 41 - "The Crusaders" male quartet, from left to right, Wayne & Gail Yoder, D. Paul & Dennis Miller in 1945.

I never did feel sufficiently confident to accept this assignment. I discussed it with our quartet members. I realized it would tie me up every Sunday morning and that it would limit potential appearances for our quartet. I had had several interviews with the personnel of the Episcopal Church and even though they

indicated to me that a lot of the singing was chanting and really not much real performance, I still did not feel qualified, nor was I willing to obligate myself for every Sunday morning. So, after considering the pros and cons, I decided to decline the offer.

Our male quartet comprised of two sets of brothers, Wayne and Gail Yoder, Dennis and Paul Miller, was rather an important institution in our camp life. After having organized and after giving a few programs, we realized that we needed calling cards to hand people when they inquired about programs. We had a batch printed with The Crusaders male quartet in the center, "CPS Unit No. 58, Farnhurst, Delaware" in the upper left hand corner, our telephone number, Wilmington 34366, in the upper right hand corner, then the names, Wayne and Gail Yoder in the lower left hand corner, Paul and Dennis Miller in the right hand corner. I still have a few of the cards left among my souvenirs.

I kept a rather detailed record of all of our programs and appearances during our CPS days. Our first appearance was April 14, 1943, and our last was January 6, 1946, three months short of three years. During that time we had worked up a repertoire of 36 songs, which we could sing from memory. Our programs and appearances included many church services, in the area of Delaware and eastern Pennsylvania, radio broadcasts, the Ohio Mennonite Church Conference, a 9-day furlough tour appearing in nine churches in Pennsylvania and Ohio, among many others. I have a record of 96 appearances we made during those two years, nine months. Our activities can best be described by simply listing the dates, places and the nature of the program, as is found in a multi-page table in Appendix III, page 337.

The four of us have gotten together only once since CPS days, at the 1979 reunion at Grantham, Pennsylvania. At that time, we were noticeably rustier, and less confident, Wayne commented publicly that his high voice cracked more than when he was younger, but it nonetheless, seemed like old times. We sang a few numbers at our Saturday evening meeting, and also at the Sunday morning service.

One additional observation I make today which was not made at the time of the event, is that we sang at two sessions of the evangelistic services of a prominent, nationally known evangelist,

Bob Jones. It was November 19, 1944, at Faggs Manor, Pennsylvania, that we sang four numbers in an afternoon session, and five numbers in his evening session. At that time, we realized that he was a good speaker and evangelist, but did not realize the popularity to which he would rise in the future.

With this itinerary, it concludes the part of the CPS Story which relied mostly on the two scrap-books and one notebook, in which fortunately and for some unknown reason, I had kept record. I also have some recordings of our quartet, and another of couple of my solo numbers. (Realizing my singing voice today, it's almost ridiculous for me to think I ever sang solos. However, one number I recall vividly having done was at the Beatrice country church after CPS. I made a few comments before I sang and later Lewis Penner, my brother-in-law complimented me for having explained what I was going to sing. Anne was my accompanist.)

The records of our Crusader's Quartet have "The Glorious Gospel" on one side and "Nearer My God to Thee" on the other. One record has the label with titles torn off, so I do not know what it contains. The small record with my solo numbers has "Now the Day is Over" on one side and "'Drink to Me Only with Thine Eyes" on the other. Ralph Cole, one of my draftee colleagues, was my accompanist. I thought at the time that they were good recordings. They are on 78s and were, at least then, played with the old steel needles. I have some un-used needles, but no player that will play the records. I also have a quite good collection of classic solos of some of the old timers, operas and symphonies, all of the 78 speed. The problem with these old recordings is that it is difficult to find players in our modern technology to play these old records.

Anne's Visit

Another incident even more momentous in my life came about because of my responsibilities as assistant director. In that role it was my responsibility to meet official guests when they visited the unit. This included ministers who came in to visit boys from their home congregations, or to preach or counsel with our fellows or MCC representatives who were sent to take care of various types of administrative and other duties, plus a wide variety of other visitors.

In the summer of 1945, the MCC sent Miss Anne Wiebe, of Beatrice, Nebraska, to various CPS camps in the east, including Farnhurst, to help with the camp music programs. During the school year she was teaching music and directing choirs in Hillsboro High School in Kansas. She was considered an outstanding music teacher with a good reputation. So the MCC called her to help CPS camps with their music. Her visits included several days with the Farnhurst Unit. It was my responsibility (or opportunity) to meet her at the bus, carry her suitcase, arrange for her lodging & meals, and schedule meetings with the fellows in our unit.

Our music program was already quite active. We had a good men's chorus organized and were making occasional public appearances. The Crusaders Quartet was organized and had been active for more than a year with a variety of appearances, including a series of radio broadcasts over WILM, the Wilmington radio station. Miss Wiebe commented that there didn't seem to be much for her to do here. Nonetheless, we scheduled a few meetings with our men's chorus, and the quartet. She was helpful with suggestions, directed a few numbers with the men's chorus, but she felt that she hadn't been of much help to us.

She was aware that MCC had the policy of requesting reports of her activities, and said she couldn't imagine what I could include in my report. I offered to send her a copy of my report if she gave me her address. She gave me the address, I sent her a copy of the report, and she responded. I responded to her response, and before long, we had a correspondence going. It continued and developed into something more than just correspondence, which, even after sixty-two years finally came to an end. Yes, this obviously became an important guest for me. (A later update: After 62 years, 6 months, our marriage ended with her death February 5, 2010.)

Sometimes one has to wonder what a difference it would have been if one little decision way back had been different. For example, what difference would it have made in my life had I told Sanford Shetler back in Sideling Hill Camp that I would not assume the leadership role when we transferred from Sideling Hill to Delaware State Hospital? I was seriously considering doing just that. Those are questions that can never be answered.

Our Family & CPS

My brother, Dennis, and I were in the same Units during our total period of service. We both registered about the same time and even though I was two years older, we were both of draft age and by the luck of the draw his number came up before mine, so he was inducted a few weeks ahead of me.

My brother, Emerson was two years younger than Dennis, and because of his age, did not register when Dennis and I did. Emerson was first inducted into Camp Luray in Virginia, October 1, 1943, and later transferred to the school for the mentally retarded at Exeter, Rhode Island. When Dennis and I were in Delaware, my sister Ruth and her husband Abe Willems, and Emerson were in Rhode Island. Dennis was inducted December 29, 1941, and discharged December 18, 1945. My dates were January 14, 1942, and January 24, 1946. Emerson was discharged June 29, 1946. Interestingly then, after our discharges, Dennis and I were together on a cattle boat, mentioned above, tending more than five hundred bred heifers which were being shipped to Austria as part of the Marshall Plan designed to help the rehabilitation of Europe after the war.

After being discharged from Delaware State Hospital and had returned from our three week on the cattle boat, Dennis and I both returned to our home in Berlin, Ohio. I worked at the pottery factory In Fredericksburg, Ohio for six weeks, then Dennis and I both enrolled in summer school at Goshen College. We continued in college through the next year, and graduated in the same class in 1947. After graduation we parted ways but always felt close to each other because of the six years we were together through this rather significant period of our life.

Miscellaneous Inclusions

Before closing in on my CPS Story, it is important for me to include a number of other items. One incident relates to a testimony from Roy Bucher regarding some of the things he says I did for him but which I was completely unaware of at the time. Recently (January 2004) in an email exchange he described this incident. I had told him I was writing up my CPS Story and would like to include his story. At the time of this writing he was having some serious health problems, kidney dialysis three times a week and not feeling well a big part of the time. The incident can best be described by simply copying his email.

Roy Bucher's Letter

January 8, 2004

Dear Paul:

I haven't felt very well the last several days, and did not get to my computer. I received your interesting letter and today I am feeling stronger, so I want to take time to answer your question.

The matter you refer to was in my first few weeks at Sideling Hill. You know of course that I grew up in a conservative home and church. We never had audible prayer in my home, and at church the young people did very little in the church I attended. I was used to lead singing but that was it.

I was not allowed to go to high school so I had only 8th grade education. I really wanted to go to Eastern Mennonite High School but my folks opposed. I wanted to get involved, so when I got notice to report to Sideling Hill it was not a sad day. It was a real happy day. This was going to be my Eastern Mennonite High School.

We had as you may remember a mid-week prayer service at Sideling Hill. I thoroughly enjoyed the first evening I attended and decided then that I was going to say something publicly some evening, for the first time in my life.

You and I were on the same working crew. We went to Midway on the Turnpike. We brought rocks down for a rip-rap waterway. For some reason you and I worked together.

On Wednesday evening my time had come. Remember I was still this conservative Dutch boy from Lancaster County. I stood up in the meeting and said, "Today the *vorld* is shouting *wictory*, *wictory*, but we will never have *wictory* without Christ." Then came chuckles. I was hurt, deeply hurt. I didn't think that was such a bad thing to say.

I slept very little that night. The next day we were on the job. I brought stones to you and you placed the stones in place. About noon I finally got up enough courage to ask you – Why did they laugh last evening when I said what I did?

Then I remember you stopped working and stood up and said, "No they didn't laugh at what you said, they were amused with your Pennsylvania accent. I asked what I was doing wrong. You said I had my *v*'s and *w*'s mixed up. This was a shock to me. I kept thinking about it as I brought more stones. I came back to you and asked what I can do. You said if you want help I will help you. I said please! And that was the beginning of a new life for me.

Fortunately we went to Delaware together. Those were further years of growth. Then you gave me the opportunity to take the GED tests. Goshen accepted me on the basis of those results.

I wanted to be a minister, but my home church used the lot, and we never say we want to be a minister. We wait for the Lord to call through the lot. They were so disappointed when I returned home without my plain coat, and shocked when I told them I was going to Goshen College to prepare for the ministry. My parents were disappointed as were Betty's. So we really went on our own.

College was very hard for me in the beginning. I had to learn how to study. My professors were very understanding and gave me extra help when needed. At Goshen I earned a BA, BRE, and ThB. Later at Winona Lake Le Tourneau seminary I earned a MA Th. Then I started clinical training for chaplaincy. I went to the University of Chicago Medical Center, Christ Community Hospital and later to Doylestown, Pennsylvania for a quarter advanced training....

In retirement I took interim assignments in eight different churches. One I really enjoyed was Walnut Creek, Ohio. I was at Metamora, Ill for fifteen years. (Roy describes in some detail his pastoral experiences including "volunteer pastoring" in Florida for 15 winters where they presented him with a gift of $1200 as a farewell gift when he left. Then he continues:

"We have a lot of memories, looking back gives me a great deal of encouragement. Sometimes I wonder had it not been for CPS what would have happened to me. I keep going back to that rip-rap at Midway. I have told this story many times; so many people have heard your name even though they haven't met you.

As I look back over my life, most of the things I did, but I never applied for. Pleasant Hill called me when I left Goshen. Metamora called me out of Pleasant Hill, Doylestown called me out of Metamora, and the hospital called me while I was at Doylestown. I was drawn in to all these assignments. This was also true of the interim assignments. Only twice did I negotiate salary.

I remember you and I had different opinions and theological views. I am glad you are happy in the church there.... No matter what your views, I can't thank you enough for what you did for me. Thank you again and God bless you and your dear wife.

Love,
Roy Bucher

Bob Kreider's Visit

Another visit was somewhat impressionable among our boys at the time, but is of an altogether different nature. Robert Kreider was the overall director of the Mental Hospital Units in the east, operating out of the MCC office and made periodic visits to the mental hospital units. He came on one of his official visits, performed his duties, and in the afternoon went with one of the other fellows to get some exercise on the tennis court.

The superintendent, Dr. Tarumianz had put up the tennis court on the hospital grounds mainly for his son, Alexis, to use, but he gave permission for us to use it, with the understanding that we follow the court regulations. Bob had not brought his tennis shoes along, so he decided to play in his street shoes, but to stay in the back court so as to not mark up the surface.

It so happened that Alexis, Dr. Trumianz's son, walked by and saw Bob playing tennis in street shoes. He reported this to his father and the next day his father, called me to his office and "raised the roof." He reprimanded me severely for allowing one of our boys to play on the tennis court without tennis shoes. He instructed me to make it clear to our boys to never let that happen again. If we'd ever be caught again on the court with street shoes we would be denied the use of the court.

I checked with our fellows, and learned what had happened. It was not one of our fellows but rather Bob Kreider, administrator from the MCC office, who was playing without tennis shoes. I reported this to Dr. Tarumianz. He heard me but didn't re-track anything from his original demands.

Although we did not consider it a particularly serious matter, we felt that we should communicate the incident to Bob. So, we bought a pair of size 13, tennis shoes, then, all of the fellows in the unit autographed them with indelible ink, and we sent the shoes to Bob, with the story of what had happened. I've always felt that Bob didn't consider it much of a joke. I have mentioned it to him several times in the years since it happened, but he has never been able to laugh about it.

A Patient's Poem

The following lines were written by one of the patients at Delaware State Hospital. From the message of these lines it appears that the CPS Unit did make some difference. Even though it is not a classic in its structure, it does however, convey the message that the CPS men were appreciated. Also, it is important to remember that this was done by one of the patients.

> A big change has taken place
> In the Hospital here
> That has taken away

All the worry and fear.

They have got some new help
They're a fine bunch of men
And there's surely a difference
Between now and then.

They call them COs
And a fine Christian bunch
Who believe in kindness
With no kick or a punch.

The bunch they had before
Should be down in a mine
With a club and a pick
They surely would shine.

But you couldn't expect
Any more from their kind
Who were just a dumb bunch
With an unchristian mind.

So we can be thankful
They sent the COs
For it's more like home
As everyone knows.

By George H.
Ward C6-2

Communion at Farnhurst

At this point I will place into the record another item which
might have appropriately been included in the discussion of the
religious activities of the unit, but which since it has been handled
as a separate matter, will be included apart from other unit
activity.

Muriel T. Stackley, editor of *The Mennonite*, the semi-monthly
publication by the General Conference Mennonite Church,
Newton, Kansas, wrote me and asked that I submit to her an
account of my experiences related to communion in our unit

which included boys from different Mennonite denominations as well as non-Mennonite churches. A pastor in Kansas who had been a draftee serving in another mental hospital in the east was aware of the communion experience in our unit and mentioned it to Muriel, and she in turn requested that I write it up for her. The letter I had sent her is as follows:

December 14, 1988
8 Wilmette Dr.
Normal, IL 61761

Muriel T. Stackley, Editor
The Mennonite
722 Main St.
Box 347
Newton, KS 67114-0347

Dear Muriel:

Some time ago you inquired about my experience with communion in CPS among GCs and MCs. My response to this query, I'll bet, is different from anything uncapped so far and also different from what you might be looking for. It really is not in the mode of the Brunk articles and may be of no use to you, so please feel free to use or not use it, as you will. Even so, I think about it occasionally and think I mentioned it to Loris Habegger not too long ago, who in turn mentioned it to you.

CPS Unit #58 was located at Delaware State Hospital, Farnhurst, near Wilmington, Delaware. We began as a somewhat self-chosen unit of 25 fellows at Sideling Hill Camp on the Turnpike in Pennsylvania. The unit expanded to 35 and later to its maximum of 45. Although I am not certain of the distribution of (we called them) OMs, GCs and others, I am aware that the unit was predominately OM (Old Mennonite). We had probably 8 to 10 GCs (General Conference Mennonite), two Lutherans, one non-affiliated and the remainder OMs. I served as assistant director of the unit (The superintendent of the hospital was considered the director). The fellows were mostly from Ohio and Pennsylvania.

One day I received a letter from the bishop of my home church, D.D. Miller, Berlin, Ohio, asking if he and another bishop, John E. Lapp, of

Souderton, Pennsylvania, could come in and have a communion service with our group. We discussed it among members of the group and decided to invite them to come.

From the very early formation of our group at Sideling Hill Camp, we were a closely knit and congenial group and seldom gave thought to what church backgrounds we came from. One or two had actually come from the Amish but did not hold rigidly to traditional Amish practices. Some came from the more conservative Mennonite churches in Pennsylvania and some from the Brethren in Christ, then some from the less conservative OMs and GCs in Ohio, and two of our group were Lutheran. The differences were never emphasized, and as we lived, worked and played together we had become a cohesive and compatible group of fellows and wives.

The two bishops came in. At their suggestion we had a preparatory meeting which was traditional in the OM churches, to precede the communion services. We were literally unprepared for what was to follow. The two bishops were not only OMs but were conservative OMs. They seemed to assume that communion would be with only the OM boys and wives. In our cohesive group this didn't sit well. So, in order to work out the differences between the bishops and the CPS group we called a special meeting of all the boys and the bishops to discuss the matter.

The meeting was held in one of the larger rooms in Kent Hall, our living quarters. I remember the scene so well, boys sitting on the floor lined the walls and occupied most of the floor space, and the bishops sat on chairs at one end of the room. The bishops mentioned that it is the policy in their church to have closed communion. This would mean that probably half of the group would not be permitted to participate in the communion service.

The point was made loud and clear that we were a group, in a sense, communing together every day for several years, sharing our problems, joys and concerns, and it did not make sense, nor would it be acceptable to us to disqualify all who were not OM. A special case, the fellow who was not affiliated with any church was a cut-and-dried case for the bishops, but was in our opinions one of the best boys in the unit. He was older and more mature than most of us. He was intelligent, thoughtful, considerate, and all of this was associated with a keen sense of humor. He couldn't commune with us, yet others among our OMs who were considered to be of more questionable character could be included. The GCs and Lutherans were not to be included. No! This just did not fit together. The bishops listened, I'm sure they were surprised and even shocked at what they encountered. It was no doubt a new experience for them. After hearing what the fellows had to say they had a brief huddle, and then announced that we would not have a communion service. Instead they conducted the church service, but no communion.

Times have changed in the forty-four years since that experience. I am not certain just what the official position on open and closed communion is among some of the more conservative Old Mennonites, but I know it is open in many places. And I think it is open to anyone who wishes to participate.

A footnote: In this account I am using OM for the group usually called MC (Mennonite Church) today. I feel that the MC label is historically inaccurate and ethically poor judgment and should not be used to specify one particular branch of Mennonites.

Footnote two: I was raised in a conservative Old Mennonite home. The conservative bishop from my home congregation in Ohio who visited our CPS unit was my father. We had a good father-son relationship until we started talking religion. After CPS days and the ensuing graduate school my father and I were increasingly farther apart in our religious philosophy, but had a very fine relationship in the more traditional father-son roles.

Muriel, it has been interesting for me to write about this experience. I would appreciate getting your response to this experience. You are in no way under any compulsion from me to use it in print.

Sincerely,
D. Paul Miller

Muriel responded, "Thanks for writing up the CPS experience; fascinating. I would like to print the story in the opening months of 1989. What intensifies the poignancy for me is that the bishop was your father. That authenticates the commentary and, I believe, qualifies you to speak to current goings-on..."

The main substance of this letter appeared in the March 28, 1989, issue of *The Mennonite*.

Demographic Information

Before concluding our CPS Story, it would be good to include some of the factual information from a few sources. One of these sources was compiled and published by the National Service Board for Religious Objectors, 941 Massachusetts Avenue, N. W., Washington, D.C., titled *Directory of Civilian Public Service, May, 1941 to March, 1947*. This directory lists the names of all young men drafted into Civilian Public Service, their home address, birth date, all camps in which they served; their induction and discharge dates, church affiliation, and occupation.

Together, the draftees were affiliated with 235 different religious denominations. The denominations with the largest number of assignees are as follows:

Table 4: WW II Draftee Denominational Affiliation (1947)

Mennonite	4,665
Church of the Brethren	1,353
Society of Friends	951
Methodist	673
Jehovah's Witness	409
Congregational SA	209
Church of Christ	199
Presbyterian	192
Northern Baptist	178
German Baptist Brethren	157
Roman Catholic	149
Christadelphians	127
Evangelical & Reformed	101
Southern Baptist	45

The government provided 151 camps between 1941 and 1946, serving 11,996 draftees. Over 2,000 of these served in 41 mental hospitals in 20 states. Camp No. 4, at Grottoes, Virginia, was the first MCC camp. It was opened May, 1941, and remained a stable base camp, closing May, 1946, only after a significant number of discharges had been issued.

Here's a list of the agencies which were approved for CPS units and which employed conscientious objectors during the war years: The Agricultural Experiment Station, Bureau of Reclamation, Coast and Geodetic Survey, Fish and Wild Life, Foreign Service and Relief, Farm Security Administration, General Hospital, General Land Office, Mental Hospital, National Park Service, Office of Scientific Research and Development, Office of Surgeon General, Public Health Service, Puerto Rican Reconstruction Administration, Training School, and the Weather Bureau.

Although approved for COs, the Foreign Service and Relief Agency was never given congressional approval for COs to work abroad during the war years. The last camp to close, according to the Directory listing was No. 151, a Mental Hospital Unit, Roseburg, Oregon, which closed in December, 1946. According to the listings, CPS Units were assigned to a total of eighteen different governmental or public agencies.

Each of the three church groups sponsoring the camps, appointed the camp directors from among their church personnel. These directors along with the other staff members were under the supervision of the National Service Board for Religious Objectors, which had an office in Washington, D.C.. Paul Comly French was General Secretary of this group. The group was in turn responsible to General Lewis B. Hershey, who was in charge of the Selective Service System of the U.S. government.

Dr. Gordon, one of the psychiatric doctors at the hospital requested an informational statement on our unit for a report he was to present at the Delaware Psychiatric History Conference. I kept copies of some of these reports in my files, and also have copies of the speeches I presented at the three anniversary celebrations. It is from these pages that I have gleaned much of the material presented in the pages above. However, as I review these once more I note a few additional items which might be worth mentioning.

In January, 1944, we were a 35-man unit. We had been working at the hospital for fifteen months; average age was 25 years, 6.4 months. The educational grade level was 11.08 years. That is at the level of just beginning the senior year in high school. Eleven had only grade school education, twelve had high school experience, seven of those graduated from high school, twelve had college experience, two of those graduated from college, and one had done some graduate work.

The average length of total service time in CPS was 19.68 months. With fifteen of these months at the hospital, this meant that on the average, each had spent 4.68 months in a base camp or other unit before being transferred to the hospital. At the time of this report, January, '44, sixteen of the thirty-five were married, just under half. And on that date, six had been discharged or transferred to another unit.

The record for those discharged or transferred from our unit is as follows: Paul E. Zimmerman, discharged March 7, 1943, physical disability; Martin B. Martin, enlisted for 1-A-O, June 28, 1943, later discharged from service for physical disability; Eugene Basinger, transferred to Goshen Training Unit, June 14, 1943, later transferred to State Hospital, Howard, Rhode Island; Daryl Frey transferred to the Goshen Training Unit, then after that unit was discontinued, transferred back to Farnhurst; Harold Martin, transferred July 21, 1943, returned to Sideling Hill Camp; Joseph Bush, enlisted for 1-A-O, December 1, 1943, discharged from service, physical disability; Clair Kaufman, discharged December 11, 1943, physical disability. As these individuals left the Farnhurst Unit, new draftees were transferred in to fill their positions.

The Farnhurst Unit #58, originated October 14, 1942, with 25 men. In March, 1943, it was increased to 35. In January, 1944, the unit increased to 40, and in May, 1945, the unit strength reached its peak of forty-five. Of the original group, five were married, and the wives were employed at the hospital. When the unit numbers reached forty-five, twenty-three were married, twenty-two single. Thirteen of the twenty-three wives were employed at the hospital as office clerks, switchboard operators, and attendants. Some of the others were employed at various jobs in Wilmington or other places in the community.

Occupations before induction show that approximately half were farmers or dairymen, eighteen per cent were teachers or students, twelve per cent were in industrial occupations, and the remaining twenty per cent were in miscellaneous occupations including carpentry, photography, postal carrier, miner, office clerks and store clerks.

The latter report, dated September, 1945, is the most recent report available in my file. At that time, the unit was anticipating discharges. One of the items requested by MCC in the reports was "Basic Needs of Men in Our Unit." In the report dated September, 1944, the need reported was "The ability to live it out and still do good work." It appears that the need was apparently being satisfactorily met. I was discharged January, '46, left the hospital for the cattle-boat in early March, the unit continued to operate until the end of the fourth year, closing in October, 1946.

IV - Senior Olympics

Introduction

Sixteen years after the fact, my recollection is that my first participation in Senior Olympics was the State Meet in Springfield in 1982. I base this on the fact that I have a "participation medal" dated 1982, the meet in which I did not place in any event. I will discuss that meet in more detail later in this chapter.

My first participation in the Mennonite Senior Sport Classic was in Goshen, Indiana, June, 1998. It was here that my brother-in-law, Dale Stutzman asked me two (what he said were) important questions: (1) "How did you get started in Senior Olympics?" and (2) "Have you done any journaling of these activities?"

Up to that point I had never given any serious thought as to how it got started, and I had never kept a record of the activities. Obviously Senior Olympics have become an important part of my life story and I attribute the beginning of journaling to my brother-in-law Dale Stutzman. This explains why the beginning of this story began in 1998, although I am including activities that I participated in from the actual beginning of the events, based on information inscribed on my medals plus my memory.

I have had a strong interest in athletics from as far back as I remember. In high school I would watch the coach tape the ankles of the football boys during the noon hour of the game day. I'd keep track of the baseball teams, professional, high school and college. In CPS, I participated in all sports, baseball, softball, basketball, tennis, horseshoe, and you name it. I bicycled to school when teaching in Mankato State and later to Wesleyan, and our family did a lot of water skiing, camping, and other outdoor activities when the kids were at home.

In more recent times, about 1981, I started running 10ks and my first Senior Olympic competition was 1982. So, responding to Dale's suggestion, I began drawing from my memory and in this chapter, I describe as well as I can, the activities in my Senior Olympic up to that point and then plan to relate further events as they occur.

In these pages I am including my exercise program which in turn led to the competition. The exercise program combined with a vegetarian diet makes up an important part of our lifestyle. Anne and I have been disciplined to a vigorous exercise program (Four Seasons, 5:00 to 7:00 am five days a week) since retiring in 1982, and are still at it at this writing, 2003 (Revised March, 2005). The exercise program for me involves 45 minutes in the weight room, ten minutes stretching then working with 18 different machines for upper, middle, and lower body conditioning, half hour walking or running in the gym, then swimming 20 to 25 lengths, to the Jacuzzi where I do some final stretching before showering and going home for a breakfast of hot cereal, orange juice and toast. Anne's program is much the same except she has given up swimming and recently uses the tread-mill and recumbent bike instead of walking in the gym. In the early 1980s she was swimming but eventually decided to give that up. She takes a coffee-break between her weights and cycling/treadmill. And we often wonder just how long we will be able to continue this program.

As I update my story (March, 2005) Anne walks from machine to machine in the weight room with what she calls her stick. It's actually a nice sophisticated cane. People at Four Seasons know us well and are very friendly and helpful. They help her on and off the tread mill; get coffee for her, and the like.

The friends and the social relationships motivate us to continue this program. We have been continuous members since it opened in 1962.

Naturally health is an important motivation. The environmental factor is also important. Eating lower on the food chain contributes to a sustainable planet and theoretically should alleviate hunger in the world; also I'm convinced it reduces our medical expenses. And to be involved in organized competition is a strong motivating force to keep me in good physical condition. And Anne seems to be just as strongly committed to the program as I am.

As mentioned earlier, Anne has also been involved in Senior Olympic competition, however, to a more limited extent. She has two State records in the women's 1500m walk race which still stand to date, February, 2005, in the '75-79,' and '80-84' age categories. In 1989, she set a state record in the '75-79' age category, with a time of 12 minutes 22 seconds, and in 1994, in the '80-84' age category, another record with a time of 13 minutes flat. Both records still stand sixteen years later. Although she has not competed since, she has always accompanied me to my meets and has been my most constant and loyal supporter. Now to some of the Senior Olympic meets as they occur.

My first participation in Senior Olympics was in 1982. I had never kept written records of the events until 1998. I had events and dates inscribed on the medals I received, but the suggestion to do journaling, I attribute to my brother-in-law, Dale Stutzman.

How It Got Started

Now to question one: "How did it get started?" I told Dale my story from the time I began my Senior Olympics competition. He said that should be recorded. I took his advice and here is my story: Bill Dunn and John Bertsche, two good friends from Normal, approached me on different occasions around the years 1980 and 1981, encouraging me to run with them. They were getting up early in the morning, taking a good run, then shower, eat, and go to work. I had high respect for both of these fellows, and I finally succumbed to their suggestion, and started getting up at 5:00 am and running.

My next door neighbors, Sandy and Jo Adams, both good athletes, gave me some good advice as to how to get started running. They said to run a little then walk. Run for perhaps ten to twenty minutes, and then walk until you feel ready to run again. I did this for several days, working into it gradually, and it was obviously getting easier day by day. Before long I was running five miles and felt that I could run all day if I had time and would run slowly.

The difficult part was getting out of bed so early in the morning. In the early stages of my running, I would get out of breath easily. Also, I recall that in my first runs, one of my feet would often nick the other as I jogged along. My first runs were slow, and gradually both these problems cleared up. My route was from our 8 Wilmette Drive home, north on Adelaide to Gregory, west to Parkside, south to College, and out in the country toward Farm & Fleet, then back home, approximately five miles. I'd shower, eat breakfast and go to school, usually to an 8:00 am class.

After doing this for a month or two, I had lost twenty to twenty-five pounds. I was weighing 155 to 160 before I started running. I got down to 135 pounds. I had to have adjustments made on my clothes, and since I had lost so much weight, people would often ask me if I was feeling well. I guess the weight loss made me look sick.

Along with Bill Dunn and John Bertsche, I registered for and ran my first 10k at a Flannigan, Illinois celebration, summer, 1982. I was rather apprehensive wondering whether I would be able to run the distance. I recall that in that race Bill had finished ahead of me then came back to meet me and ran the last half mile with me. That support was meaningful.

It was at this event that I met a man, Bob Morse, a medical patient of John Bertsche, who suggested I enter the Senior

Olympics at Springfield. I had never heard of the Senior Olympics before, but it sounded interesting. At his suggestion, John and I stopped at his home on our way home, picked up Senior Olympics registration forms for both John and me.

It was just eleven days before the events were to take place. I registered to do the 50m, 100m, the 200m, and the standing long jump, and put the form in the mail. That evening I went to the high school track to practice running the dashes. After the second evening of fast running, my quads were so sore I could hardly walk. I soon realized that I would not be able to heal up and be in shape to do the dashes in Springfield.

Consequently, I called Annette Fuchs, director of the Illinois Senior Olympics, and asked her to shift me to the distance runs which would be more in line with what I had been training for in my jogging. I entered and ran the 800M, 1500m, and 5K races, and kept my long jump entry. On the day of the meet, I did all the events and didn't place in any of them. At that meet I saw many winners getting their awards and wearing the medals around their necks, and I was envious. I wanted so badly to get just one medal, but failed to place in any of my events in that first meet. I did receive a small participation medal, which was embarrassing to me at the time, but which I prize highly today.

I talked to Bob Keck, the IWU track coach about my sore quads. He said, "Paul, meet me in the weight room and we'll go over a weight program for you." This was my introduction to working out with weights. Keck lined up a series of weights for me and suggested regular workouts. I followed his advice and have held rigorously to weight work ever since. I soon realized that weight training contributes to muscle strength and is very important in an exercise program.

My failure to place in that first meet was a motivation. I felt that if I would train properly I would do better. I continued my conditioning, mostly jogging, weights, and stretching, where we were members at Four Seasons. Six weeks before my track events, I would begin conditioning for the sprints. I would do fast running on the Four Seasons track.

On the Four Seasons track I worked on the dashes, and the second year of my Senior Olympics was a different story. I don't have the details here, but the "Results & Records Book," which was published annually along with my bag of medals would show the details. I have participated in the State Meet every year since I learned about the events. And for a number of years in the 1980s and '90s, I felt confident that I would place either 1st or 2nd in the dashes. One competitor, Francis Hitchell from Peoria and I would share 1st and 2nd pretty much equally in all three dashes. I'd win some and he'd win some.

One year Dennis came from Goshen and entered several events. He placed second and got a silver medal in the 1500m walk race. He entered the dashes but stopped with a pulled hamstring in the 100k He also did the bike races but didn't place. A year or so later Ruth and Abe, also from Goshen, came and entered several events. Abe got a silver medal in the 5000m run and Ruth also got a gold in the 5000m run. She was the only female entry in that and walked most of the race.

After I got acquainted with the State Meets, and started going regularly, I gained a lot of confidence and began winning medals. There was a period when I was in my 60-64s, the 65-69s, and in my 70s, I felt pretty confident in the dashes and the bike races. At one time I broke the state record in the 50m. It was then broken the following year. I held the state record in the 200m dash for seven years, 1987-93, at 32+ seconds. I've had several of the bike records, and since I'm in the '80-84' age category, I hold all of the five bike records for several age categories. The 10k bike record eluded me for some time. One year when I was all set for it, it rained and was omitted. Then two different years the timing was not done right. For example, in 1999, after I had really finished, the volunteer, an older lady said, "You have two more laps to go." I did the laps but had 8 miles on my computer rather than the 6 plus it should have been. As an aside, my 10k in the time trials in the Nationals in Orlando, 1999, I had a time, three minutes faster than the state record in Illinois, the record I've been trying to establish.

In the State Meet, September, 1999, we had poor attendance. We assume it was due to the fact that all qualifications for the Nationals in Orlando had been completed in the 1998 State Meet the year before, so this one was relatively meaningless to many people.

John Bertsche missed this State Meet for the first time in many years. He and I usually went together and had been doing this ever since I began participating in 1982. The reason John did not participate was that he was invited to participate in a medical meeting in our "sister city" in Russia and that conflicted with the Senior Olympic dates. Loren Moser, another friend from our church, who biked with us all summer was interested, he registered and went with me and entered the bike races. I won golds in five bike races (1/2 mile, 1 mile, 5k, 10k, and 20k), also the 100, and discus; 3rd in the 1500m walk race and 2nd in the 50m dash. All told, I received 7 golds, 1 silver and 1 bronze. Loren got silvers in his four bike races. He competed in the '50 - 54' age category and had one fellow he just couldn't beat. I considered this meet as a sort of warm up for the Nationals in Orlando to be held the following month, October 19-29.

I have participated in the Illinois State Senior Olympics every year since my introduction, except on the occasions where my injuries prohibited participation. I continued to enter the Illinois State meets regularly. For a number of years in the 1980s and '90s, I gained a lot of confidence and I felt that I would place either 1st or 2nd in the dashes.

Currently, I'm listed in the 2009 Record Book with eleven State records. The record events are cycling, 5k, '85-89' age category, 10:40 seconds; '90-94,' 10:53; 10k cycling, '85-89,' 23:34 seconds; and '90-94,' 25:23 seconds; race walk, '85-89,' 11:03 seconds, and '90-94,' 12:53 seconds; 50m dash, '85-89,' 10.43 seconds, '90-94,' 11.34 seconds; 100m dash, '90-94,' 22.9 seconds; 200m dash, '90-94,' 53.32 seconds; standing long jump, '90-94,' 4' 7.25.

Here is a summary of my experiences to date (2009). Up to 2009, I have a total of 225 medals and ribbons: 156 gold; 46 silver; twelve bronze; five 4th place ribbons; three 5th place ribbons; and three 6th place ribbons. At the National level, I have seven golds; five silvers; two bronzes; two 4th place ribbons; one 5th place ribbon and two 6th place ribbons.

At the National level, my cycling events have been more productive than the track and field events, seven gold, five silver, and 2 bronze medals, all since I've been in the 80 and above age categories. In my first National competition, Baton Rouge, 1993, when Brenda was with us, I had a 7th place (no ribbon but listed on bulletin board) in the 100m dash, along with the 5th and 6th place ribbons in cycling.

Over all, at the National level, I have two 4th place ribbons, in the 200m dash, and 3000m walk race, a 6th place ribbon in the 100m dash, a bronze in the 1500m walk race (my first ever medal in the Nationals) and two gold and two silver medals in the cycling events. 1999 was the year I got two National Records in the 20k and 40k road races.

From 1982 to approximately 1993, it became a pattern for John Bertsche and me to attend the meets together. He entered the distance runs and I, the short races. My regular entries were the 50m, 100m and 200m dashes, 1500m walk race, standing long jump, and discus. John's events were the 800m, 1500m, and 5k. He would do the 10k the Saturday before the Track and Field events on Sunday. He set the state record in the 10k, at 40:31, in 1993. That record is still standing in 2010. After John had heart problems, his doctor advised against his competing, and since the early 1990s, Anne and I have been attending the Senior Olympics without John.

The Role of "Four Seasons"

The Four Seasons Health Club has been important in the lives of our family since it opened in 1962. It has also been vital in keeping both Anne and me in good physical condition, and enabling us to participate in the Senior Olympics. Harlen Bliss was the builder/realtor from we bought our house on Wilmette Drive when we moved to Normal in 1960. He was co-owner of

Four Seasons Health Club when it opened and convinced us to take out family membership. At that time we did it particularly for our children, for swimming, playing in the gym and the like. Our kids used it a lot, particularly in the summer time and weekends year around. We all used it enough that we felt it worthwhile to continued membership.

After the kids left home, Anne and I still used it enough that we maintained membership. Once we were both retired in 1982, we began using it on a daily basis. After experimenting with different times for our exercise, we liked the early morning time best. We established the habit of getting out of bed at 4:15 am, start the cereal cooking before leaving, dressing for our exercise, and getting to Four Season by the time the door opened at 5:00.

Usually there were 20 to 30 people waiting in line when we arrived. We would go downstairs work in the weight room 45 minutes, go up, Anne would get her cup of coffee and visit with friends for a few minutes, I'd go to the gym, later Anne would join me, we'd run/walk for 20 minutes or so, then for a number of years we'd both swim. Later Anne became more or less frightful of swimming and discontinued. I'd usually swim 20 or 25 lengths; sometimes we'd use the Jacuzzi, then shower and leave for home at 7:00. We often commented about how good we felt after our workout, and became convinced that to get out of bed that early in the morning was worth the effort.

We followed this program for many years. Friends often commented how foolish we were to get up so early, when we were retired and didn't have to. Nonetheless, we continued this schedule until it became difficult, then finally impossible for Anne to physically negotiate the steps. Limitations came on gradually. Anne began using a cane to walk from machine to machine in the weight room. She would occasionally latch on to a friend, lock arms, in getting off the treadmill, and walking to the next machine. She began using a cane to help in her walking. She'd joke about her "stick." Actually it was a sophisticated cane we had purchased. Then she'd hang on to me going up the steps.

The critical turning point came when I had a bicycle accident, could not take care of Anne, she had to go to a nursing home for exactly one month, June 1 to July 1, 2007, and it was at that time that we quite drastically "rewrote" our fitness program. After I was sufficiently recuperated, I started going to Shirk, Wesleyan's fitness center. We bought a treadmill, put it in our living room, Anne used it faithfully for a number of years, and after having fallen the second time, she gave up on the treadmill.

I then wrote a letter to Four Seasons Health Club indicating that we would discontinue membership and explained why. Harley was the man who we were well acquainted with and who pretty much ran the operation, although he was not the official head of the organization. The letter follows:

July 7, 2007

4-Seasons Association
Attention: Harley
904 Four Seasons Club Road
Bloomington, IL 61701

Dear Harley:

Sometime ago we received the notice that it was time to renew our membership. Last January we renewed for only 6 months and I think our membership expires July 1, and it appears that the time has finally arrived when we must close in on it.

You are no doubt aware that we are long-time continuous members; in fact I question whether anyone else can match our tenure in your association. We joined when Harlen Bliss was co-owner of the club when it was a privately owned operation. He says it was in 1962. The sign out front has the date, 1965. I think that is when the Association took it over from Harlen and his partner. From these figures it appears that we have been continuous members for approximately 45 years.

It is needless to say that to give up membership is not an easy matter. In fact it is a quite emotional experience for both Anne and me. We don't do it without some deep regret and perhaps I might say with reluctance. Four Seasons Health Club has been an important factor in our lives for many years. We have developed many good friends there and it has been important in our lifestyle and general good health. Indeed we do appreciate what all the people involved have done for us and what it has meant to both Anne and me.

The critical events that cause us to make this move at this time is that I had a bicycling accident in which I broke 3 ribs and got bruised up quite badly. The emergency room doctor put me in the hospital for two nights, and gave me a wide battery of tests. During my recuperation I have not been able to take care of Anne so she had to go to a nursing home. That all happened about a month ago. At the time of this writing I am pretty well healed and Anne came home July 2. We hope we can take care of our own necessities at least for a while. I personally have been working out at IWU's Shirk Center. That works real well for me, and the cost difference is significant. It appears that Anne will simply have to give up this kind of activity.

Harley, we could name many good friends that have come from our Four Seasons experience. I think of Rick, Kevin, & Bob, Randa, Bill McNamara, Steve & Brenda, Roger & Scott, John, Judy, Mary Sweet, Stan Giesen, and Peggy who so faithfully visited with Anne while she had her coffee, and we could go on and on. Those I didn't name, please forgive me.

Again I say thanks for the role 4-Season has played in our lives. Personal greetings and farewell from both Anne and me.

Sincerely,

D. Paul Miller

Shortly after I wrote this letter, we had a knock on our door, and a lady was here to deliver an "edible arrangement" (a large fruit bouquet) from the board of Four Seasons Association, with a note expressing thanks for our long membership and regrets for our inability to continue. I sent a follow-up letter thanking them for the "edible arrangement."

Anne and I maintained contact with a number of our good Four Seasons friends until her death, and I still have occasional contacts with those friends. It was hard for both of us to give up Four Seasons. I have been using Shirk Center regularly, five days a week, and have developed a number of good friends who come in early in the morning. I have appreciated particularly getting acquainted with Norm Eash, the Wesleyan long-time football coach. Also to bump heads with some of the varsity athletes has been special for me.

To give you some notion of the type of friends I have developed at Shirk Center, at the time of my 92nd birthday, I was in the rear of the fitness center involved with my regular program, when one of my friends, Chad Beatte, a burly six-foot-two, 240 pound, former quarter back on IWU football team, came to me and said, "Paul I need your help." I couldn't imagine what I could do to help him. He said "Come with me." We went to the front of the room; there were a bunch of people who sang Happy Birthday to me. Then Norm Esch opened the cabinet door and pulled out a package, handed it to me and said "Happy Birthday."

It was an IWU athletic suit, shirt and pants, normally issued to the athletes who participate in the Wesleyan sports. The whole event was an emotional experience for me and I appreciated it deeply. Incidentally, prior to this occasion I had been wearing my Four Seasons shirt every day, and some of my friends would jokingly jibe me for continuing to wear my Four Seasons shirt. I guess they thought I should be wearing an IWU shirt. And I have worn it every day since I received it.

The foregoing discussion includes more than the information I gave Dale on how it got started. In general, I have brought our exercise program pretty much down to the present time. Now we'll look at some of the specific events in our Senior Olympics.

State Senior Games of Illinois, 1982-2010

The Illinois Senior Olympics has been the basic part of my Senior Olympic experience. As mentioned above, I was introduced to the Illinois Meets in 1982, I have participated in the annual meets every year since except one, or maybe two years, I was unable to participate because of injuries. I have had five injuries which has affected my participation. (These will be described later) The exact dates and meets it affected is somewhat vague, since I did not keep copious details until more recently. E. g., I recall it affected my national meets twice, and I think the State Meet only once.

I remember clearly that I called the National Office when the meet was scheduled at Baton Rouge in 2001. With a doctors statement they refunded my registration fee. Also I recall that I had some communication with Greg Moore, one of the officials, regarding my national records in the cycling road races.

More recently I had to cancel the Louisville Games. That cancellation is more vivid in my mind because it is more recent, 2007. Louisville would have been a relatively short drive from home and at that time, Anne and I had motel reservations and planned to drive. That cancellation was due to my cycle crash right here on the MRC grounds. I was riding around the circle and making a turn at a pretty good speed, in front of Oyers house and simply fell. My friend, Russ Oyer took me to the ER. After giving me a battery of tests, the hospital reported a concussion. I have no memory of what or how it happened. Since I didn't hit any car or anything else, and have no memory of anything causing my fall, I have been somewhat concerned as to whether I blacked out then fell, or whether the fall with the concussion caused me to lose all memory of events leading up to the fall. I've been riding now for three years and have had no black outs, so it appears to have been the latter, the concussion caused me to lose memory.

One year I did the cycle races in Springfield with my wrist in a brace because my big roto tiller backfired on me and cracked my wrist. That injury, however, apparently did not affect my cycling. The races all went well.

For a number of years the bicycle races were held one weekend in September, with the Track and Field events the following weekend. Later the cycle races were scheduled earlier in the summer, June or July. I am told that the shift is because officials from the National Cycling Federation were available in June or July and no longer available in September. So currently the cycling races are in the summer, track and field in September. And without fail, never once did I participate in a meet, State, National, or Regional, without Anne accompanying me. She has been my most loyal supporter and at every meet. As I write this, my 2010 events will be the first I will have participated in without her.

The point I intended to make when starting this section is that to list each state, and the few regional meets individually would take too much space, and become monotonous and boring. For that reason I have made a more or less summary statement of those meets. I've had fewer Mennonite Meets, they and the Nationals have been more special, so I'm describing these in more detail in the following pages.

Mennonite Senior Sports Classics

Goshen, Indiana, 1998

June 24-27, 1998, the first Mennonite Senior Sports Classic (Senior Olympics) was held at Goshen College, Goshen, Indiana. It was at this meet that Dale asked the two questions, alluded to earlier, and that got me started with keeping this record.

I had competition activities each day, Thursday (25th), Friday and Saturday. In the Mennonite Meet, participants were divided into 10-year age categories. The banquet with opening ceremonies was Wednesday, the 24th. Anne and I made our headquarters with Ethel and Dale Stutzman, my sister and her husband, who lived on 14th Street, close to the college. We attended the banquet Wednesday evening then the following three days I participated in ten events, 50 & 100m dashes, discus, 50 yard swim, (back, breast, and free-style), the 5000m walk race, and finally the 1500m walk.

Both walk races were moved from 4:00 pm to 7:00 pm, mainly because of the heat. Also some of the walkers complained about walking on the chip and grass path where the races were originally scheduled. The 5000m was moved to the high school track where we had had the track and field events earlier in the day. The 1500m walk was kept on the chip and grass path near the Recreation Center where it was originally scheduled. The officials in charge indicated that they couldn't move both of the races to the high school because the grounds people had worked so hard to prepare the "chip & grass" track, and they just couldn't let it go completely unused. It was a bad track for race walking but for the short race it worked out OK.

Finally, Saturday morning we had the bicycle races. They were run on roads south of Goshen that had been marked out rather carefully. They were staged as time trials. They lined us all up, youngest to oldest, then started each in thirty-second intervals. It was well administered and run in a professional manner. In each of the 10K and 20K races, I was lined up last. The only competitor in my age category was just ahead of me. In each race I passed him within the first half mile even though he had a 30 seconds head start on me. I got gold medals in both races and passed up quite a number of people in the younger age categories. For example, in both races I passed up Truman Herschberger about two-thirds of the way through the race, who won the gold in the '70-74' age category for both races.

In the ten events I got seven gold and three silver medals. The silvers came in discus, back and freestyle swim races. The others were gold. In most events I had only one other competitor in my age category. I keep saying that the real race at my age is lifestyle, the race of survival. A vegetarian diet and regular exercise and conditioning contain the secret. The ranks get thinned out as one goes up the age ladder. In the MSSC events there were a total of four participants in my age category, the 80 to 89 age group. Most of these were in other events, swimming, golf, and discus.

The most rewarding and enjoyable for me were the two dashes and the bicycle races. In the dashes they had two heats, first, all the '50s' age categories, seven in all. The second heat, the one I was in, included the 60s, 70s and 80s, seven or eight runners. One, a 60-year-old ran away from the field. I placed second overall in this heat for both dashes. The races went real well for me, and I was satisfied with the times, 8.87 for the 50, and 17.62 for the 100. The official timers rounded off my time and it was printed in the papers at 17.70, but told me I was actually timed at 17.62.

The interesting thing about the 5000m walk race is that one of the men in the 70s walked my speed and about the second or third round we started visiting. We spent probably the last 8 or 10 laps getting acquainted with each other. As we walked and talked we kept up our fast pace, about six mph. His name was Ezra Beachy. He was wearing long pants, said he felt self-conscious in shorts. He had come from Amish background, lived in Iowa as an Amish lad, and then later joined the Mennonite church. I told him I had lived with Freeman & Bertha Beachy when on sabbatical leave from Illinois Wesleyan University. He said he had some Beachy relatives in Arthur, Illinois but had lost touch with them.

When I learned about his Amish background I could understand why he felt self-conscious wearing shorts. He got a bronze medal, third behind the two Herschbergers, Gene and Truman, who were the fastest walkers overall. Gene had placed second in the nationals a few years earlier. I had known Gene and had walked with him when we were in Phoenix for two weeks several years ago. My times were pretty much what I had done in the past, 39:24 in the 5000, and 12:27 for the 1500.

In the bicycle races the layout of the courses made the 10K actually 11.8K in length. The officials explained that this was necessary so the start and finish line could be at the same place. The 20K was exactly 20K. My time in the so called 10K was

24:54, which was really meaningless when compared with my past 10K times. The 20K time was 43.0 minutes about what I have done in the past.

Before entering the events I never anticipated winning the swim events or the discus. For some reason, however, I did get a gold in the breast stroke. I think the other fellow in my age category scratched, if so that left me the only entrant. I enjoy throwing the discus but seldom practice it. Although I had no idea who any of my Mennonite competitors would be, I must admit that in my mind beforehand, I would have been disappointed if I had not won gold in the other events.

After the events were all over, and we were sitting around the table, it was then that Dale asked me the questions alluded to above. I discussed this with him and the others present, in some detail. When I told him I had never thought particularly about how I got started and also that I had never done any "journaling," he responded "You should." That was sufficient motivation to get me going on this chapter in my life.

Goshen, Indiana, 2000

The second Mennonite Senior Sports Classic was again held in Goshen, June 29 to July 1, 2000. Anne and I went to the banquet on Thursday evening, then the following two days I participated in 8 events: 50m and 100m dashes, 1500m walk race, 5000m walk race, three cycle events 20k, 10k, 5k, and also table tennis.

Summarizing the meet, I got gold medals in all of the events. Competition was low. I had one competitor in the cycling events, and one in table tennis. In the whole meet a little less than one hundred participated. Anyone affiliated with any Mennonite agency was eligible. It is discouraging to participate when we have so few in my age category.

As in the meet two years earlier, Anne and I stayed with Ethel and Dale. They are very cooperative in preparing the proper food, allowing freedom for us to come and go, and also supporting me by attending every event. My brother, Dennis and his wife Anne, along with one of the Farnhurst CPS buddies Ray Miller and wife, attended the track races. An interesting aside is that Dale took videos of all the events I participated in, and then gave me the tape, so I have that in my possession.

This Mennonite event is fun in a different way compared with other meets. It becomes important to me particularly because you rub elbows with Mennonite people in a different context. The officials responsible for the meet say we will need to get approximately twice as many participants if we want the program to continue. It is entirely possible that this is the last Mennonite meet that will be scheduled.

Harrisonburg, Virginia, 2003

Anne and I drove the pickup since I felt that it was better to have my bicycle inside, also we had a lot more room for baggage and supplies. I participated in the 50m and 100m dashes; the 1500m walk race, three bicycle races and the discus.

As in the two other Mennonite meets, registration was low, I won my events, which under the circumstances of low competition became less important, but I met many interesting people and made new friends.

Picture 42 - Brenda, Dad and Mac (left to right) following their Mennonite Classic victories in Goshen, IN, June 1996.

My former Farnhurst CPS buddy John Martin and his wife Helen were at the meet. John and Helen are among the younger of our Farnhurst group and have been serving as our Farnhurst CPS historians. They had been living in Florida, and were visiting their children living in Harrisonburg at the time.

Goshen scheduled another Mennonite Sports Classic for 2005. I registered for it, but received a notice three weeks before it was to take place, indicating that due to insufficient registration it was cancelled. They indicated that the Mennonite Senior Olympics programs would be discontinued because it seemed impossible to stir up enough interest to make them financially feasible.

It was meaningful to me when Rich, Brenda, and Mac participated with me in the Goshen Senior Sports Classic. They were in the area for a Wiebe reunion in Michigan the same week and decided to participate. Rich participated in and won the cycle races he entered. Brenda and Mac and I were in the same walk race. All walk racers were together, and then they sorted out by age categories after the finish. All three of us won our race competition, but we have to admit there was very little competition. Brenda, however, had serious competition in the running long jump, and I think it was on her third jump when she out-distanced her rival and won the gold. This was one of the more exciting events for spectators. I think she also won gold in her table tennis match.

It was equally meaningful to me that Don did not participate. At that time he attended the reunion but had responsibilities staying with his family caring for his recently adopted daughters, and transportation schedules with his responsibilities did not permit his family to attend the Senior Olympics at that time.

The National Meets have always been special events for both Anne and me. Although Anne did not participate in them, she always indicated that she enjoyed attending and supporting her husband. Also, I enjoyed and appreciated her loyal support. In the following pages, I'll give a run-down first of some of my state meets and then of the National events we attended.

State Senior Games of Illinois, 1982 – 2010

September 10 & 17, 2000

The qualifying meet for the State of Illinois was held in Springfield September 10 to 17, 2000. The bicycle events were held on September 10 and Track and Field at the Lampier Stadium a week later, September 17. The bicycle races were transferred to a new location this year. Previously they were in Lincoln Park using an oval nine tenth of a mile around, and it had two sharp turns, one on a downhill. In the years I have participated, I have witnessed a number of accidents and I think it was primarily for safety reasons that a new location was found. The new location had an excellent course on new roads near the campus of The University of Illinois Springfield. It was referred to as "the 11th Street extension."

I participated in all five of the cycling events, 20k, 10k, 5k, 1-mile, and ½-mile sprints. I think it was because of the new location that I did three of the races in record time. Previously, I held the records of four of the five races they stage, and have been working to get the record in the 10k that has eluded me since I am in the '80-84' age category. The first year I was in this age category, the 10k was rained out. It was the second year in this category where, as I alluded to earlier, the volunteer who was keeping track of my laps told me, after I had actually completed the race, "you have two more laps to go." I did the extra two laps, won the race, but in a time of 27 plus minutes. I had done that race in Orlando in 18 minutes and was confident I had done it here in less than 21 minutes which was the posted record at that time.

The 10k was scheduled to be run first, and interestingly, they had some problem synchronizing the timers at the finish line which was approximately a mile away from the starting point. At the finish line the timers gave me a time of 20:18 seconds which was a minute and 5 seconds off the record, and this seemed realistic to me. When they gave out the awards, they quoted a time for me of 16:43, a time I could never have done. I mentioned this to Sheila Shields, the director of the Illinois Senior Olympics. She said there was some confusion in getting the timers at the finish line synchronized with the starters, and they would have to work things out. So I am not sure what will be done with the times they will eventually give me. I think the 20:18 is the correct time. I did the mile in 2:57, which is 23 seconds off my old record set the previous year. Then, for the one-half mile, I beat my former record by a little over one second. For both the mile and the half-mile races we had a slight breeze advantage and most of the race was on a good road, straightaway.

My good friend and biking partner, Page Coleman, was one of my good supporters at the cycling events. All told, I felt very good about the events, with the exception of the timing on the 10k. The course was a big improvement over the Lincoln Park course, the weather was ideal, cool but not cold, and most of the time we had a cloud cover. Anne and Page were good support and all five races went well, no crashes, and no flat tires. Five events, five gold medals, and I'm qualified for the nationals. (Update, February, 2005: Unfortunately, it appears that all records of the meets for 2000, and 2001, have been lost. The director, Sheila Shields simply was not qualified to run the meets, and her results were simply dropped from the files. We now have two good co-directors who are doing a good job but have no books recording the events and records for the two years mentioned above

Track and Field, 2003

In the track and field events, I achieved my goal, even beyond expectation. I realized the records were within reach but didn't know just how I would respond when the time came.

I should point out here that it has been the policy of the State Meet officials to list records of out-of-state participants separately from state residents. As it turned out, I achieved State records outright in the 50m, 200m dashes, and the 1500m walk race. I have the state record in the 100m but a man from Indiana had a faster time than mine set in 1987. I was .46 seconds slower. So in all the events that I participated in I have state records for '85-89' age category and overall records for all but the 100m.

When records are kept it has been policy in the past to give the best time for Illinois residents, and then list separately the times for out-of-state participants. An Indiana man had a 20.51 time and mine was 20.95. You will note that my challenge for next year is to cut .46 second from my "this year's" time. All the other track times were overall records for this age category.

Another note of explanation is in order here. The director of the State Of Illinois Senior Olympics had resigned and Sheila Shields was appointed director in 2000. Being new in this role and apparently incompetent, we have not had any publication of "Results & Records" that have been compiled and distributed to participants in the past. For the years 2000 and 2001, nothing whatsoever has been distributed to participants. I inquired by phone calls and emails a number of times and of no avail. Shields is on some kind of medical leave and did not appear for the 2003 events.

Two new women, Deborah Staley and Selvarine Jones, were appointed co-directors, to replace Sheila Shields. We are not informed as to whether this is a permanent appointment or simply interim. I became quite well acquainted with Deborah Staley and have put a lot of pressure on her to keep records and distribute the "Results & Records" to participants. This is important to me. This is the period that I participated in the 80-84 age group and did some good races with record times and my fear is that these may never be recorded. For example, in 2000, I did the mile in 2:57. In the 1999 record book my record for 80-85 is listed as 3:20. It is a disappointment for me to not have the results and records recorded correctly, published and distributed but none of this has happened in any of Shields years. She was so disorganized and mixed up and it appears that she never could get things straightened out. The co-directors this year have gleaned some semblance of results from Shield's files and have published results for 2002 events. This publication contains no records and no introduction, history or other explanations that had appeared in earlier publications. It is my hope that we can get permanent director(s) and get the files organized and distributed for this year and years to come.

This is the extent of my information as of the date October, 2003.

Track & Field, 2004

I am doing the summary of this State Meet, February, 2005. As of this writing, we have reservations made for a motel in Pittsburg, June 5 to June 10, and plan to make the trip. Brenda tells us she would like to attend these events, and assist her parents. She would indeed be helpful and we would appreciate her coming, but I say when we are unable to function on our own, it will be time for us to re-evaluate our program.

Update, March, 2005, after the Records and Results book came out for the September, 2004 meet: I mentioned above that I had established State records in all three of the dashes in the State Meet, September, 2003. When the Records and Results for that meet came out, I noticed that my old friend and former competitor, Francis Hitchell of Peoria was listed as the record holder in the 100M at 19.86 seconds, from the 2000 Meet for which I had been informed, data were lost because of the confusion with Sheila Shields being in charge. I had been told that all records for events in years 2000 and 2001 were lost. I inquired via email to Deb Staley, the current co-director. She informed me that an assistant that was helping her go through the old records and results had dug up some of Shield's records that appeared to be acceptable, and that Hitchell's record was included and listed. That took away my record which was .65 second slower than his. I had participated in that meet and although I don't remember details of that race, obviously he beat me. I had a silver medal in that race consequently no state record. I still do, however, hold the State records for the 50M and 200M dashes in the '85-89' age category, these along with records in the walk race and all the cycle events.

I should mention here also that since we have the new directors a new policy has been adopted for the 2004 State Meet.

They decided to eliminate the one-mile and ½ mile cycle events, and to discontinue timing the road races. This brings the state events in line with the nationals, i.e., no cycle races shorter than the 5k, and road-races not timed. I had a number of the State records for all of the short races along with most of the time-trials, and 20k road-race listed in the 1999 records and results book. The latest Records & Results Book, 2004, lists times and records for only the 5k and 10k cycle time-trials along with the race-walk and two running events.

I have no record of the 2005 State Meet. I think I skipped it because of my injury.

Illinois State Meet, 2006

I participated in the Track & Field Meet, September 17, and the Cycle Events September 23, & 24. I have given up on the discus throw because of my rotator cuff surgery problem. In Track & Field, I did the 1500m walk-race, the three dashes 50m, 100m, and 200m, and also the standing broad jump. I received gold medals in the walk race (12:51.7), 50m (12.02), 100m (23.47), 200m (57.0), and silver in the standing broad jump (4'8"). This qualifies me for all of these events in the Nationals in Louisville, Kentucky, June/July, 2007.

I also participated in the four cycling races, two on September 23, and two September 24, and placed first for Illinois riders in all four events. An out of state man from Atlanta, Georgia, John Taylor, beat me in all of them. My times were 5k, 11:59.82; 10k, 26:42.67. These were both time trial races. I placed first, again for Illinois riders, in the 20k and 40k road races. No times are kept for the road races.

I am qualified to enter any of these events in the coming Nationals, in 2007. Policy limits participants to two age categories in National competition. I plan to do the cycling; then either the walk races or the running events, but am not allowed to do both the walking and running events, along with the cycling.

As I'm writing this in March, 2007, (just now getting caught up) I'm planning to do the cycling with the new bike the kids bought me for my 90th birthday and Christmas. It is a Trek, Madone SL, I'm told, the same frame Lance Armstrong's Discovery Channel Team used in the Tour de France. It is a really good bike and I am anxious to test it in competition. I'm not expecting too much in National competition this year. I'm 89, will be 90 the month just after the Nationals close in July, this year, but I still have to compete in the '85-89 age category.' There will be a number of new 85 and 86 year old "youngsters" just new in the '85-89 age category.' And every year does make a difference.

Another interesting turn of events is that I learned recently that the State cycling meet this year was to be held in May. It's really too early to get into any kind of good physical condition that early in Illinois. Weather is too cold. By March 19, I have been on my bike only two times so far this spring.

On approximately May 5, 2007, I did some real damage to my left wrist, cranking the roto-tiller. It backfired and twisted my left hand way back really hurting it severely. I went to the doctor at Convenient Care, Carle Clinic. There it was x-rayed, no broken bones but ligament damage. They put on a wrist splint and told me to check with our primary doctor in a week. Later my doctor said that upon examining the X-rays closer, they found the wrist was actually cracked.

I was concerned about the State Cycle races coming up in two weeks. I recovered sufficiently to do the races but with the wrist brace. Since my age category in the State Meet determined the age as of December 31, the year of the meet, I was in the '90-94' age category. In the 31 years of Illinois Senior Olympics, no participant in this age category had ever entered the cycle events So to simply finish the races would be State records. I did only the 5k and 10k time trials. I figured the longer races (29k & 40k) were more than my wrist was good for.

The 5k was, with the exception of a ¼ mile jog, against a brisk head wind, start to finish. Time was 16: 01, quite slow, but a state record. The following day for the 10k, we had a similar wind; however the route was to the 5k point and back to the start line; against the wind out, with the wind on the return. On the return I had good speed, most of it 18 up to 20 mph. My goal was to do it in less than half an hour. Actual time was 25: 53, faster than my 2006 time of 26:42.67. Both races were State records, the first races with my new bike.

I felt I was in good condition for the Nationals coming up June 22-27. However, on May 28, 2007, I had a cycle accident while riding around here on the MRC grounds. As I mentioned earlier, I had no recollection of the fall, do not know if I blacked out ahead of the fall or whether the fall knocked the memory out of my reach. Russ Oyer took me to the emergency room at BroMenn. They kept me two nights and gave all kind of tests trying to determine why the fall. X-rays showed three broken ribs although all other tests showed up positive, so the reason for the fall remains a mystery. I simply cancelled the National races scheduled for June.

It was necessary for Anne to go to a nursing home while I was recuperating from my fall. Rich came down and helped process that. We had many telephone conversations with Don and Brenda, one a 5-way conversation with Rich's telephone technology involving Rich, Brenda, Don, Anne & me. As of this writing, June 19, 2007, Anne is still in Manor Care nursing home, 510 Broadway here in Normal. I'm living alone at home while in the process of healing the broken ribs. I have had some problems with pseudo-gout while recovering, but again, as of this writing, I'm looking forward to being sufficiently healed so we can bring Anne home in a week or two. I've gone to Shirk Fitness Center two days this week, had some good workouts and it feels good to be back into some semblance of conditioning. At this point I'm looking forward to and hoping to be able to compete in the State Track & Field meet next September.

Illinois State Meet, 2007

My first year in the '90-94' age category, 2007, I entered 7
events, resulting in 7 state records. Events, the old records, and
my new records are as follows:

Table 5: Illinois State Meet Record (2007), D. Paul, age 90.

Event	Old Record	My Record
1500m Walk Race	14:19.83	12:52
100m Dash	23.65	22.09
50m Dash	12.58	11.34
200m Dash	no record*	53.31
Standing Long Jump	3' 7"	4' 5"
5k Time Trial	no record*	16:01
10k Time Trial	no record*	25:53

*Indicates that in the 31 years of Illinois Senior Olympics,
no one in this age category ever participated in this event.
It is assumed that these events are too much for a ninety
year old.

Cycle races were held May 19, 2007. (In the Illinois Meet, age
is considered as of December 31, in the year of participation.)
Richard Hirschler, and our friends, Paul & Esther Andreas were
here for this meet. I had given Richard a copy of the seven
events with the old state records, and as the events were run, he
wrote down my times and the distance in the standing long jump.
When completed we were pleased to see that they were all state
records.

Since all seven of my Senior Olympics events this year were
State records it was sufficiently rewarding for me personally that I
had the medals engraved professionally. Otherwise in the past
years, for State Meets, I engraved the medals with my hand
engraver.

Illinois State Meet, 2008

In 2008, I entered only four events. I missed the cycle races because of a scheduling conflict. Earlier, I had registered for Anne and me to attend the Builder's Retreat at Camp Friedenswald. We had arranged ahead of time, to have the most convenient lodging possible at the Health Center, near the dining hall and meeting places, because Anne was in a wheelchair. Also we had arranged to pick blue berries at a favorite spot in Indiana on the way. The day before we left I realized that the cycle races were scheduled for the same weekend, and I simply did not have the nerve to cancel the Builder's Retreat. Unfortunately, this was the qualifying year for the Nationals, so I am not qualified for the cycling races which have always been my best events. Since 1999, I have always won medals in cycling at the National level. I've never done so well at the Nationals in Track and Field so we will probably not attend the Nationals next summer in San Francisco. I have further regrets since Don has offered to assist us if we would get to San Francisco.

My events, times and distance for September 21, 2008, at age 91, are as follows:

Table 6: Illinois State Meet (2008)

Event	Result
1500m Walk Race	13 minutes, 48 seconds
100m Dash	28.35 seconds
50m Dash	12.45 seconds
Standing Long Jump	4' 7 ¼ " (a new State Record)

A few days after the Track and Field Meet, I received in the mail a plaque from Deb Staley, Coordinator of the Illinois Senior Olympics, which states "Illinois Senior Olympics presents D. Paul Miller the Skinner High Point Award for the 2007 Games, Men's 90-94 Age Division." It is a beautiful plaque with the inscription on a brass plate mounted on a finished walnut panel.

Also on the plaque we have under a glass plate "2007 Illinois Senior Olympics," and a picture of Abe Lincoln. Deb sent an accompanying letter stating that she was sorry she hadn't given this to me at the Track & Field Meet.

Illinois State Meet, Bicycling, 2009

Cycle races for the State Meet, had a change of venue this year. The place west of Chatham, where the races have been held the past few years, was not available for the cycle races this year, so they were brought in with registration at the Elementary School, just on the east side of Chatham. I had received a packet from Debbie Staley with maps of the new courses, a sheet with a confirmation of the events for which I was registered, and on the other side of the confirmation sheet information including the location of our new venue.

When the packet came in the mail, I saw the maps, looked at the confirmation sheet and laid it aside thinking the maps were for people who did not know our regular course. So when Anne and I arrived at the old place on Saturday morning, it was dead, no one around. We asked for information at several places, including the high school, and a park where people had congregated, but no one knew anything about it. So I was about ready to give up and go home, hoping to check one more place where I had seen a bunch of cars in a parking lot on the way in. Sure enough, here it was, and by this time we were about fifteen minutes from starting time. But we got Anne situated with some friendly people at the registration table, got my bike and gear lined up and I took off for the starting line. I was the last one registered so, I had about half an hour before my turn came up in my first race, the 5k Time Trial.

It was a straight course; we had a slight wind to our back, so I felt motivated to go for the record. Two years earlier I had set the State Record at 16:01, mostly one direction and against a good head wind. Slow time. The 10k that year was done in better time at 25.53, since we came back on the course, to the finish line, with the wind.

On the new course this year, the 5k was a straight shot, start to finish. With my good bike that the kids had bought me earlier, the new course, with a slight favorable wind, I felt motivated. I averaged (if I figure correctly) nearly eighteen miles per hour. Time: 10:55. More than five minutes off the State Record I had set two years earlier. It's a big difference but given, the wind factor, along with the new course and my good bike, I'm confident the time is correct.

The next day, I did the 10k, with a time that appears more realistic. My old record was 25:53, while the new time 25:23, thirty seconds off the old record. With both races being State records, I felt rewarded, and also felt the times were respectable, probably better than I can ever hope to do in this age category. Also, I was thankful that, even though we had some difficulty finding the new registration place, we didn't miss out on the meet

Illinois State Meet, 2010

For track and field, held in September, I was registered for four events. I got in two before it rained. It rained so hard that the meet was eventually cancelled. I did the 1500m Walk Race in 13:06. That is 21 seconds slower than last year. Then the Standing Long Jump, 4' 3" which is four inches less than last year at 4' 7 ¼ ", which is the record for my age category, which I set last year.

Picture 43 - D. Paul at the start of the 10k time trial at the Illinois Sr. Olympics in 2010, at the age of 93.

I was disappointed that I could not do the 100m, and the 50m dashes. I trained quite rigorously in Shirk Center for approximately 6 weeks beforehand. My training involved track work in the gym rather than the elliptical. I think I will now go back to the elliptical. I feel the elliptical saves my knee and hip joints. I'll probably not run any significant amount until I get ready for the meet next September, 2010.

Even so, am quite sure I would have been slower this year, had I run them. I hear one loses about one percent a year. I think at my stage of life, I'm losing more than the one percent. Even so, I feel I could have done the 100 in around 30 seconds. Last year it was 28.35. And the 50 in 13 seconds, something. Time last year was 12.45.

The 2010 State Senior Olympics meets have all been affected by rainfall. The cycle races scheduled for July 17 & 18 were held as scheduled. Rich drove down from Evanston to support me in my races. I ran the 5k time trial on the 17th, and qualified for the Nationals to be held 2011 in Houston. I elected not to do the 40k road race held the same day because it is longer than I feel like racing at my age. On July 18, I was scheduled to do the 10k time trial and the 20k road race. We were all set to get the meet on the way but a threatening rain storm had been looming all morning. Before the races began, it began raining with lightning and thunder. We all waited until about 10:30am and with no apparent let up, the official called the meet off.

Debbie Staley, director of the Illinois Senior Olympics, notified me that she had contacted the National Senior Olympics office and because of the circumstances were permitting her to qualify me for both the 5k time trial and the 20k road races. So I am now qualified to do three cycle races in the Nationals next year, 2011.

The track and field meet was scheduled for September 19. I was registered to do the 50k, 100k dashes, 1500m walk race, standing long jump, and discus. Two of these events, the 50m dash and standing long jump, are not included in the National meet. Again, interestingly on September 19, we again had threatening rain and lightning storm. I drove to Springfield in the rain. When I arrived it was raining and all the participants were notified that the again, the meet was cancelled for the day with a probable makeup date to be announced.

I was later notified that the make-up date was to be October 10. I was scheduled to attend Brian's wedding October 8, and to be gone the weekend including the 10th. So I figured I would not qualify for any of the Track and Field events. However, I later received a notice from the National offices that I was qualified to do the 100m dash and the 1500m walk races, the only two I was actually interested in entering. Apparently, my friend Debbie, the State Director, had pulled strings for me to get me qualified for those two events.

So as the situation now stands with the latest on Senior Olympics as I finish this report, I am qualified for the three cycle races, 5k and 10k time trials, the 20k road race, and in track and field the 100m dash and 1500m walk race. The Nationals are scheduled for June, 2011, and if I am feeling up to it at that time, I hope to participate.

The National Senior Games

Picture 44 - Paul and Brenda in Baton Rouge, LA in 1992.

To date, 2010, I have attended five National meets, Baton Rouge, 1993; San Antonio, 1995; Orlando, 1999; Hampton Roads, 2003; and Pittsburg, 2005. I missed the 2001 meet in Baton Rouge, and also the 2007 meet in Louisville, Kentucky, both because of injuries described earlier. Brenda was with Anne and me in Baton Rouge. Rich and his friend (no longer around) were in San Antonio with us. And Don met us in both Orlando and Hampton Roads. Brenda was with us again in Pittsburg. For the Pittsburg meet she flew to Bloomington, and then drove most of the way for Anne and me traveling to Pittsburg. She also drove the entire time in Pittsburg, to and from our cycle venues. She was very good in negotiating the city traffic and reading the maps to our events. I feel the National meets have been special so will report them individually.

Baton Rouge, 1993

This was my first National Senior Olympic meet. I was very happy to learn that Brenda was planning to be with us there. She flew to New Orleans where her cousin Marilyn (Harms) Jeppeson who lives in Slidell, Louisiana, met her at the airport and drove her to Baton Rouge to be with us. We had lodging in the University dormitory. It was adequate but more primitive than motel living. I took our camp stove along so would be able to do some cooking, although we found good food at the University cafeteria and used the stove very little.

In this meet, in the '75-79' age category, I placed 5th in the 20K bike race with a time of 37:40, and 6th in the 5K bike in 8:28. Since they awarded ribbons 4th to 6th place I received two ribbons for these events. I entered the two walk races and the two dashes and did not place high enough in any of these to receive an award. I did qualify to run in the final heat of the 100m dash. Of the nine entries in the final heat I finished 7th. Brenda and I both saw my name posted in 7th position in the final bulletin board posting.

As an aside, while we were being placed in positions for the various heats for the 100, I noticed that one of my spikes had been lost from my track shoes. I had additional spikes but they were in our dormitory room where we were lodging. I told Brenda about it and she came to my rescue, ran to the dorm, up seven flights on the elevator, got my sack of spikes and came back puffing. I had just enough time to set the spike and be ready when our heat was called. It was really good to have Brenda there to help, also it gives us a chance to visit and get acquainted in a special atmosphere.

In the early bike races I did not feel particularly happy with my 5th and 6th place ribbons. At that time, I figured I should place higher and hopefully win a medal, in some of my walk and running races still ahead. However, as time wore on and as the other races were completed the ribbons in the biking looked better all the time. I do not recall my position in the walk or running races. I only know I did not win a medal or ribbon, and I also felt they were not worth remembering.

The events were scattered over a week or more. In some of our days off Brenda, Mother and I did some sightseeing. Among other activities, we visited some historic plantations and an alligator farm. One other event which I'll never forget was that when taking Brenda to the airport with the bike on the top rack I drove through the entrance with a low bar above and it hit the bike and tore it from the rack and damaged the rack. We held up traffic while we were picking up the pieces and somehow got the bike in the car, took Brenda to meet her flight, then went to a bike shop and got the rack repaired so we could travel to our Illinois destination. That was my first National Senior Olympic meet.

San Antonio, TX, 1995

Even though I was in the upper part of the '75-79' age category, I enjoyed the events of the Baton Rouge meet to the point that I wanted to continue attending the national meets. I figured it was beneficial for me to participate, a diversion, and enjoyable for both Anne and me.

Rich was with us in San Antonio. This was a meet in which I did not receive a single award, no medals, and no ribbons. As I recall, I did not enter the running events but only the biking and race walking. Even though I was registered for four cycling events, I did not do the 20k thinking that this would give me a better chance in the 5k to be run the same day. Apparently it didn't make much difference; at least I did not place in any event in this meet.

If my memory serves me right it was the 5000M walk race in this meet where I was among 150 participants who were disqualified for a "bent knee." This resulted in a great deal of controversy and complaint to the Senior Games office. Since that time the race walk judges have been more lenient. After the 1500M walk race I inquired of the time-keepers and was told that I had placed 10th. So after two National meets I learned that it was not easy to place. All told I had received a total of two ribbons for a 5th and 6th place in biking at Baton Rouge. I was hungry for a medal.

Orlando, FL, 1999

Before leaving for Orlando I told people my goal was to get at least one medal at a National Meet. This was my first really successful National Meet, at least from the standpoint of medals. Significant was the fact that it was my first year in the '80-84 age category.'

At the National Senior Olympics in Orlando, Don had taken quite a few pictures. I put together a spiral bound book which included copies of the pictures Don took along with a journal of the day-by-day activities during the two weeks October 19-29, 1999, we were in Orlando. I gave a copy of this to each Brenda, Rich & Don.

For the Nationals in Orlando, I had made reservations for Anne and me to stay at a Travelodge Motel in Kissimmee, a five-minute drive from the Sports Complex of Disney World. Several months earlier I offered John Bertsche to share our room if he wished. When the time came to get serious about plans he told me that he had health problems, a heart valve condition, and his doctor suggested that he not compete, so he gave up going to the Nationals in Orlando. I should add here that John and I went to the State Meets in Springfield together for many years, 1982 to 1998. The Orlando Meet, 1999, was the first time we did not go to the meets together.

Anne and I left on Saturday, October 16, in our Toyota Tacoma pickup with the bike in the rear along with our suitcases and some food I decided to take just in case we had trouble finding the proper food. We decided to take the pickup because they were predicting rain, and a hurricane had gone thru parts of Florida about that time and I hated to have my bike on top of the car in the rain. Also, it is easier and handier to secure it in the back of the pickup than on top, when stopping at motels, restaurants, and the like.

The first day we drove to Montgomery, Alabama. We wanted to stop in Birmingham but due to the NASCAR races near Birmingham, all motels were filled so we kept driving until we finally found a bed in Montgomery, at 10 pm, 750 miles that day. We took our time Sunday, drove leisurely, ending up in Gainesville, and on in to Orlando Monday morning. First competition was to be Tuesday. We picked up my packet at the Registration Office and walked around getting acquainted with the Sports Complex so we'd know where to go the next day.

My first event was the 100m, scheduled for 9 am. The order of events was oldest to youngest, men first then women in each age category. The 100m had three heats. I ended third in one heat. After the race they told us the clock wasn't working for that heat and it'd have to be run over the next day at 8:45 am, 15 minutes before the finals were to begin. We were there; I did the re-run, placed 2nd, time 18.50. That was enough to qualify me for the finals, although some of the better runners were not aware of the re-run and were permitted to run then compare times to determine awards. Later, in the pm, we had the preliminaries for the 200m. I did that in 39.81, again good enough to get into the finals. The track had 9 lanes so 9 qualified for the finals.

Picture 45 - Richard & D. Paul at the Sr. Olympics in San Antonio, TX in 1995.

On Wednesday morning I woke up stiff and sore. Looking back I wonder if it wasn't imagination and anxiety. I was concerned about the day ahead with three races: The 100m re-run, then the finals in both 100m and 200m. I went out to the parking lot at the motel, tried to loosen up but was discouraged to the point that I went to the drug store not far from the motel and bought a bottle of "extra strength Tylenol," took a dose right there in the store, then two more during the day and really felt fine thru all the races. I got a 6th place in the 100m finals, a 4th in the 200m. Ribbons in both and I felt good about the day.

Also, I was surprised at how fleet-of-foot I felt in all three races, considering how I felt when I got up in the morning.

In the 200m we had nine lanes, nine finalists. I was assigned lane 8. One fellow was ahead of me in the staggered start. I looked back at the seven others; all had eager looks on their faces. In the race, I came around the curve into the straight-away pretty well in the lead pack but back a few places from the front runners. In the 39 plus seconds it took me to run it I had time to think about maybe overtaking some of those leaders. I held my own but was about a yard out of third place and finished for a 4th place ribbon.

The dashes were finished on Wednesday. I had no events on Thursday. Even though it rained quite a bit, we drove to Lake Minneola, about 28 miles from the Sports Complex, where the bike races were to be held, on Thursday. We drove around the lake and sized up the bike race courses but did not ride the bike that day.

The Walk Races

The walk races were scheduled for Friday and Saturday, with the 5000m on Friday and the 1500m on Saturday. The course for the 5000m was laid out in the parking lot of the Sports Complex. The course was exactly one kilometer, so we had to do the course five times to get our 5000m. I thought I had the technique under control but got a warning early in the race: bent knee. They had a bulletin board placed on the course showing warnings the various participants had received as the race progressed. As I was entering the final lap, I noticed that I had two warnings, ("three warnings and you are disqualified") so I became very conscious of technique.

Fortunately, the one judge said "Your left knee is bent." This gave me an important clue. I began to realize that the left knee was the one that had a fractured patella a couple years earlier and was in a cast for six weeks, from a fall, climbing Long's Peak. So I gave special attention to that left knee and survived the race with no further warnings, and placed 4th. The attention to the bent left knee actually slowed me down significantly. The next day in the 1500m, I had no warnings, and finished 3rd - my first medal. It was a real victory for me to finish the race with no warnings from the judges.

We had nice weather both Friday and Saturday of the walk races. The Thursday before we drove out to the bike course again and I rode the course three times to become familiar with all the turns and hills we'd have to encounter. That proved to be a wise move.

Sarasota at Dunns

I had the course well in hand when we did the cycling the following week. We finished the 1500m race by 10 o'clock, but

Picture 46 – D. Paul at the start of the 10k time trial in Orlando, FL.

wanted to pick up my medal. We waited several hours. For some reason the results were delayed and we finally left for Dunns about 2 pm without the medal. Had a good visit with Bill & Irene, went to Sunday School with them, and then returned to Orlando for the Parade of Athletes at the Citrus Bowl. We were in the Citrus Bowl from 4 pm to 9 pm. It was cold. The cold temperature record was broken on two or three different days while we were there. After I, along with the several hundred other Illinois participants, was seated, I left the stadium and went to the pickup to get my Gortex jacket. I got lost and had to have a policeman help me find my pickup, but did get the jacket and returned to my seat while the meeting was still in progress. Walking distances were always great and crowds caused lots of confusion, particularly when

Picture 47 - D. Paul at the start of the 5k time trial in Orlando, 1999.

Anne and I were separated. I was with the Illinois delegation and she a spectator somewhere in the crowd, but we survived it and got home around 10 pm.

Bicycle Races in Orlando

Monday we went to the bike course again. We met Don at the airport in the evening. Got up early, 4:00 am, Tuesday morning, drove to Clermont where Lake Minneola and the bike venue were located, ate breakfast, a big bowl of oatmeal, at a restaurant called The Clock, and got down to the course before

daylight. Got the bike out, checked the tires and got in line to get my packet and a chip to put around my ankle for the electronic timing.

Incidentally, chips were used for both the cycling and the 5,000m walk race. For that you tied a chip around your ankle and the timing sensors picked up the beginning and the finish

Picture 48 - D. Paul (left) on the silver medal podium, with a 2nd of 8 places in Orlando, FL.

times. To me it appeared to be an accurate system but I got the report that it did not work for some people so they discontinued using it for subsequent meets.

The 40k road race was my first event. It went well. I was motivated. Got in a pack with five or six cyclists and stayed with them, exchanging the lead occasionally. The officials started age '50s' categories first. Five minutes later, 'all 60s;' then 'all 70s and older.' It was to my advantage to have the two '70s' age categories in my group. I found out later that the group I worked with in drafting was all in their 70s.

Picture 49 - Anne & D. Paul at the San Antonio Sr. Olympics in May, 1995.

Perhaps the highlight of my Orlando

experience came when I saw the results posted, D. Paul Miller, first, averaged 18 plus mph. A few hours later, I did the 5k time trial and got a silver in that event. On Wednesday, we had the 20k road race in the morning and the 10k time trial in the afternoon. Like the first day, I got gold in the road race and silver in the time trial. There was one fellow, a Mr. Jukes from Canada who beat me by 9 seconds in the 5k, and 11 seconds in the 10k. My fastest race was the 10k. The average speed posted on the bulletin board was 19.8 mph.

Picture 50 - D. Paul and Don in Orlando, FL, 1999.

All the events were electronically timed. Approximately half an hour after the event was completed, the results were posted on the bulletin board, then, reasonably soon after the posting, the awards ceremonies were staged. The Olympic song was played at the beginning of each ceremony. Since an award ceremony was staged for each age group, and for each race we heard that recording so many times we got tired of it.

After the cycling races were completed I had 2 gold, 2 silver and a bronze medals, with two 4th place and one 6th place ribbons, eight events, eight places, lowest being the 6th place in the 100m dash. Don took quite a few pictures of the cycling races. We have no pictures of the running and walking events. I

Picture 51 – D. Paul (middle) drafting in the 40k road race at the Sr. Olympics in Orlando, FL.

had the pictures Don took put on a computer disk, printed the pictures, each with a brief description, then with an opening statement about the Orlando experience, including a daily journal for the time we were in Florida, and a closing statement, I had books bound and gave each of our kid a book.

It was very helpful to have Don there to assist, checking schedules, progress of the races so I'd know when I was due, someone to take my sweats, and the like. After the cycling events and award ceremonies, we ate, then dropped Don off at the airport and checked in to the motel for our final night there. We got up and started driving Thursday morning about 4 am, got in a big day, stayed overnight at Nashville, and on home Friday by 2 pm. All told it was an excellent experience. Anne was good support for me throughout, and I think she really enjoyed being a part of it. I was sufficiently pleased with the outcome that I'll probably try it again someday.

Hampton Roads, Virginia, May 26 – June 9, 2003

(An update: At the awards ceremony, they announced me as winner in the 5000m walk race. I questioned the first place, and wondered about the fellow who beat me in the 1500m, earlier. The announcer said, "You won, get up on the stand." So I did. When the results book came out later, I noticed that one person had a time better than mine in the 5000m and I was listed in second position. So it appears that my medal should have been silver rather than gold.)

In the Illinois Qualifying Meet, the cycling and track dates were September 21, and September 28, respectively. I entered all the cycling events, 5k, 10k, 20k & 40k. The short races ½ mile and 1 mile were omitted this year for the first time. It appears that they might be eliminated permanently. That would make sense since none of these short races are held in the Nationals.

Picture 52 - D. Paul before the 1500m race walk in San Antonio, TX in 1995.

Of the four races scheduled this year, the only one that has ever been run by someone in the '85-89' category is the 5k in 1991. Sam Dorman did it in 13:16. My time was 11:29, which takes almost 2 minutes off the old record. The other races, 10k, 20k, & 40k were all records simply by virtue of finishing. However the 20k and 40k road races were, for the first time, not timed here this year. Apparently they did not time these because in the Nationals, they were not timed this year. I think this lack of timing in the Nationals is a first this year. The 20k and 40k in Orlando, 1999, were timed and I did both in record times. So, in the State Meet I have record times in the 5k (11:29) and 10k (23:34.33) cycle events, and the only person 85-89 to have ever done the road races.

I was qualified for two running events, the 100m and 200m, two walk races, the 1500m and 5000m, and the four cycling races, 5k and 10k time trials, and the 20k and 40k road races. The NSGA (National Senior Games Association) ruled effective this year for the first time that an individual could enter in only two sports. I elected to enter the cycling and walk races. The walk races are not considered Track & Field events, but an individual sport. Two factors contributed to my decision to omit the running events. One, running is the most damaging to my physical body. It stresses the knees and hip joints more than the race-walks and the cycling. Two, in the past I placed higher in walking and cycling than in the running. Consequently, I entered the cycling and race walking.

Anne and I drove the Tacoma pickup. With this we could lock the bike inside and it would be dry in the event of rain. We left Sunday, May 25; started around 3:30 am in order to avoid the Indy 500 traffic in Indianapolis. All went well. We sailed thru Indianapolis around 6:00 am, on to Louisville and east thru beautiful country in Eastern Kentucky, West Virginia, and ended in Lexington, Virginia around 6:00 pm, a good day's drive.

We called our friends Bill and Julie Smith, former colleague and friends from Wesleyan. Spent some time in their home, then slept in an Econo Lodge motel, and drove on into Norfolk arriving at our formerly reserved Econo Lodge around 11:00 am. After lunch we went to the Pavilion Convention Center to pick up my registration packet and get Anne a companion pass, then went to the cycling venue at Northwest River Park in

Chesapeake, 40 miles south, drove the course and back to the motel.

Don came from California to help us. He was very helpful with the cycling and then helping Anne while I was participating. The first day, Wednesday, I won the 5k time trial by eight seconds in 11 minutes, 10 seconds, and the 40k by a wide margin, having teamed up with some of the younger riders. The American Cycling Federation supervised the road race and did not keep individual times. We had some bad accidents near the finish of the 40k. I passed the scene of a two-man crash before the last turn of the race, then after the last turn eight cyclists went down, six were taken to the hospital in ambulances, one seriously injured rider with a punctured lung and head injuries was taken in a helicopter. He and another rider were in intensive care at the hospital. Thursday was a day off. Anne, Don and I went to Williamsburg to see the historic sites, and then Friday I had the 10k time trial and the 20k road race. My time on the 10k was 20:00, more than a minute less than my nearest competitor. In the 20k, I teamed up with a group of six riders in a younger age category and stayed with them until the last half mile. In the road-races, I was with a group of 93 riders, 70 and over males and all the females. My fastest time was the 10k averaging 18.6 mph, and my slowest was 17.1 in the 40k according to my odometer.

The 1500m walk race was held on the Norfolk University track, a beautiful facility. In presenting the awards the announcer said "Paul Miller with a time of 11.27 just broke the national record of 11:57, then second place broke that record and the winner broke them all." In other words three of us finished with a time faster than the old national record. I got the bronze medal. That was on Monday, June 2, and the 5000m walk race was Wednesday, June 4. The latter was held on the Little Creek Amphibian Naval Air Base. They had a 1 kilometer course marked off on a large concrete area and walked us around that five times. In this race I was surprised to get a gold medal in a time of 40 minutes, 8 seconds.

In the days off, Saturday and Sunday between the biking and walk races, Anne and I spent quite a bit of time at the Naval Air

Base, watching both men's and women's softball games and also some basketball. During our stay we ate most of our meals at Golden Carol or Mi Hogar, a Mexican restaurant, lunches at Subway and breakfasts on competition days at Holiday Inn restaurant where the waitress, having served me previously, would bring me an oversized bowl of oatmeal with side dishes of raisins, honey and milk.

Immediately after I received my award for the 5000m walk race, we ate lunch and started driving toward home at 1:30 pm; drove 366 miles to Beckley, W. Virginia, and on home the next day. We arrived home at 8:00 pm.

All told it was a successful venture: six events, six medals, five golds, one bronze. No car trouble except on the Air Base parking lot I backed into another car and was delayed over an hour filling out police reports. Don's presence was important. I think he enjoyed participating in the activities of his parents, and it was indeed a big help to both Anne and me. We were somewhat unhappy with the Econo Lodge motel. It was old, poor lighting, no extra towel for Don until I picked one up at the office, and only one hand towel, no shampoo or hair dryer, etc. Breakfasts were orange juice, coffee and doughnuts. We'd get the orange juice and coffee but not the doughnuts. Then when we checked out they offered to redeem the book of stamps (a stamp for each day in the motel) total worth $50.00, the desk clerk tried to get me to sign the credit card without giving the fifty dollar credit. I refused to sign but went to the room and got the original receipt given me when we checked in and by the time I got back she had a fifty dollar credit prepared for my credit card. It was obvious that the desk clerk was trying to get away with the $50.00 we were to get credit for. We were ready to move on and decided to avoid Econo Lodge in the future.

A report of my participation appeared in *The Daily Pantagraph*, June 7, 2003, issue. The week before we left, a full-page spread of Anne and my lifestyle activities and Senior Olympic plans appeared in the May 22, 2003, issue of the *Normalite*, a weekly newspaper.

As an aside, earlier we had done some leg-work in tracking down some Amish built dining table and chairs which Don and Sharon are planning to buy. Anne and I decided to buy a captain's chair for the set for them as a reward to Don for his help at the Senior Olympics. He had been with us at Orlando four years earlier. He is very knowledgeable about bicycles, and with the limitations of his aging parents, it was good for him to be with us to drive, help with the cycling races and helping mother. The next Nationals in 2005 are to be held in Pittsburg and 2007 in Louisville. Whether or not I'll participate will have to be determined later. At this point it looks favorable.

Pittsburg Nationals, June 3-18, 2005

We drove from Normal to Pittsburg. Brenda accompanied Anne and me and did most of the driving. We stayed in a Day's Inn located at 1150 Banksville, Pittsburg. The motel had been reserved ahead of time and it turned out to be a good motel but at a bad location considering the distance we had to drive for the cycle events. One advantage to this motel was that a restaurant with good food choices was located just a block away.

The cycle venue was located at North Park, Pearce Mill Road, Allison Park, Pennsylvania. Brenda figured out our driving and did an excellent job of getting us to the races on time and mother placed at strategic locations so she'd be in best position to see the races.

I was registered for the four cycle events, 5k and 10k time trials, and the 20k and 40k road races. I got silver medals in the 5k (time 11:58.36) and 10k (27:36.93) and also the 20k road race. A Larry Johnson from New Mexico, who had turned 85 in March, beat me in all three races. The 20k road race was the worst race I had ever run. It was hilly and had one long steep hill probably ¾ mile upgrade. I got down to 3 and 4 mph and could barely keep pedaling. I passed six or so cyclists who were walking their bikes up the hill but even though dead-tired and puffing, I managed to keep upright. When I learned that the 40k the next day was to do this same route twice, I decided to cancel. Had I known that we would be involved with such hills, I would have used my red Cannondale which has a triple gear in front. Having checked out of the 40k allowed us to leave for home a day earlier.

I was not qualified in the Nationals for the walk races and track events this year. The qualifying State Meet, September, 2004, was held on the weekend of Anne's ninetieth birthday celebration when the kids were all here, so I skipped the qualifying State Meet.

Rich had flown into Pittsburg for, I think, the last two cycling races. Brenda picked him up at the airport, and was very helpful in doing all of the driving in the Pittsburg traffic. All in all, the trip was successful and I think we all enjoyed the experience.

Broken Patellas, Cracked Ribs and Pelvis

Since I missed several meets because of injuries, it seems appropriate for me to give some detail of the accidents and injuries which affected my attending several meets. Injuries involved were two cracked patellas, separate incidents at different times, two cycling accidents landing me in the emergency room, and a stupid accident falling while reaching for my water bottle in a ride with Don at Lake Bloomington, also landing me in the emergency room.

My earlier comments (the most serious competition at this stage is survival) have been definitely reinforced in my Senior Olympics experiences. I have had two broken patellas, one in each knee in recent years, the cracked pelvis, and two cycling crashes. The broken patella in my left knee occurred during the D.D. Miller Reunion, June, 1999, in the Long Peak climb, slipping on wet rocks. It healed sufficiently so that I was well conditioned during the summer with the Menno Riders to participate in the Orlando Nationals in October that year. I am convinced that the two warnings for "bent knee" I received in the 5000m walk race were related to the broken patella in the left knee. One judge commented during the race "number 647, your left knee is bent."

The cracked patella on my left knee occurred February 16, 2001. This caused me to cancel my registration to the Nationals in Baton Rouge. The knee simply did not heal sufficiently for me to participate. Also, I was registered for the Mennonite Sports classic in Harrisonburg, Virginia to be held in June, 2002, and had to cancel that meet.

My cracked pelvis occurred when I was riding with Don when he visited us that summer. I was in good riding condition. We were riding around both lakes and through the park at Lake Bloomington, June 2, when I reached for my water bottle, and ran off a drop in the road into the ditch fell pretty hard. I couldn't get up; Don carried me over to a picnic table in the park near where my fall occurred.

It attracted attention of a group picnicking nearby, where a Good Samaritan offered to take us and our bikes home in his pickup, then Don and Anne took me to the emergency room. I was x-rayed, the report, a cracked pelvis. I stayed in the hospital two nights, and got around with a walker, and the soreness lingered longer than I had hoped for. I had to give up going into the boundary waters on the canoe trip excursion scheduled with Wilderness Wind in Ely, Minnesota, that we planned with Don and Sharon.

Even with my limited physical condition, we still took the Wilderness Wind trip. Anne and I, with a friend, Terry Wiebenga, from our church, met Don and Sharon in Minneapolis, then drove on to Ely. Anne and I stayed in a cabin at Wilderness Wind while Don, Sharon, Terry, and a guide went on the 4-day canoe trip into the boundary waters.

My pelvis healing was sort of touch and go but I did compete in the State Senior Olympics in September, 2002, with a hip less than one hundred percent healed. Eleven events, with eleven gold medals. I repeat: the ranks thin out as one goes up in the age category. Competing in the '85-89' age category, I had no one in my age category in the six biking events, so just finishing them qualifies me for the 40k, 20k, 10k, and 5k in the Nationals next summer. Only two events were listed as having had participants previously, the one-mile and the 5k. I beat the times for both of these and the others were records by virtue of simply finishing them. No records had been recorded in my age category previously for the 40k, 20k and 10k cycle events.

In the track and field I had five events, the 50k, 100k, 200k dashes, the 1500m walk race and the discus. In all of these except the 200k, we had two or three others in my age category. The competitors were all slow enough that I won the races, so am now qualified for the Nationals to be held the last week in May & first week in June, 2003.

The results in the State Meet events just completed in September are: cycling, 40k (1 hour, 39 minutes); 20k (53: 2); 10k (23:12.2); 5k (12:33.5; 1 mile (3:36.36); ½ mile (1:42.0). All six were State records for this age category. In track and field the results are 50m (11.5s), 100m (26.28s), 200m (58.86s), 1500m walk race (12:27) and discus (53 feet, 1 inch). This is the completion of my report to date, October 13, 2002.

The short cycle races, one mile and one-half mile have been dropped from the Illinois State Meet's schedule, since none of these are scheduled in the Nationals. So now the scheduled cycle races in the Illinois Meets correspond with those scheduled in the Nationals, four races only, 5k and 10k time trials, 20k and 40k road races. Also, the other change that has occurred is that the road races are no longer timed, but they record places only.

Senior Olympics Concluding Statement

In the twenty-eight years of my Senior Olympic participation, two of the many meets I took part in, stand out as special to me personally. Both have been described in some detail earlier in this chapter. I mention them here again because of the special nature they are for me. One is the National Meet in Orlando, 1999. This one is particularly special because it is where I received my first medal at the National level. The bronze in the 1500M walk race was the very first National medal. Then it is hard to describe my thrill when I saw my name posted on their electronic bulletin board with two first places in the cycle races, and also posted was the 18 mph plus average speed. In that same posting I was listed with two silver medals. Later I realized the golds were both National records

The other special meet was the Illinois Meet in Springfield, 2007. This was the first year after I reached 90. My unspoken goal was to get records in all my events. I say unspoken because I was reluctant to mention it, and then maybe not accomplish my goal. As stated earlier, my nephew, Richard Hirschler, and two other friends, along with Anne, were witnesses to the events. I had seven events and seven State records. And this was special for me.

Another item which bears repeating in my concluding statement is the fact that Anne has been my most loyal supporter through the years. She never missed a meet, not one, State, Regional, or National. This year, 2010, is my first competition without my most loyal supporter. I miss her.

As I sign off, July, 2010, I admit that my hip and knee joints become more and more sensitive, particularly in my running events. Cycling goes well; also the walk race causes no particular problem. So in the best interest of my physical condition, I may eliminate running from my competition program. I realize furthermore, that the time will come when I will discontinue all my competition. As I look into the crystal ball, I see that even after I discontinue competition, I may still be able to carry out my exercise program at Shirk Fitness Center.

V - Rocky Branch & Hedgewood

Our Introduction to the Clark County Woods

Our first information about "Rocky Branch" came through my colleague at Illinois Wesleyan, Greg Gardner, who was a CPA, and doing a tax assignment for Clinton Tribby, the owner of "Rocky Branch," who was in trouble with the IRS. Greg met me in the hall at IWU one day and asked if I'd be interested in one hundred acres of woodland in Southern Illinois. He gave me the telephone number of Tribby; we called him, made an appointment for Anne and me to meet him at a restaurant in Kansas, Illinois.

We met; he then drove us to his woods. We walked most of the borders, into Den Holler, saw the clear streams, the limestone out-croppings, many deep ravines, saw many beautiful views, and really were impressed and liked it from the very beginning.

The Purchase

Tribby was asking fifty thousand dollars for the 127 acres. That seemed reasonable but Anne kept saying, "But there's no income, all woods, nothing cultivated, no crops." I realized that but we both really liked the place. We left the matter ride, making no decision. Greg kept pressuring us, and Tribby called us a number of times encouraging us to buy it because of our interest in keeping it in its natural state. Greg and Tribby kept after us. Finally I told them I'd make an offer and they should feel free to reject it. I offered forty thousand.

They accepted the offer and Greg even offered to work out an option to buy. We put five hundred dollars down; in six months we were to make a decision. If we buy, the five hundred is applied to the purchase price, if we don't buy Tribby keeps the five hundred. In six months our decision was to purchase the property. The warranty deed was delivered; we closed March 31, 1981. I often think of how near we came to not buying, and how important that one questionable-at-the-time decision was in our lifetime.

We hear that Tribby owed the IRS twenty-five thousand dollars because he had never reported his bull-dozing business income since he began, as an eighteen year old boy, and now had voluntarily turned himself in. He took care of his obligations to IRS, we own the property, and the more we worked with it the more we fell in love with it.

The Cabin

After we purchased "Rocky Branch," we made an effort to meet the neighbors. It seemed to please them that we purchased the property. One of our first contacts was with Chuck Sanford. Chuck offered us a small shed located at the site of the abandoned buildings on the land he bought from Millhouse. These buildings had been the residence of the Millhouse family. He had constructed and used this "shed" as a cabin in his park in the Den Holler area to be described later. It had a window on each of the four sides, also a chimney to accommodate a heating stove. It was still in stable condition but needed a roof and windows repaired. He offered it at no cost and said he would help us move it to our "Rocky Branch" property if we were interested. We accepted that offer and went to work on the cabin. We put hickory skids under it and Chuck dragged it down to its present location with his farm tractor. We put on a new roof, gutted the inside of the rotten cardboard siding, pulled out a million (more or less) nails that were holding the cardboard siding, and repaired the windows.

I made bunk beds for four mainly from boards salvaged from the old buildings, put in a wood-burning stove. I cleaned up and painted an old table in the cabin, acquired some chairs, and metal cabinets that other people were discarding, we later moved a privy near the cabin and have found the facilities to be extremely useful even though primitive. When we were putting on the new roof, Rich visited us and helped mostly with the patchwork around the chimney. We salvaged four folding chairs from Don's dumpster at his place on High Street in Denver, hauled them home, painted them a bright orange, and have used them in the cabin to the present time.

We have never locked our cabin. We figured we didn't have any really valuable items inside, and that if people wanted to get in it would be easy for them to tear down the door or break a window and cause more damage than with an unlocked door. Over the years we have missed a few items like a kerosene lantern, an iron skillet, and a splitting maul, and naturally are disappointed that our trust-the-people policy has some flaws, but the damage is obviously less than a break-in would have been.

Occasionally someone will ask us where we got the name "Rocky Branch." While we were restoring the cabin, a motorcycle with two people drove into our lane and up to the cabin. They introduced themselves to us indicating that they had grown up in this area and years ago had stomped the woods of "Rocky Branch" many times. That was the first time we had heard the term "Rocky Branch," and we decided at that time that was the name we were going to use to identify our woods. We have learned since that there is another area named "Rocky Branch" several miles southeast of our property. When the State Biologist, Mary Solecki was preparing the report for the Illinois Nature Preserve Commission, described below, she identified our property as "Miller's Rocky Branch."

Nature Preserves

We had couple unsolicited calls from the Department of Conservation, Division of Natural Heritage, regarding our interest to register our property with them. Their interests seemed to comply with what we had in mind for keeping it in its natural state. Consequently we registered Miller's "Rocky Branch" as an Illinois Natural Heritage Landmark, and were given signs to erect on the property and a framed plaque signed by Governor Jim Edgar, and other officials, dated November 15, 1997.

Later we were approached by State Biologist, Mary Solecki, regarding our interest in putting the property into a more legally binding agreement under the Illinois Register of Land and Water Reserves. We spent several sessions with her visiting in our home and she with my input developed the proposal, which we signed and which was considered for approval by the Illinois Land and Water Preserve Commission, in Springfield, on February 1, 2000.

Anne and I attended the meeting in Springfield at which this proposal was considered. The state biologist, Mary Solecki showed a series of slides, discussed the general features of the property such as the clear-water streams, out-cropping sandstone cliffs, deep ravines and many beautiful views, answered questions raised by commission members, after which the commission members voted unanimously to accept the proposal. The agreement was set up with the provision that it is binding for ten years, and may at that time be discontinued with the unanimous consent of the owners. This agreement is also binding on any future owners in case of a change in ownership.

More History

(The following is a copy of the report I wrote for Mary Kay Solecki, the State Biologist, at her request, to be used for her report to the Land & Water Preserve Commission, presented February 1, 2000.)

The scenic aspect of Den Holler has been appreciated and enjoyed by many people over the years. From the Depression era until after World War II, a park and picnic area existed near the entrance to Den Holler. Two overgrown brick fireplaces and an old well casing are the only remaining signs of the park.

Mr. J. E. Millhouse, who owned this land from 1937 until 1962, had a small one-room cabin in the woods at the bottom of the hill near Den Holler. This area was at one time used as a place for picnics and community celebrations on 4th of July, Labor Day, Memorial Day, and so forth. The cabin was moved to Mr. Millhouse's adjacent farmstead in the 1940s. The woods was purchased by Mr. Clinton Tribby about 1962. Mr. & Mrs. Miller purchased the woods from Mr. Tribby in 1981. At that time Mr. Charles Samford owned the land and farm buildings adjacent to Miller's "Rocky Branch". Mr. Samford offered them the cabin, which was in need of repair. The Millers renovated the cabin and moved it to its current location nestled on a ridge top overlooking the forest.

Four wells are found at scattered sites in the forest. These are the remains of early homesteads which have since disappeared. A house sat near two of the wells on what is frequently referred to by local residents as Lowry Hill. A cabin was once located on another hill near the south entrance of the pipeline. In order to keep out the family who had a habit of simply moving into and occupying the cabin, Mr. Millhouse burned this cabin before he moved to California One old well which still has a concrete base is located at the foot of the ridge south of Lowry Hill, and the fourth well is located in Den Holler.

Mr. Tribby farmed the bottomland area one year in the 1960s. He said that the deer and raccoons got more of the corn than he did so he discontinued farming this area. The former crop field is now a young forest with many tall, dense trees, predominately black walnut.

The Millers have owned and enjoyed this woods for over 17 years. The cabin and forest offer a rustic get away from their home in Normal. The Millers visit here often, hike the trails, and share the beauty of the forest and cliffs with friends and family. Mr. Miller has hunted here.

Historical Information

Much of the following information is taken from my book, sort of a diary, where I kept record of my visits to "Rocky Branch," and recorded work done, experiences with neighbors, and the like. Without that record I would never remember much of the detail of twenty years ago.

In the early 1980s, when we bought the property, Casimer Trefz lived in the farmhouse where our lane meets the hard-surfaced road where he was born and raised. He has lived there all his life, so he is quite aware of happenings in the area. He was a very likeable fellow and we were good friends and have spent lots of time together, hunting and visiting, until he passed away in the late 1990s.

Casimer informed me of some of the experiences he had with James Millhouse, the owner of "Rocky Branch" before Clinton Tribby. He says Millhouse had a nice park which was open to the community for celebrations on holidays, July 4th, Labor Day, etc. He erected a small cabin near the foot of the hill, south of where the cabin now stands, near the mouth of Den Holler. He had dug a shallow well for drinking water, and erected two brick fireplaces in the area for roasting wieners and heating food. This park was open to the community for many years, until he eventually closed the park because community people became careless, leaving the gates open and no longer having respect for the property.

One can still see remains of the park. The two brick fireplaces, and the heavy well casing covered with a rusted-out barrel still remain in the Den Holler area. Casmier related how he with his 4-horse team pulled Millhouse's cabin from the park, to where it was located when we arrived on the scene in the early 1980s.

Casimer also described the Lower Hill residence across the creek and in the northeast corner of our "Rocky Branch" woods. Three wells and a bit of junk including parts of an old cast iron stove are the only remnants of that residence that remain today.

The largest well is lined with stone, is thirty-two feet deep and well preserved. I have covered it with a grated wire gate to avoid the misfortune of someone falling into the well. Another smaller stone-lined well approximately 150 yards southwest of the large well, has been partially filled in with soil, but is still easily visible. The third well which appears to have been part of the Lowery residence is down the hill south toward the creek, in the bottom, and has a concrete platform cover. One can only presume that this well was used to furnish water for livestock that was probably penned in that area

Casimer recalls when a horse fell into the large well and they tried to chain him out, broke his neck and they had to pull out a dead horse. In those days a wagon-road came in from our present lane, down the hill across the West Big Fork Creek, where the banks are low, and out the road at the northeast corner. The buildings of the Lowery residence were located east, northeast of the wells.

According to Trefz, another small cabin once stood just a little northeast of where the pipeline enters our property on the south border. This was in the 1920s when Roy Chilocotte owned the land. Trefz recalls when each summer a Negro family would move into the cabin, then leave during the winter and return again each summer. It appeared that this family moved in voluntarily, without paying rent or having any kind of formal agreement or permission from the owner. Chilocotte had relatives in California, and planned to join his relatives. Before leaving he burned the cabin so the Negro family would not be able to move in and cause potential problems for the neighbors after he was gone. He sold his goods on auction and gave Casimer clock which he (Casimer) still had in his possession as he reported this information to me.

When we bought "Rocky Branch," Chuck Samford owned the farm adjacent to our property. It had old abandoned buildings about one quarter of a mile east of the hard surfaced road. Among the abandoned buildings, was the cabin which he no longer had any use for and was still in good condition, however, was beginning to deteriorate. This was the cabin Millhouse had constructed in his park in the Den Holler area described above. It had a window on each of the four sides, also a chimney to accommodate a heating stove. It needed a roof and windows repaired. He offered it at no cost and said he would even help us move it to our "Rocky Branch" property. We accepted that offer and went to work on the cabin. We put hickory skids under it and Chuck dragged it down to its present location with his farm tractor. We put on a new roof, gutted the inside of the rotten cardboard siding, pulled out a million (more or less) nails that were holding the cardboard siding, and repaired the windows.

Chuck also related some experiences of Wesley Hogue who in 1917, lived just one-fourth mile south of our lane entrance, and one mile west of "Rocky Branch" This was the year a devastating tornado ripped through the area Chuck took me to Marshall to visit Wesley Hogue. Hogue related that he was living with his parents and four siblings when this devastating tornado ripped through the area on May 26, 1917. It flattened buildings and laid destruction in an area one-half mile wide, between Charleston, east through Terre Haute, and on east into central Indiana

According to Wesley's story the tornado flattened their home except the kitchen wall where six family members including Wesley, were sheltered. They pulled carpets over their heads to protect themselves from the hail. In that storm the rock cliff at Den Holler broke off and formed a dam which in turn formed a lake that was good for fishing until some years later the dam washed out and only the stream remains.

It happened that I was working at "Rocky Branch" on May 26, 1992, and had my radio tuned to the Champaign Public Radio Station, "WILL." At that time they gave a documentary describing that tornado on the 75th anniversary of the storm. It was fascinating for me to listen to the documentary, and from what they reported. It appeared to be every bit as devastating as Wesley had described it.

In 2006, Doug Ulrich, a brother of Jeff Ulrich was deer hunting at Rocky Branch, walking along West Big Fork Creek, near the center of the property, when he spotted an item in the water which, when retrieved, turned out to be a tooth of an American mastodon.

At the time we realized it was an unusual find but were not able to identify it. Consequently we made an appointment to see the curator of the Illinois State Museum in Springfield, Jeffrey Saunders. He immediately identified it as the 3rd molar of the upper jaw of a mastodon and showed us a similar tooth they had on display in the museum. The mastodon which roamed the area from about 4 million to 13,000 years ago, as an adult, stood 8 to 10 feet tall at the shoulders, and weighed 4 to 8 tons. Their teeth had blunt cones ideally suited for browsing on herbs, shrubs, and trees.

As curator of the museum, Mr. Saunders was sufficiently interested in the specimen that he wanted to see the area where it was found. Jeff Ulrich and I made arrangements to meet him at our cabin at a later date. We roamed the area but found no further remains of the mastodon. The specimen is currently in the hands of Jeff Ulrich.

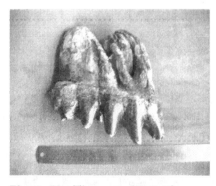

Picture 53 – The mastodon tooth, which is more than eight inches wide.

Timber Stand Improvement (TSI) Program

Shortly after we purchased the property, we contacted our State Foresters, Bob Blair and Bob Wagoner, seeking information on caring for our woods. They walked through the woods with me and recommended that we get started on a TSI program. I completed the necessary forms, November, 1981 requesting forestry assistance, and returned them to the Clark County Department of Natural Resources on January 23, 1982.

In a notice dated May 28, 1982, the USDA (United States Department of Agriculture) indicated that our request for a cost-share TSI had been approved. This allowed us payment for the Torodon and gas, plus $4.50 per hour for labor. Blair and Wagoner had already marked the trees that needed to be culled out, and Anne and I had begun our girdling and treating marked trees on forty-nine acres, mostly in the south 80 acres, and some in the area north and east of the cabin.

Picture 54 - Anne & D. Paul (left to right) splitting wood at Rocky Branch in 1990.

Anne and I worked many hours, hard and long, staying in the woods all day, girdling and applying Torodon on the marked trees. This involved pulling our garden cart with chain-saw, gas, oil, drinking water, lunch, and the chemicals, through the woods, up and down the ravines. I would girdle (saw about an inch deep around the circumference of the tree), then Anne would spray the Torodon in the sawed area. This would kill the trees that we were culling out, and give the good trees better growing conditions. The dead trees could then left to deteriorate in the forest or used for firewood.

Picture 55 - Anne unloading the trailer at Rocky Branch in 1985.

We completed the work for our first TSI before the deadline, June 1, 1984, a period of a little over two years. We received payment, approximately eleven hundred dollars, for work that we wanted to do even without any cost-share. In the following years we did a number of TSIs without any pay because of a lack of funds for the program.

One very memorable experience occurred on our first trip to the major area in the south eighty acres. The only access I could see to our marked trees required that we cross the stream at Den Holler, and then proceed up a steep hill about 30 or 40 yards to the top, pulling the loaded cart. I lifted the cart up the bank at the stream, then began the struggle up the hill, I pulling and Anne pushing. We'd inch our way a few feet then stop to rest, holding the cart from rolling back down. We had to go under a big tree that had fallen across our path. Several times the cart almost got away from us, but we finally managed to get to the top.

Once at the top, we made a quick and definite decision not to return the same route home. In fact, we left the cart with supplies in the woods that night and walked west to the Murphy residence on the road, and took our lane home. The walk home was an extra two miles but better than to try that hill again. Also, the occasion afforded us the opportunity to meet the Murphys, who informed us that we could drive right back to our woods with our pickup by going through their pig pen. Later we used the grass lane at the edge of their field, back to the pipeline and to our project.

Picture 56 - Timber Harvest at Rock Branch in the spring of 1992. D. Paul & Anne are standing in the front of one of the loads ready for the trip to the mill.

Today (2010) as I look back on our experiences in the early 1980s, realizing my limitations and Anne walking with a walker, I marvel at the work we did twenty five years earlier. When we had our major lumber harvest described below, we were told that the TSI work we did twenty-five years earlier, was a major contributing factor to our abundant lumber harvests. And, with the physical work, we would be tired at the end of the day, eat and sleep well, even on our bunk beds, and both Anne and I really enjoyed those years working together in the depth of nature.

In later years when Anne and I hiked the Den Holler area, we would look at that hill, and marvel at how we struggled to get our cart to the top on that first morning. It was sufficiently important to us that after Anne's death, when Jeff Ulrich and I were at "Rocky Branch" to meet our forester, Bob Wagoner, we buried a portion of her cremated remains at the foot of that hill.

Lumber Harvests

Picture 57 - Anne on the logging bridge in 1992.

Our first lumber sale was a selective harvest of the 14 acres in the northeast corner of our property. The forester marked and we sold 225 trees with an estimated 37,000 board feet of lumber, to the Weston Paper Co., Terre Haute, Indiana, in June, 1990, for $10,230. The contract allows the buyer two years to remove the trees. The weather was not cold enough to freeze the ground to handle their big equipment, so the harvest was not begun until May 25, 1992, and finished June 4, 1992.

The second harvest was again a selective harvest but included the entire property except the 14 acres which was harvested a few years earlier. Also the bottom area on both sides of the creek was not included in the second sale. At the suggestion of the State Forester, we engaged a private forester, Ken Hoene, to mark and market the trees.

Hoene advertised them in various forest and lumber magazines. Interested buyers were to submit sealed bids to him. On August 26, 1994, we had the meeting to open the sealed bids. Hoene had marked 705 trees, with an estimated 200,000 board feet of lumber, which took 64 semi-truck loads of logs, and sold for $76,300, less 7% for the forester's commission, and 4% for the State. The logging operation was begun March 16, 1995, and completed April 2, 1995.

Mini-Tree Harvest

In September, 2008, Anne and I went down to check on the condition of the walnut logs Jeff Ulrich and I had sawed from a large walnut tree that was down from high water in the tributary near the mouth of Den Holler. I sawed couple pieces off one of the logs and brought them home hoping to be able to work on them on the lathe in our shop at MRC. They still seemed pretty solid even after having been down for 4 or 5 years.

While there I noticed that a large number, probably two dozen, of the Tulip Poplar trees between the trail to the creek and the bluff to the south had been uprooted. It appeared that a real storm had gone thru and blew them down.

Picture 58 - - Skidder dragging logs over the bridge.

Neither the forester, Bob Wagoner, nor the

lumberman, Bennie Joines, had an explanation of why or how the trees had been uprooted, other than, as I mentioned, a severe wind storm.

Picture 59 - Knuckle-boom handling a 45' log.

I later contacted my forester, Bob Wagoner, who indicated that it would be well to clean them up. He contacted a lumberman, Bennie Joines, who lives in Hindsboro, Illinois, and who runs a small lumbering operation with his own Bobcat and truck. Joines, the lumberman, said that since poplar trees aren't choice trees and are not worth much on the market, he would clean them up for the logs. So that's what we decided to do.

He told me when he would be working on the project, so Anne and I went down to meet him and check on the job. While there, I offered him the walnut logs that had been down for several years. He loaded them and took them out. While there I had him pull out the roots of the walnut tree that I had been wanting to retrieve. He took the logs and root-stump up by the cabin entrance, sawed off some of the root branches, loaded it into the trunk of our Corolla and we brought it home. In that condition it weighed approximately 150 pounds. I trimmed off all the dead and rotted wood and got it down to a good solid piece of burled walnut root 20" x 15" x 15", that weighed 130 pounds. Now, in November, 2008, I'm not sure just what I'll do with it. I hope to cut it in slabs and do some lathe work with it. At this point I can only imagine that it will have beautiful grain when finished.

In a later telephone conversation, Bennie, the lumberman, told me he got two truckloads of logs, sold them to the Amish to make crates. He received a check of five hundred dollars for them, which he says was a bit more than expenses, but not much more since he had to move his equipment fifty miles and work three days with the project. Thus ends the story of my Mini Harvest.

New Tree Planting, 1997

One other item to mention here is that we planted approximately 150 new trees in the area north of the cabin, on April 24, 1997. We planted only trees native to Illinois, Oak, Walnut, Ash, Tulip Poplar, and Cyprus. Our son Don was here at the time and met our forester, Bob Waggoner, Don Samford, owner of the adjacent fields, and Brent Walters who farms Samford's land. Our son Don helped with this tree planting operation.

Unfortunately even after six years the new trees are not doing too well. Most of them are alive and trying their best to grow but the pesky deer keep nipping them off at the top. Currently I am collecting soap to hang on the trees. I am told that deer do not like the odor emitted by soap and will not bother trees with soap tied to them. I have the Four Seasons janitor Loren, collecting soap that's left in the locker room for that purpose. I hope to use it this spring when growth begins.

I requested soap from several motels in the area and got a good response from Holiday Inn and Motel 6. I have many boxes and bags with hundreds of the small bars of soap that apparently the motels would otherwise simply discard. I have also requested friends and neighbors to save their mesh bags they might get at the grocery stores with onions, oranges, and the like, and have used these to contain the small bars of soap to be tied to the trees.

Last spring I tied soap to approximately half of the small trees at "Rocky Branch" and some out at Hedgewood where I have also planted several hundred small trees. It appears that the soap does have a deterrent effect with the deer and I hope to tie soap on the remaining small trees this coming spring.

In the summer of 2004, I went back to check on my trees and found that every one of the bars of soap was gone. The empty mesh bags were still tied to the trees but no soap in a single one. It appeared that some animal, probably a squirrel, had chewed a hole in the bag and eaten the soap. However, I am not giving up. I have a bucket full of bags with soap which I plan to try again this spring (2005). It appears to me that the soap does have some deterrent effect, if only I can keep it on.

The attempt to save the young trees we planted is discouraging. A few of the trees seem to be getting taller than the deer can reach to nip off, but then in the rutting season the bucks rub and tear up many of the larger trees.

Since we are getting older and Anne's difficulty in walking has developed, our activity at "Rocky Branch" has become considerably less. We visit the property occasionally, but Anne because she is unable to negotiate the steps, is unable to stay overnight in the cabin. I still like to join the three young fellows who have become pretty much regulars in the deer hunt. I am not the ardent and successful hunter I once was. I pick the easy spots for my stand; hunt from the cliffs or from my hunting tent. I do not hesitate to take the extra deer that one of my hunter-friends, Kevin Lee, shoots and gives for me.

Many People Enjoyed Rocky Branch

On three different occasions we had an open invitation for our church friends to enjoy our woods, July 4, 1984; July 4, 1990; and May 30, 1994. On each occasion we had notice in the church bulletin two weeks in advance, and had from 25 to 32 people respond. Each occasion involved a hike to Den Holler, the burial site, and the big well, the beaver dams and a Heron rookery, then return to the cabin for our meal at 4:00 pm. Each family was instructed to bring meat or meat substitute to be grilled over an open fire, and a dish to share. We provided drink and watermelon. There was free time for visiting and for the kids and some adults to enjoy the creek.

June 8, 9 & 10, 1990, all of my Miller siblings and spouses, Ruth and Abe, Dennis, Emerson and Ruthie, Dale and Ethel, all except Dennis' Anne, spent a three day family celebration. Abe's brought and slept in their camper, Anne and I slept in our pickup, then with tents and the bunk beds, we had beds for everyone.

Picture 60 - Reunion of siblings and spouses at Rocky Branch. left to right, D. Paul, Abe, Dennis, Ruthie, Dale, Ethel, Ruth, Anne. Emerson took the picture.

In the fall of 1983, Hilda and Cornelius Krahn, Erna and Orlando Harms, spent and overnight. Again, Anne and I slept in the pickup, and our quests enjoyed the bunk beds. At that time we had a heavy layer of fallen leaves on the ground which was made a big impression on our guests.

In 1985, we invited our bridge group to celebrate the end of our season at "Rocky Branch." At that time we had Big Red, a Honda three-wheeler, which people enjoyed riding. Another attraction was swimming. At that time that the beavers had built eleven dams along a one-half mile stretch of the creek, and we had quite a number of water holes deep

Picture 61 - Anne and Paul hauling wood at Rocky Branch with 'big red'.

enough for swimming. Bill Dunn took a picture of Bill Smith and me in our birthday suits, and later had the photo made into a put-together puzzle.

Russ Oyer, Gerlof Homan, Dean Reeser, and Freeman Beachy, along with all of our grand kids, and a teen ager, Chris Reeser, for whom I served as mentor in our church program, have spent time with me doing various jobs such as cutting trails, making fire wood, and girdling some of our marked trees.

Also a significant part of our experience is that Anne and I alone girdled 49 acres of trees in the mid-1980s. This became a significant factor when it came to our major harvest some years later.

In addition to these people mentioned above, we have had a dozen or more deer hunters. On one hunt Tom Yoder shot two deer, in my hunting years I have taken nine deer, and Tim Waltner tells me he has taken eight big bucks with nice racks. Our policy at present is that we are limiting hunters to three young men, Tim Waltner, Kevin Lee, and Jeff Ulrich. In return they are doing work helping eliminate honey-suckle at Hedgewood.

90th Birthday Celebration

Picture 62 - Paul & Anne relaxing during Paul's 90th birthday celebration at Rocky Branch.

The kids said they were all coming in to help me celebrate my 90th birthday and wondered what I would like to do to celebrate. Naturally, I chose to go to "Rocky Branch." Brenda said she'd make up the invitations. She did an elaborate job with a printed and decorated sheet with red envelope to send to the people I had listed. Forty-three people attended. We all met at the cabin, took a guided tour, beginning at 1:00 o'clock, to Den Holler, the burial site, and the pioneer well, back to the cabin and had a big picnic dinner with the group.

Each family was asked to bring their own meat or meat-substitute and a dish to share. The kids furnished a fabulously

big and elaborately
decorated cake, and
everyone had an abundance
of food to eat. Our three
kids and all the grandkids
were present. All told, it
was a great and once-in-a-
lifetime experience.

Our Intentions for Rocky Branch

Picture 63 - D. Paul and Brenda
ready for the birthday cake at
Paul's 90th birthday celebration.

The "Rocky Branch"
property has afforded us many enjoyable experiences over the
years. The neighbors in the community have frequently
expressed satisfaction for the interest we take in the property and
for our interest in keeping it in its natural state. Before we
acquired it, they realized the possibility of some rowdy group
coming in, or a land developer getting hold of it. We heard also
that there were rumors of a group from Chicago wanting to
establish a nudist colony on the isolated property. It had the
potential of adding some real problems to the community. With
the relationships we have developed locally, these kinds of
problems have been avoided.

In addition to the recreational aspects, it has been important
to us for the income received from the lumber harvests. The
harvests have been and we hope will continue to be under the
supervision of professional foresters. The foresters of the
Weston Paper Manufacturing Co., Terre Haute, Indiana,
volunteered to prepare a 20-year program for the timber. Two of
their foresters spent several days detailing an in-the-field analysis
of the 127 acres. Their report is available in a separate document,
has been examined by the Illinois Department of Conservation
foresters, Bob Blair and Bob Waggoner, and it meets their
approval.

Blair and Waggoner are the foresters with whom we have
worked closely in the TSI (Timber Stand Improvement) program

since we acquired the property. We plan that for any future harvest we will continue to work with them in marking the trees and also in marketing the timber. This is a service rendered by the Illinois Conservation Department, free of charge, except that when a harvest sale is made, a four percent tax is taken off the top of the sale dollars, to help finance this service.

Finally, it is important for us to maintain this timberland for environmental reasons. Forests help clean the air and reduce pollution, prevent erosion, and provide a habitat for wild life. It is important for the welfare of planet Earth, to keep as much land as possible in its natural state.

Consequently, we feel that it would be best to protect "Rocky Branch" and keep it in its pristine state. Also, because of the interest our kids and grandkids appear to have, we hope to keep the ownership in the family. If for logistic reasons, it is not feasible for the family to maintain ownership, and if all family members would agree, a final decision to sell the property should lie with those who own and are responsible for it.

Our intention is to embark on a program that will enhance nature and contribute to the welfare and long-range needs of our environment and at the same time meet the needs and interests of those who have the ownership and responsibility for the property.

This statement of our intentions was prepared July 1, 1993, and was signed by D. Paul Miller and Anna B. Miller and a copy was submitted to each of our three children at that time.

Today, January 13, 2000, our philosophy and general feelings regarding the eventual future of the property, remains unchanged. I made some revisions to the original statement. I made a few editorial changes and described some developments, most of which have occurred since I wrote the first statement. Those changes have been incorporated into the above statement.

What about the Future?

Another important development is that we have made arrangements for Jeff Ulrich to assume supervision responsibilities for our "Rocky Branch" and Hedgewood properties, once Anne and I are no longer around and the kids are in Salt Lake City, California, Evanston, or somewhere else other than near here. A copy of that agreement, listed as an amendment to our wills, has been given to each of the children, to Jeff, and I have retained a copy. My attorney tells me that, in its present form it is not legally binding, but we are letting it stand as is. Apparently it is serving the function we intended.

What If?

"Rocky Branch" has proven to be a really good "event" in our lives. When I look back on the purchase of that property, I feel that we have been exceptionally lucky to have acquired it. In addition to all the enjoyment we have received from it with our family, kids, grandkids, groups of friends, hiking, picnicking, wood cutting, sawing, and burning, deer-hunting with friends, and the like, we have harvested and sold logs for more than twice the original purchase price, and still have a good forest. I often think of how near we came to not buying it. We had to be encouraged and almost coaxed by both Tribby, the owner, and Gardener, the colleague who was doing Tribby's tax work to buy it. I made the offer, expecting them to refuse it, but they accepted. What if?

Hedgewood

Even with all the good features of "Rocky Branch," I felt that something was still lacking. I needed something in the nature of "Rocky Branch", but to which I could go to in just a few minutes, spend little or much time, and return home without traveling so far. So checking the various possibilities, I found the Deer Ridge Estates owned by Carl Grieder, the sod-farm man near Carlock. He had a number of lots for sale and some of them were quite heavily wooded. I purchased one lot for twenty thousand dollars.

It was too much money for approximately three acres but absolutely the only property of this nature available within our vicinity. Deer Ridge Estates was in a development with thirty or so lots, and with this location, I felt that in the long run it should not be a bad deal even from the standpoint of investment. We had the closing on it June 11, 1997, and called it Hedgewood because of the almost unlimited number of Hedge trees growing there.

Soon after my purchase, our friend, Jeff Ulrich, purchased Lot 16 joining ours along the hard surfaced road. Also, I learned that he wanted to sell his lot. I saw these two joining lots located along the highway to be a desirable piece of real estate so purchased it for twenty-three thousand dollars. We closed on this second lot, January 26, 1999.

I then contacted our district forester regarding the possibility of doing a TSI (Timber Stand Improvement) program on these lots. I learned that five acres was the smallest number of acres that could be put into a TSI program. So from this standpoint it was important for us to have purchased the second lot. The first lot was approximately three acres and the second four acres, so our property totaling seven acres did qualify for the TSI.

An important additional factor was that as subdivision lots, the taxes were very high, more than nine hundred dollars per year for the two lots, too high to justify this as a "playground." However, when the property was approved for the TSI, with the forest management, the taxes were reduced so low that we have paid zero taxes.

One of the first things I did after obtaining the first lot was to contact a construction man to build a road so I could drive into the property. When I acquired the property it was so densely populated with trees and underbrush, and just plain trash that had been bulldozed into a big long pile just south of the entry lane, that we could hardly walk through it. On our first exploration into the lot, Carl, the owner showing the property, and I, had to use tree trimmers to work a path to even walk onto the lot. After I had done some clearing I contacted the owner of the 60-feet right-of-way just north of our property. Half of the lane is on his property. He welcomed the road if it would be put in at no cost to him.

The construction man did the grading through the little gully and the stream in the bottom, then hauled in crushed rock and recycled road material to make a road with very dependable footing. The billing indicated that we hauled in 80.16 tons of A S Millings ($492) and 38.24 tons of recycled road material ($241), a total of 118 tons of surfacing material. For the complete project I wrote him a check of $1538.20. This was a major investment in addition to the high cost of the lots, but I have never regretted it. We use it constantly.

At this point I have been working with the forester. We have planted several hundred small trees, and are working diligently with friends needing firewood to remove the many large hedge (Osage Orange) trees. Jeff Ulrich and Tim Waltner have been chief among the wood-cutters. In the winter, 2002-03, we spent four or five mornings cutting down large hedge trees and sawing it into firewood lengths. Jeff and Tim haul it out and plan to burn it. We are really getting that bottom area opened up so the newly planted trees can get light.

In November, 1997, Rich came for a visit. He and I cut down the big Box Elder tree in the bottom. We had to maneuver with the long mountain-climbing rope and a "come-along" to get it to fall away from a nearby hedge tree. We got the job done and that opened up a lot of sun light for the smaller trees. Gerlof Homan, Russ Oyer and I have spent several mornings stacking and burning much of the smaller brush that was lying down and the honeysuckle that I had cut earlier.

The TSI program has cost shared shelters for fifty trees each year for the first three years. We have planted around four-hundred small trees but have put shelters on only one hundred fifty in the three years of the program. For three years in a row, Anne and I have picked up bushels, three or four, five-gallon buckets, each year, of walnuts and have scattered most of them and planted some in the bottom along the stream which I transplant after they get a good start. It appears that the squirrels get the major share of the walnuts. A few grow and I have transplanted and sheltered probably couple dozen walnuts. Eventually I would like to remove most of the hedge trees on the two lots, and then continue to go after the honeysuckle and multi-floral rose.

I usually mow the lane and bottom, couple times during the summer. One drawback is that it is so easy for the tires on the mower pick up hedge thorns and cause flat tires. I then have to buy new tubes or plug the tire to the tune of ten or twelve dollars a throw.

I have cut a lane that crosses the stream and goes up the hill to join the two lots. This enables me to drive from one lot to the other in dry weather, and that is only with the 4-wheel drive vehicle.

John Bertsche and I had cut many, many big Honeysuckle in the woods along the highway, but apparently used an ineffective herbicide and most of it seems to grow back from the bottom. We hope to get out again this spring (2003) and go after the younger growth and use Torodon. It appears that there is no other way to get rid of the pesky Honeysuckle. I had worked with John in his woods in his TSI program as exchange labor.

My long-range goal for this property is to get rid of most of the hedge, box elder, and any "junk" trees, clear out the Multi-floral Rose, and Honeysuckle, and have the ground cleared to the point that one might walk almost anywhere in the two lots. I will probably continue to report activities in Hedgewood as we continue to work there.

As of March, 2005, Jeff Ulrich and I have done most of the hedge cutting for the last couple years. We are getting the area just south of our entrance pretty well cleared out, and are now starting on the south lot near the Deer Creek Estate entrance.

May, 2010 Update

Times have changed. Anne passed away February 5, 2010. Although I'm still active and in good physical condition, and since we moved to MRC, I have sold my tractor mower, trailer, and use our woods less and less.

My deer-hunting friends are helping me with work at Hedgewood. They do this as pay for hunting privileges at Rocky Branch." A party in Clark County offered me three thousand dollars per year, for the privilege of bow-hunting only, at "Rocky Branch." However, I prefer to keep strangers out of "Rocky Branch" if my deer-hunting friends will help with eradicating the honeysuckle.

I spent a morning with each of Jeff, Kevin, & Tim, sawing honeysuckle and putting Torodon on the stump, and would like for them to continue the project without me helping.

I have spent several mornings this spring (2010) clearing and burning some of the dead honeysuckle we cut last fall. That sort of work is about as much as I care to do anymore. After all I am 92 years old.

VI - My Impressions of Haiti

Going

This is my report of experiences in Haiti, January 6-16, 1994. I was a member of a work team from the Normal Mennonite church who volunteered to go to Hospital Albert Schweitzer, Dechappelles, Haiti, to work. The team consisted of Joe Haney, Lois Jett, Earl Kaufman, Franzie Loepp, D. Paul Miller, Doug Poag, Larry Reeser, and Meredith Schrocer. We were asked to pay our own expenses, including airline ticket, the wages of a Haitian worker who was to work with each of us, plus room and board, and the exit fee of twenty-five dollars. The work team was organized by the staff of Hospital Albert Schweitzer, mainly through the efforts of Bill Dunn, who is Executive Director of the hospital.

The group gathered at the Mennonite Church and left at approximately 7:00 o'clock Wednesday evening, January 5. Plans were to stay at the Howard Johnson Motel near the O'Hare airport in Chicago. Our flight was scheduled to leave O'Hare at 6:25 am Thursday morning. Originally we had planned to get up early Thursday morning and leave around 2:00 am. Weather reports on Wednesday, however, predicted snow and ice which was to make driving hazardous, so we decided to leave on Wednesday evening, stay overnight in Chicago and thus be ready to leave on the early flight.

When we arrived at the motel we received the message that our 6:25 flight had been cancelled. Franzie Loepp got on the phone, contacted Bill Dunn who was working out of his headquarters in Sarasota, Florida, and between him and the American Airline, the schedule for our group was changed, we were transferred to a 7:00 am flight to La Guardia airport in New York, were to transfer to the Kennedy Airport, and there catch a flight direct to Port au Prince.

Three taxis were to be furnished by the airline to transfer us with baggage from La Guardia to Kennedy. After an extended wait two taxis showed up. One of the drivers became impatient and rather than to wait for the third we got all our bags and people in the two taxis, although, one of the trunks was so full the driver had to tie down the lid of his trunk with a rope because he couldn't get it shut and latched.

Arriving Port-au-Prince

We made the connection in plenty of time. Since we had our tickets changed I do not have a record of the exact time of our departure for Port-au-Prince, however it was after eleven am. We arrived Port-au-Prince at 4:00 P M, and although we thought we had had some problems with our scheduling, change of flight, not getting the third taxi, and so forth, we found that the confusion really began after we reached Port au Prince.

The station was flooded with red caps all wanting to carry our bags. Since the Haitians speak Creole and very few speak any English, communication was difficult. We stacked our baggage on a pile, guarded it carefully and finally got the message across to one of the red-caps that we were going to Hospital Albert Schweitzer. He apparently knew where to find the person who was to meet us there. Kathy Troyer, who was carrying a sign outside the exit gate, was told by the red cap where we were and she was allowed to come into the area where our bags were stacked, although normally she would not be permitted in our baggage area

Kathy could speak Creole and knew how to handle the mob of red-caps all of whom wanted to get in on carrying our luggage. They all seemed anxious; yes even desperate to make a little money. Kathy asked us about our ability to carry our own things and then made it clear to the red-caps that we would hire one and only one to help us take everything to the vehicle to Hospital Albert Schweitzer, ninety miles away. We carried our luggage including two large boxes and one small box of plumbing supplies Joe had brought along for his plumbing work, loaded our things and crowded into the van, ten of us, eight of the work team plus Kathy and the driver, a native Haitian. At the customs check, the officials wanted to keep one of the large boxes of plumbing supplies, actually as a bribe for them letting the other box through. Kathy became very adamant; pointing out that for them to keep part of our baggage was illegal. They said, you can come and pick it up tomorrow. She made it clear that we were not going to drive ninety miles back to Port-au-Prince to pick up the box we had with us now. They seemed to realize that they were not getting anywhere with Kathy, and finally let us go with all our baggage and plumbing supplies.

It is unbelievable how difficult it was to get away from all the people, mostly, but not all red-caps who wanted money. Some kept their hands in the door of the van so it couldn't be closed, some held the sliding windows open, and finally when we did get the windows and doors closed one fellow stood on the back bumper and refused to get off. The driver accelerated in reverse and stopped suddenly several times in an attempt to throw him. Although it took some time, the maneuvering finally threw the last one off and we sped away. It was after we got some distance from the crowd that Kathy asked the driver to stop to check something she was not sure about. We soon learned that we could not stop near a group of people without them rushing to the car wanting to sell us something or begging for money.

The trip to the hospital was something else. The first sixty or so miles had fairly good roads, black top, fairly narrow, directly through several towns and villages with people, people everywhere. Coming out of Port-au-Prince the traffic was heavy and the driver was very aggressive. It seemed to me that he would take real chances, getting out and passing other cars and trucks with headlights coming very close from the opposite direction. Sometimes he would come very close to hitting, but always got by without a scrape. We were later told that it was sort of an unwritten law that the larger the vehicle, the greater the right-of-way.

The roadsides were crowded with people walking or riding donkeys, many, mostly women carrying baskets, buckets, etc. on their heads. On this first stretch of road, several of us commented that we were surprised that the roads were so good. But we were soon to learn what we had been warned about before coming, rough and bumpy roads. We left the black top, some said only twelve, some said twenty miles from our destination. But words cannot describe how rough the roads really were with deep pot holes extending great distances, gullies, holes, and ruts, and more holes and ruts. The driver would have to look for the best holes to take and which to dodge, whether to hit holes straight or at an angle so as to not get hung up.

Albert Schweitzer Hospital

We arrived at our living quarters, "Kay 11," at about nine o'clock. It was a house with three bedrooms and one bathroom. The women, Lois and Meredith were assigned to one bedroom, the six men were divided into the other two bedrooms, three in each. The two bedrooms occupied by the men were at one end of the house with the one bathroom between. The women were at the other end of the house. The one bathroom for the eight of us caused some inconvenience but with everyone considerate and cooperative, we had no serious problems.

We were informed that work hours are from 7:00 am to 4:00 pm, with an hour off for lunch. Breakfast was to be served at 6:00 am, and the evening meal at 6:00 pm. Various activities were scheduled around the work program, some in the evening and some during work hours. Details of these activities will be described later.

After breakfast the first morning, Kathy took us for a hurried tour over the grounds and through the hospital so that we would have some idea of where we were when work assignments were made. Kelly Harmon was our work supervisor. He with the suggestions of Franzie and Joe assigned Doug, Lois and Meredith to the paint crew. Earl and Larry were to put together some steel shelves, Joe and Franzie were to start on the bathroom they were to construct in the house we lived in. I was to assist them in a sort of "gopher" role.

The bathroom project required some major plumbing outside, with cement work probably twenty or twenty-five feet long, four or five feet wide, with a trough at one end for the maid to do the washing. The bathroom inside required breaking up the floor for the waterlines, making intricate plumbing connections and tiling the shower with their crude one-inch thick tile blocks.

My major assignment was to haul and sift sand. The sifting was done through fine screen (a sheet of regular window screen) which was placed inside a sifting box with quarter-inch screen. Fortunately, I had taken a pair of leather work gloves along. The Haitian worker, Michlet, who was assigned to me, and I, each took one glove and with the gloved hand rub the sand through the screen. The gloves were nearly worn out by the time we left. But we had a nice pile of fine sand left even after the plastering was completed.

Franzie laid the concrete blocks to enclose the shower and make the wall to contain the sink and stool. These blocks then had to be plastered. Electric wiring was done to provide light switches and outlets for electric shavers and dryers. They have 110-volt current so we could use our appliances without adapters. The plumbing and masonry work was fairly well completed when we left but some overtime hours had to be spent to finish and clean up the project.

In addition to hauling and sifting sand I ran many errands to the garage and shop area to fetch tools, a water hose, screws and bolts, electric wire nuts, etc. etc. All equipment and supplies had to be kept behind locked doors and gates so the Haitians couldn't steal them. On our last day of work, I was assigned to the paint crew. Most of my paint work here was to paint the high sloping ceiling in one of the hospital wards. This was done with the use of a ten-foot step-ladder and paint roller attached to a six foot pole. It was challenging and a real adventure for us to do the work. Under the circumstances of inadequate tools and because we could not communicate with the Haitians assigned to work with us, we were all relieved when we finished our last day of work on Thursday evening, and looking forward to our day of rough-road travel on Friday, seeing Port-au-Prince in the daylight, and flying home on Saturday.

We had arrived at the HAS compound on Thursday evening, January 6, worked Friday and Saturday, had off Sunday, then worked Monday, Tuesday, Wednesday, and Thursday, spent Friday and part of Saturday traveling to Port-au-Prince, and "touring" the city and meeting our plane at 2:08 pm. Before going into the Port-au-Prince adventures, I shall go back and describe some of the things we did and enjoyed during the week at HAS.

Near the end of the work-week, Kathy distributed questionnaires and asked us to fill them out in order to give her a notion of some of our reactions, and to help her in making plans for future work teams. Ours was the first work team assigned to HAS. It appears that the idea of work teams originated with Bill Dunn. It was only natural that when organizing his first work crew, he would go to the church he was acquainted with, Mennonite Church of Normal, and approach the people he knew. Planning for the work team was in process for probably six or eight months. At least I had gotten some wind of it some months in advance of the actual announcement and request for volunteers. The following work team scheduled to come to HAS, I think, in February, was to come from Kathy's home church, Oak Grove, Smithville, Ohio.

On Kathy's questionnaire we were asked to indicate the three most enjoyable or impressive experiences we had during our stay. My number one was the motorcycle ride I had with Larry, who was a good mechanic and the person in charge of the garage area which contained the hospital's trucks, vans, pickups, tractors, and a recently donated wrecker along with supplies and equipment that would go to make an operation like HAS run.

My second most enjoyable choice was the visit to the market in *la Verrettes*. Third was the visit to *Ceneque*'s church Sunday morning. *Ceneque* was the Haitian pharmacist who had come to Illinois a year or so earlier, stayed with John Bertsches and was invited to our place for a meal one evening. He invited me and anyone of our group interested, to visit his church. Other experiences could have been mentioned but we were asked for three. Two others experiences I recall readily were, one, our pickup ride, ten or twelve people in the back of the Keith Flanagan's two seated Toyota pickup to Plassic where HAS has a dispensary, and two, our walk with Kathy after we quit work at 2:30, to a nearby school and to see the home being built by a Haitian who is working at the Hospital.

The Motorcycle Ride

It was sort of by accident that I even got in on the motorcycle ride. Joe Haney and Earl Kaufman, because of the nature of their work specialties, worked more closely with Larry than the rest of us. Earl had taken a ride with Larry earlier and after that ride, came in all excited about what he had seen and experienced. The next day, Joe got a ride. He too was excited about it. Earl had arranged to go again but because of his rash and swollen leg and ankle and he not feeling well, asked me to go to the garage and tell Larry he couldn't go. I went to the garage. Larry had already left. I talked to his wife in the office. She said he was home and tried to describe where they lived. I tried to find it, had some difficulty, but my Haitian friend, Renald, realized my problem and came to my rescue. He said, "The man with the motorcycle, I show you." He did. Larry was checking the oil on his bike and when I gave him the message that Earl couldn't go, he right away asked me if I'd like to go. I was pleased for the invitation, he got a cushion to put on the back for me to sit on, and we were off. We went down rough roads, across the canal on a narrow steel bridge probably eighteen inches wide and eight or ten feet long. He had to make a turn just before hitting the bridge but he did that with no problem. We continued on the rough roads past people, goats, donkeys carrying heavy loads of produce such as sugar cane, lumber and the like, pigs tied with ropes around their necks (I never could figure out why the pigs didn't slip the rope off their round heads).

Keith visited as we traveled. He said early that he was hoping to cross the river today. He had never done that with his motorcycle. It was the big river in the area, *Riviere De l' Artibonite.* When we reached the bank of the river, we had a nice view. People were wading across, but we had a rather steep bank to descend to the water. It was so steep he asked me to get off and he'd pick his way down with the bike. When he got to the river bottom on the gravel, he asked me to climb back on, hold your feet up and hang on. Couple young boys waved us over to a shallower part of the river and we got across, about knee deep, with no problem. We then drove along the bottom 'til he found the trail that led up to the town of Petite Riviera and on up to the Fort de la Crete a Pierrot, a French fort that was built a century earlier. The view of the river and valley, miles in both directions, was fantastic, the most beautiful view I saw in Haiti. The city, pronounced like *'teet riviera,* had beautiful paved streets, paved with light colored octagon shaped tile. The streets were paved with this beautiful tile because, according to Keith, some politician who lives in this city had some influence with the dictator some years earlier, and fraudulently gotten the paved road he requested, obviously a good example of corrupt politics.

We descended from the Fort to the road below, drove along the river to the dam. Here we crossed the river on the dam, a crossing Earl had fussed about several days earlier. It was a crossing about a block long; the top was about fifteen inches wide. Larry said to me, "Sit up close to me, don't put much weight on your foot rests (a little jerk could throw us off balance) and it goes better, it's easier to control if I go faster." So I followed his instructions and on the dam top we went. He was very steady and actually I had no fear at any time. On the one side, had we gone off, was a cobblestone descent probably at a forty-five degree angle to the water. On the other side was a drop off, at some points probably three to five feet to the ground and some places less. It would have been bad, even dangerous, to have gone off on either side. We continued over rough roads, thru mud holes. Couple times I had to get off and walk so he could make it thru. On one of these occasions, running over the rough pot-holes filled with water, I stumbled, fell and got some scratches on my legs. (Kathy was always concerned about scratches and cuts getting infection, but this was my second fall, once when running with Bill Dunn, but I healed up okay with all my scratches.) We went up a steep hill where Larry said that on a different occasion he almost lost a Haitian boot-black, a man he was hauling, he had almost slid off the back going up the hill. We got in shortly after 6:00, just in time for supper. It was a great experience.

La Verrette Market

The work team took a morning off to visit the Wednesday market. The big market is scheduled only once a week. Here the experiences and observations are almost beyond description. People, people everywhere, walking, sitting on the ground with their small supply of wares to be sold, rice, beans, sugar cane, molasses, ground corn in many grades, hardware, dishes, meat, scads of it out in the hot weather, it's hard to understand how they can eat it and survive. In one hut, I bought a machete, the type the peasants use to cut rice, etc. I paid eight Haitian dollars, approximately three dollars, sixty cents for it in American currency.

On one occasion, Earl and I stood and watched an old woman picking up rice kernels out of the gravel, one by one. She apparently did not have money to buy from the good piles, so was getting what she could pick up, for nothing. She'd pick up one kernel at a time, put it in her other hand and then when that hand was full, put it in a small container she held. Kathy bought several things, molasses, some vegetables, and sugar to use in our cooking. The market experience, travel and all took us all morning. We traveled in the pickup that had to be pushed to start. On the way home we picked up an old lady who was walking in our direction with a heavy load. She was grateful for the ride. We saw lots of pathetic sights but all told it was a good day.

Ceneque's Church

Ceneque was a Haitian pharmacist who had visited the states a year or so ago. He stayed at Bertsches, worked at the hospital, and thought he was working for his keep here in this country, but I'm told was a definite liability. While visiting in Normal, he came to our place one evening for a meal, and he felt that he knew me when I arrived at HAS. He gave me a special invitation to his church. I was sort of crippled from the fall I had when running with Bill Dunn the morning before. Our whole group attended the hospital church service, and it was announced in church that *La Grande Mellon*, the daughter in law of Dr. Mellon (his son Billy's widowed wife), was driving to *Ceneque's* church, I talked to her about riding with her. She was driving a Peugeot. She said she had a space reserved for me. Larry Reeser, Kelly (our work foreman), another lady and I rode with her.

The church had lots of activity and participation. People would stand, clap, wave their hands above their heads, sing, pray loudly, and kneel in prayer, and so on. We had about three sermons, at least talks, and the same number of musical solos. At one point in the service, Ceneque introduced each of us individually and asked if I wanted to say anything. I commented that I was glad to be here and thought later that I had missed the opportunity to tell them that Ceneque had been in our home in Illinois. Anyway, it was a good day and we were all glad we had the opportunity to ride rather than to walk the rough and busy road.

Our Walk with Kathy

Visit to School & Haitian Home being built: After our workday ended at 2:30 pm Saturday, Kathy took the group on a short walk, perhaps a half to three quarters of a mile to see couple things: (1) a Haitian home in the process of being built, and (2), a Haitian School. The man building the home was a

Haitian who had a job at the hospital. We were informed that a Haitian needs a definite source of income in order to build. Also, if a Haitian has a steady job and is not building, relatives, neighbors and family will feel that he should be helping them out with basic necessities such as food and clothing. When you are building, you can simply tell them you have no money to give, and they believe it. This fellow was to be building over a period of a year or more. The posts were up and tied together at the top, the tin roof was on but no walls and the floor was dirt and would probably remain dirt. Behind his house, perhaps sixty or seventy feet he was digging the pit for his privy. The hole was approximately three feet in diameter and when we were there, twelve feet deep. He said it was only half-done; he was going a total of twenty-five feet. The hole was impressive. Deep and narrow and it seemed too deep for anyone to climb down to dig. Also, much of it was rock. I asked him how the workers get down and up. He said they prop their feet and hands on the wall and work their way down or up as the case may be. He, also Keith, told us that the cost of the tin roof was about half the cost of the entire home. He told us that if several workers worked steady on a home project like his, and didn't have to stop to wait for more money to buy materials, they could put up a house in about fifteen days.

On this walk on the road along the canal we were always impressed with the things and people we saw. Many animals, particularly pigs tied up with a rope, chickens with a string around one leg, sometimes dragging a limb or weight so they couldn't get very far away. Couple girls, probably eight or ten, asked Meredith to take their picture. They posed by the well and when done went away laughing and giggling and chattering in their language. Kathy translated for us. As they ran giggling they said, "That white lady took our picture."

Thoughts

Perhaps my biggest frustration was the fact that we were instructed definitely, to not give the Haitian people money or things, clothing, food, etc. If we wanted to give, we should leave it with the staff. They knew where the real needs were. Often the clever ones who approach new people coming in, have a way to get to you to give and they are usually not the ones who really need.

A good example of this was Renald, who I mentioned earlier. He was a young man about 20. He could speak fairly good English. He was with me for hours while we were sifting sand and working around the house. He told me his mother and father were both dead, he had a sister 10 and a brother 12. He wanted to go to school. He had gone thru the 10th grade and his teacher told him he couldn't come back till he brought the money to pay. His school cost eighty Haitian dollars a year. That converted into thirty-six U.S. dollars. I told this story to the staff at the Wednesday prayer and study meeting. I said I would like to pay for his two years of schooling if they could check it out and work it thru the proper channels. They knew the boy, he had been Irene Dunn's yard boy, and they said she had put him thru school many times. They suggested I talk to Jan Flanagan who was in charge of schooling and scholarships. I learned that Renald had talked to most of the others in our group with the same story. He was clever and convincing. I told Jan that my offer stands. If he really attends school, I would pay his two years to finish the 12th grade.

Irene Dunn called me Sunday afternoon after we had returned home. We visited a half-hour on the phone. She verified the stories about Renald. I told her I'd really like to help him. He appears to have some real potential if he'd get the right opportunity. She said she always hopes he would make a change and really go to school. She and the other staff members said he would never go to school if you gave him the money. My offer was to pay for schooling. He'd have to attend and make grades in order to receive the help he was asking for.

For me it is much more satisfying to help some person I know and can relate to rather than to donate for "the cause." For example, I'd rather share a meal with someone I know than to make a donation to feed the hungry. So I remain frustrated. I would like to help but am not permitted to. And I can see that to respond to their begging only encourages more begging. I cooperated one hundred percent with the staff's request to not give to the person, yet at the same time it gives me a feeling of regret, certainly disappointment.

We are confronted with a real dilemma. In our Christian and humanitarian world we are conditioned to develop attitudes of helpfulness and service. Help the poor, feed the hungry, and give to the needy. Yet in this environment we are given instructions to "don't help, don't respond to begging, even when the beggars are all around you. If you want to give or do something for the needy, give to us, not those who ask. We'll see that it goes to the places where it's needed. I don't question the integrity of the staff." I'm sure they know where real needs exist, but I lose my motivation to give when we have to put it thru a middleman. I did leave some donations for Kathy and others of the staff to dispose of, but it would have been much more rewarding for me if I could have placed my own resources where they were to be used.

Meetings

In the next few paragraphs, I'd like to look at some of the meetings they provided for the work team, meetings that were organized especially for us. I should mention that we were informed in the literature received before leaving home that this was intended to be a worthwhile cultural experience. It was not for us to just work, but we were to share not only with the Haitians but with the staff personnel as well. Much of this report reflects the staff's willingness to take us with them into the field, to meet the people literally at the grass roots level. Some good examples of this are in the trip to visit the dispensary at Plassic with Keith Flanagan, the visit to the churches, permitting us to visit the home under construction, the motorcycle ride, the market at *la Verrettes*, and even the day to day work with some of the assigned native Haitian workers, and finally, important to me the unassigned workers who wanted to work and weren't among the chosen few, and it was they who spent time with us, talking, telling of their plight, and in reality, begging for things or money. They were with us because they wanted to get "next to" us, thinking they might gain some personal advantage.

The work team was invited to Keith and Jan Flanagan's home Saturday evening to see his slides. I personally never get too turned on with slide shows but he did have a side of the culture which was important for us to see. It made the trip to the dispensary at Plassic Sunday afternoon with him in his pickup more meaningful. His job is community relations and community development. He was a specialist, very skillful and effective in that area, although he was a trained veterinarian. He knew personally so many of the people on the road and those sitting in their front yards. His slide show prepared us for what we were to see the next day.

Bill Dunn, who at the time of our visit was residing at Sarasota, Florida, arrived at HAS Saturday evening. He appeared on the scene at Flanagan's after Keith's slide show. Couple things came out of his arrival, which are appropriate to mention here. One he asked if anyone was interested in running with him in the morning. I volunteered and was the only one interested. The next morning I looked at my watch wrong and got up an hour earlier than planned. Since I didn't want to wake the house up, I laid on the couch in the living room until Bill came at 6:45 am.

On our run I was slower than Bill but ran quite a bit of the way to *la Verrettes* about three miles away. We ran and walked. I was anxious to do it because it was good to visit with Bill and get his version of things we were seeing. It was on this excursion that I stumbled in one of the rough spots and skinned my leg and hip. He, as well as Kathy, and others of the staff, were concerned about watching it carefully so as to not get infection. It was because of my fall and Bill's concern and thoughtfulness that I got the ride to *Ceneque*'s church later that morning with Dr. Mellon's widowed daughter in law.

The other thing regarding Bill relating to our group is that he wanted us to see the Mellon home before Mrs. Mellon would return home Tuesday. So on Monday right after lunch Bill came to our house and led us thru the paths, over the canal to the Mellon house. It was quite a house, with a big patio or porch overlooking the valley and mountains in the distance. Two large and outstanding trees grew in their back yard. One was a large banyan tree which grew with extended props to the ground to prop up the weight of the large limbs. It was interesting to see the Mellon house and get the tour before Mrs. Mellon arrived.

On Wednesday Kathy took us to see Mrs. Mellon. She had just returned the day before from the states where she had her knee tended by her U.S. physicians. Earlier she had stumbled and fell and was advised by the local doctors to go have it checked in Connecticut. We visited a few minutes with her, she had her maid serve us a drink and we returned to work. I was impressed with the degree to which she had the details of the bathroom we were working on in our house, under control. She knew just where the shower was, the sink under the south window and the stool in the corner. Franzie described what we were doing and she understood every detail.

Tuesday evening we went to Jim Dutton's home for his talk on the background of Haiti. He had a pretty good grasp on the current conditions, the effect of the embargo, and so forth, but seemed to be lacking in early history of Haiti. One of my major dilemmas derives from the fact that when Columbus arrived centuries earlier it was, according to descriptions, a tropical paradise. It was occupied by the docile Arawak Indians. The Spanish then moved in settled and virtually extinguished most of the native Indians, then the French came, replaced the Spanish, and actually finished off the remainder of the native Indians, then carried on an intense slave traffic until eventually the Africans outnumbered the whites 11 to 1.

This imbalance created a situation ripe for revolution, and in time resulted in the first successful slave uprising in the history occurring 1791 to 1802. Haiti won its freedom from France in 1804. It became the first independent black nation in history. A great deal of tension and strife existed between the Spanish, French and African influences, and for some reason Haiti has never been a stable nation.

It raises the question of whether it can ever become stable and if not, why not. Is it possible for a nation of Africans to stabilize itself and become a successful and prosperous nation? Or is there a biological dimension which makes this impossible? Looking at history, and viewing the African nations which have more recently become independent, and seeing their lack of stability and ability to handle independence, one naturally raises the question of "why." One must be careful here or he/she might be considered a racist.

The eight of us went to the HAS church service Sunday morning. There it was announced that we were all invited to the Wednesday evening prayer meeting at Kathy and Virgil Troyer's home. They had passed out an article on prayer, with the "ask and it shall be given unto you," sentiment. I didn't like the article and had earlier decided not to go. Doug was going and at the last minute I decided to go along. I figured you have nothing to lose and it would provide more experiences in Haiti. They did very little with the article. A fellow played his guitar and we sang a few songs, and then had an informal discussion which turned out good for me. It was in this setting where I first voiced my frustration regarding being instructed not to give to the people we contact personally, but rather give to the staff and they'll know where the real needs are. As alluded to earlier, contributing is so much more satisfying to me if I can meet and interact with the person in need, rather than simply donating to the cause. My case in point was Renald Anilius who I had spoken to quite a bit while we were working, and I might add, my frustration never was, and still has not been resolved.

Port-au-Prince: Home Bound

We finished our work week Thursday evening and left for Port-au-Prince Friday morning in the HAS van loaded with 13 people, three staff members catching a plane, Kathy and her husband Virgil, and the eight of us, plus all our baggage. We were loaded, the roads were rough for the first 12 miles, but it was much more enjoyable going out in the daylight, and hitting the rough roads first while we were still fresh, also we had three of the hospital staff with us who could give us so much information about the hotels that were abandoned, the beaches once popular, club facilities which were no longer in service, etc. etc.

We stopped in the banana country to buy three bunches of bananas which we munched on as we traveled. We arrived at Port-au-Prince, left the people off at the airport, then went to the Olofoson Hotel for lunch, then down town to the office of Pierre Allen, the hospital's agent. We didn't go in but conditions were unbelievably bad. Streets full of people, literally packed. We'd honk for people to get out of the way so we could keep moving and they'd spread to let us by. If you stopped you were mobbed with beggars and people wanting to sell something or ask a favor. At one place Virgil had to keep driving while Joe and Kathy went in to buy a battery for his camera. He said if you stop they're likely to let the air out of your tires, then want pay to help fix it. So we drove around and came by for the third time before Joe and Kathy were out and ready to go.

We then went up to the Baptist Mission, a long drive to the top of the mountains. Here it was actually cold. With Virgil's help at bargaining, Earl and I each bought another machete, this time in a leather case. We paid 50 Haitian dollars for the two. This amounted to ten U S. dollars each. So I brought two machetes home. I also bought a set of a dozen tea napkins, hand cross-stitched, for $6.50 Haitian. The exchange rate was forty U.S. cents to the Haitian dollar. This was a quite nice shopping area; some of the group went to the restaurant and got banana splits, and so forth. From here we went to a place where Kathy bought two maps of Haiti for two U.S. dollars each. Then we went to our lodging place:

Bins Place
Missionary Guest House
Rev. Barbara A Bineta Bare
% Lynn Air International
Ft. Lauderdale, FL 33340
Tel: 011-509-46-390

Bin's Place was frugally furnished but adequate. The men all slept in one room; some of the beds had only one sheet. Port-au-Prince had no electricity when we arrived, due mostly to the embargo, so they lighted kerosene lamps. Due to a communication breakdown, they were not prepared for us to eat, so the maids had to go to the market, shop for food and then prepare it. We waited probably two or more hours. The meal, however, was good. The main dish was rice then a sort of bean gravy to put on. We also had a salad and fruit for dessert. I enjoyed the meal. Some of the group couldn't say as much because they were not vegetarians. Some felt a meal was not quite complete without meat. Even so, we had not been served much meat in our Haitian stay.

That night after the meal we had a good discussion on our experiences the past week or so. Meredith started it by asking us to share our "three most impressive experiences in Haiti." I got the impression that Kathy was somewhat disappointed that the staff's request to not give personally to the begging Haitians caused me some frustration.

We had a good night's sleep. Showers were cold; no electricity in the evening, but lights came on in the morning. For breakfast we each had a dish of cereal (kiks), and grapefruit. After breakfast we all went for a walk down the street outside the Bin's Place fence. Young kids were peeking thru the banana leaf fence, and as soon as we come out they were right with us. Couple kids spoke a little English. They followed us, one picked up a tin can and while beating time on it, they sang a simple little song in English. A 'shoe-black' come walking down a side street toward us ringing a bell. Everywhere we went we were an attraction.

After returning to the motel we met in the common room and listened to MCC representative, Gordon Zook. He described their work centering mostly in the Ranquitte area, in the northeastern part of the country. His story was also very bleak. In their work they focused on agriculture and health. He pointed out that they taught the Haitian farmers to contour and to not burn their stalks but to work plant material into the soil to give humus and fertilizer and also to prevent erosion. They discussed a variety of topics and moved from one area to another to cover as much territory as possible

They had Haitian community leaders who were to be
responsible for carrying on in what they were taught. They
reported, however, that two years after they left an area, they
would return and note that the Haitians had fallen right back into
their old methods, no contours and burning the debris. They
insisted it is easier this way. He seemed to be very pessimistic
about any long-range benefit to the Haitians. Again, this brings
up part of my frustration. I have to keep asking why? After they
actually experience increased yields, which they did, why would
they go back to the old farming methods?

Home

We left the motel for the airport at 11:15 am. Our plane was
scheduled to leave at 2:08 pm. We drove thru some of the most
ungodly streets (Virgil's shortcut), narrow, living quarters close to
the road on both sides, we almost got hung up with deep ruts and
sharp corners, but finally we got thru and to a more passable
road. We simplified our *red-cap* problems by everyone carrying
his/her own bags. The only exception was that I carried
Meredith's big suitcase. It had mine and Earl's machetes in it.
Some of our group didn't want me to carry the machete by the
shoulder strap. I think I could have gotten by but we put them in
Meredith's bag, the only one big enough to hold the long
machetes we had bought.

We waited thru long immigration lines, had some bag
checking, nothing more than a casual look, paid our $25.00 exit
fee and were set to depart. Kathy and Virgil had picked up their
son Steve who was attending school in Port-au-Prince, they
bought us lunch, and we bade good-by, left the Troyers and sat in
the hot waiting room till about 3:00 pm. On the plane, I sat with
Meredith both New York to Port-au-Prince and Miami to
Chicago. The flight to Chicago was during dark. Sky was clear
and we knew it would be cold up north. We learned by some
making phone calls that Illinois was having record-breaking
freezes. When we were half an hour from Chicago, the pilot
announced the temperature in Chicago is minus 17 degrees. So
we came from a plus 90 degrees to minus 17 in about 5 hours.
And the cold really hit us.

We did, however, have a smooth ride in Larry's van on Interstate highway. It was smooth, no ruts and big potholes. We could drive speed limit. We had a new appreciation for things we so often simply take for granted. On the drive from Chicago, I called Anne with Larry's cellular phone, told her we'd be home between 11:00 and 12:00, and that I had offered to take some of the people home so Larry wouldn't have to deliver everyone.

When we arrived at 8 Wilmette Drive, I started the Corolla in frigid weather, took Lois, then Franzie home and then drove out to Lucca Forest to deliver Joe. I got home to stay shortly before l: 00 am. Anne seemed glad to see me. She had been under the weather most of the time, sick with the flu or bad cold while I was gone, which I was indeed sorry to hear. We talked and talked, went to bed and got to sleep probably about 2:00 or 2:30 am. I was glad to be home but cold, cold, cold.

We got up in time to go to church. During the sharing period Joe Haney got up to share some of the Haiti experiences. (He was considered our leader.) He was so affected emotionally by our experiences that he broke down emotionally, big, burly Joe who is always on top, and a big talker, got to the point he simply couldn't speak. And while standing there he wiped tears from his eyes. When he sat down, Earl got up and explained more what we had done.

That evening we had Homebuilders meeting at the church. Each of the eight of the work team gave a brief talk of our impressions and experiences then opened the meeting for questions. The people who served refreshments said seventy people attended.

Marilyn Townley had asked me to share some of my experiences with a Sunday School class at the First Presbyterian Church, Normal, Sunday morning. I gave the talk. The response was good and Anne said it was one of the best talks she heard me give.

Joe Haney had eight copies made of all the pictures he took. Each of us got a big pack with approximately two hundred snap shots. I sorted some of mine out, bought an album and put the selected ones in the album. I hope this report will help to give a clearer picture of some of the things the work team did while in Haiti, also, it will hopefully help to explain how I personally, as well as others in the group were affected emotionally by the low level of living we saw first-hand.

VII - My Spiritual Journey

Introduction

This statement has been motivated by the assignment given to all the CPS men and women who worked at the Farnhurst, Delaware CPS Unit during World War II, to describe their spiritual journey. The statements were to be given as part of the 50th anniversary celebration of the Farnhurst Unit at Bluffton College Campus, August 7, 8, & 9, 1992. Daryl Frey originated the idea He along with the reunion program committee felt it would be particularly appropriate since this is the 50th anniversary, most of the members are getting up in years ('60s & '70s), and it is inevitable that CPS groups are facing an eventual dead end. Following is the story of my journey, a summary of which was presented at the Reunion program.

It began on the farm in western Kansas. I was a country boy who went barefooted all summer and even went to church on Sunday evenings barefooted and in bibbed overalls. As I look back on my early encounters with the world, I feel that I had a pronounced inferiority complex. I was not permitted to keep pace with the normal run of kids my age, particularly in high school. I didn't have as much of the inferiority feeling among my church friends as with school and neighbor kids. My brother Dennis just two years younger than me was taller and bigger than

I was and I always felt the girls as well as other people in general liked him and paid him more attention than they did me.

My father was a conservative Mennonite minister and bishop deeply committed to his calling. He was the dominant influence in our family. Mother was the ideal minister's wife, reserved and by nature retiring and a hard worker. She would cook meals for company, do chores around the farm, help with the fieldwork, and assume most of the responsibility for the family of five children. Both parents were, as I look back, deeply committed to family as well as to the church. They wanted their children to have the kind of training and experiences that would prepare them to get the most out of life. I admit that quite often their ideas of what is best for their children did not always coincide with my notions. As a high school student I often wanted to do things and participate in events which Dad would not permit.

Even though Dad had not completed his high school education, he had rural school teaching credentials and as my teacher through the fourth grade. We were told that Mom went to the 7th grade, although in recent years one of my sisters said mom had attended only to the 4th grade. Our parents said they would like to provide a high school education for their children and then beyond high school, the children would be on their own. Even so, the folks did all they could to help us after high school, particularly in our first years of college.

Dad had the greatest responsibility of enforcing discipline in major decisions in the home. Mom took the main responsibility in everyday affairs, preparing meals, permitting us to play with neighbors, go to the creek to swim or fish, and the like. Dad was responsible for a great deal of the discipline in church and conference matters, and naturally this responsibility trickled down into the family. He was very sensitive to, and tried to control his children particularly in those matters which might have reflected on his role as pastor and bishop.

Dad wore the plain coat or clergyman's garment, Mom wore a cape and a prayer head covering with strings. We children wore simple clothing, most of it homemade. Common garb for boys in our church was knee pants. Girls would not have their hair cut and usually wore it in braids. It was against the rules of the church for women to cut their hair. For a woman to cut her hair was contrary of biblical teaching. We were not permitted to wear a necktie, and I wanted to but was not permitted to wear long pants until long after I felt it was overdue. Long pants were a sort of puberty rite.

My First Conversion

About once a year, our church would arrange for a series of evangelistic meetings. During that time we would attend church every night for a week or ten days. The evangelist would preach fire and brimstone and offer the invitation at the end of the sermon for anyone who would to "accept Christ."

This might be a first-time experience for some. Young folks might, on such occasions, decide it was time to join the church, or for former members it might be a rededication. In my personal recollection of these experiences, we were assured by the evangelist and this was reinforced by the attitude of church authorities, that if we died "unsaved," it would be hell and if "saved," heaven. So in the years of our childhood and youth, the psychological pressure was great.

I personally yielded to the "call" when (as near as I can remember) I was 13 years of age. I vividly recall that even at the time I was considering membership very seriously; this whole process was enshrouded in mystery. I believed, yet I couldn't really believe without questions popping up in my mind. I couldn't quite see it, as absolute and unquestioned, as the evangelists and others said, yet the psychological pressure was so great that most of the young people as they approached puberty yielded to what was probably indirect influence from home, followed by the evangelist's message. Young people at that stage were sufficiently aware of the teaching of the church and were becoming believers at least in part because they felt they could not risk hell. In these few paragraphs I have attempted to explain the family and religious environment out of which I came.

I graduated from high-school in 1935. We had 18 members in my graduating class. After finishing high-school, I stayed out of school a year to help harvest the fall row crop while Dad took an extended evangelistic trip to the west, holding a series of meetings in Oregon and Idaho. That winter, after Christmas, I attended Short-Term at Hesston College, a six-week session of Bible study intermingled with church.

Part of the Short-Term program was more evangelistic meetings in the evening. In one of the meetings I was so moved that I again "stood" and in the conference with the ministers that followed, I confessed a "sin" which had been on my mind for some time. The "sin" was an event that occurred while in high school. I had slipped into a track meet one afternoon without paying the ten-cent admission charge for students at the gate. My friend Nelson Sanders had me hide in the trunk of his Ford coupe while we drove through the gate, then when in, and parked, he left me out. And I didn't have to pay my dime.

The outcome of my confession was that I made restitution. I sent a dime to the track coach of Ashland High School where the track meet had been held, and at that time I felt genuine relief for having righted my "sin."

The following year I attended Hesston College as an academic student. At that time Hesston was not accredited and the administration had worked out an arrangement with Hays State Teachers College to allow Hesston students to attend a summer session at Hays and, if they did satisfactory work, give credit for the work at Hesston. In this program the student could then be awarded a teaching certificate based on one year of college, plus the Hays College summer school. I did receive my teaching certificate then taught the following four years at a country elementary school in Marion and McPherson Counties, two years at Peabody and two years at Canton, Kansas in rural, one-room schools, with 8-grades, 1938-41.

The war was in progress, I had registered for the draft, had received a 4E classification (conscientious objector status), and was due to be called up at any time in the fall of 1941, consequently I did not apply for another year of teaching. Instead, I decided to attend Goshen College until my draft number came up.

My folks had moved to Berlin, Ohio, where Dad was called to be minister and bishop of several churches there. I think it was mainly because the folks were in Ohio that I decided to register at Goshen College our church school; also I'd be close home. I finished most of one semester and was called to report to my draft board for induction into camp on January 14, 1942. This was about three weeks short of the end of the semester, so I arranged with the teachers and staff at Goshen College to complete my work before leaving. This worked out OK with all courses except chemistry. I had to do some additional course work in chemistry while in camp, and eventually received full credit for my semester's work.

Summarizing my experiences to this point, I had come through two identifiable stages in my life, one, the childhood youth stage at Protection, Kansas with the influence of family and church tempered by four years of high school. (The stages presented here are not to be confused with the three conversions to be described later.) In this stage I felt in my mind that truths were readily identified, specific, known, and absolute. The Christian religion was the only "right way." For the believer, truths were equivalent to knowledge. In fact, what we were taught was accepted as truth, no questions asked.

A second stage, a sort of intermediate stage, began when I left home to attend Hesston College. When I left the restrictive home, rural, community life, I was forced to assume responsibility for myself, make decisions on my own, and at least in a preliminary fashion declare my career interests. I applied for and was hired to teach country school at Peabody, Kansas. In the next four years I kept close contact with my family at Protection, my brothers and older sister were attending school at Hesston, approximately twenty miles from Peabody where I was teaching, so I had frequent contact with my siblings at Hesston while teaching at Peabody.

My school teaching term was eight months. In April after my school was out I attended a short session, which Hesston offered in the spring, designed especially for teachers. In addition to the academic credit received, an additional attraction was the intramural track meet which I could participate in at the college.

One spring my two brothers and I all three participated in track. We took first, second and third in the three dashes (50, 100, and 220 yard), with the exception that Dennis was disqualified in the 100 because, at least in the eyes of the judges, he had interfered with the competitor next to him.

These activities were new and exciting to me. This stage in my life was different. I could participate freely where I chose, and was forced to take responsibility for my own decisions. My personal theological value system remained pretty much unchanged. I took a definite interest in dating and socializing. I was developing many male friends, and was also dating frequently.

I still maintained the belief system that I had acquired in my childhood and youth. At Hesston College I was nicknamed "bishop" by some of my close friends because of my conservative quirks and notions. I was more conservative in my theology and dress customs than many of my fellow students. I still felt that truths and beliefs were not only identifiable, but were still, specific and absolute. Little did I realize how my attitudes and general outlook on life, the world, the universe, would change in the next stage of my life.

My Second Conversion

I was inducted into Sideling Hill Camp, CPS Unit #20, on January 14, 1942, at age twenty-four. In camp we worked, ate, slept, and literally lived with men of all sorts. We had Mennonites and non-Mennonites, Amish boys, and non-church fellows, obedient and conforming, disobedient and non-conforming, liberal and conservative. I began to realize that some of the best fellows in camp were not Mennonites. Some of the "bad" boys were Mennonites. My world was expanding. I had exposure to a large number of fellows from a wide variety of places, from many different church backgrounds and these were individuals with whom I was interacting daily. I was beginning to see things in a different light.

After nine months at Sideling Hill Camp, working out-of-doors in the forestry department, I was transferred with a group of twenty-five to the Delaware State Hospital. Here we were in contact with not only our group, but with other workers, mental patients, ex-patients, intelligent people, handicapped, and sometimes simply naive people. I became aware of some of the problems that caused patients to be admitted to the mental hospital, such as alcohol, family violence, schizophrenia, manic-depression, and the like. We COs interacted with them all. We also interacted with a variety of COs in our unit.

Fortunately, and contrary to the living situation in many of the CPS hospital units, we all lived in one building, Kent Hall. The front door was at the center of the building. The living quarters for the married couples were in a wing to the right and the singles' quarters to the left. We lived close together and had daily contact in our off-duty time. We had many bull sessions and informal discussions. I realized more and more that the world out there was BIG. With friends and fellow COs we attended movies, plays, symphonies, grand operas and the like. We read, we discussed, we grew, and many of us changed our mental outlook on the world in general.

I frequently thought of the different lifestyle I was now engaged in and often I would compare in my mind, our existing experiences and changing attitudes with my earlier conservative religious background. I would sometimes shake my head in disbelief when I thought of what was happening to me. We continued in this environment for nearly four years.

In addition to our work assignments at the hospital and the cultural activities mentioned above, we played a lot of softball. Our unit had a good team which ranked third in the Wilmington league. I sang in a quartet which made ninety-six public appearances, and had weekly appointments to sing on WILM, the Wilmington radio station for a period of time. We also had a men's chorus which made numerous public appearances in the community.

Activities of these sorts continued until I was discharged January 24, 1946. I stayed on working at the hospital for several weeks. My brother, Dennis, Daryl Frey and I had applied and were approved to serve as cattle boat attendants with a load of heifers to be sent to the war stricken areas in Europe under the auspices of the Brethren Service Committee. We stayed on and worked at the hospital until our ship-load of cattle was due to depart. We took this trip in March, 1946, unloaded the cattle at Bremen, Germany, then returned to our parental home in Berlin, Ohio.

I stayed at home with my folks in Berlin, Ohio, got a job working in a local pottery factory at Fredericksburg near Berlin for about six weeks, then enrolled in and attended summer school at Goshen College and stayed on the following year, graduating with a major in sociology in the spring of 1947. I was married in the summer of 1947, taught social studies in high school for two years in Hillsboro, Kansas, then went to graduate school full time at the University of Nebraska

Here things continued to happen in my intellectual, philosophical, and theological life. I had a related minor in anthropology and economics. I studied and read about societies and cultures the world over. Horizons continued to expand. My PhD dissertation was a study of Jansen, Nebraska, which began as a Mennonite community and through the ensuing decades became thoroughly secularized.

I vividly recall that the major portion of the time spent in defense of my dissertation was a response to questions raised by committee members regarding the changes that had taken place in my own personal outlook, the changes from my conservative religious background to some of the things I was writing and saying in papers, course work and master's thesis and dissertation. My committee members seemed to be more interested in the changes that had taken place in my thought process than in the content of the dissertation. The dissertation defense was a thoroughly enjoyable experience for me and apparently was satisfactory to the committee. It was accepted and the degree was confirmed.

Graduate school was followed by teaching stints at Wayne State College, Nebraska, Mankato State College, Minnesota, and Illinois Wesleyan University, plus a one-year temporary position at Emporia Kansas. While teaching at Illinois Wesleyan we did not have regular summer sessions so I applied at various places in U.S. and Canada and with some degree of regularity for the next few years, spent six to ten weeks teaching summer sessions at Syracuse, New York, Boulder, Colorado, Kingston, Rhode Island, Flagstaff, Arizona, Johnson, Vermont, and Edmonton, Canada

The courses I was teaching forced me to continue my search for truth and understanding. Some of the courses that influenced me most were General Anthropology, Human Ecology, Social Psychology, and Criminology. After working through these along with other courses, it became inevitable that I make some significant adjustments in my personal philosophy and general theological outlook.

I moved from the simple fundamentalist conservative theology which might appropriately be described as "a state of pre-critical naiveté," to a more rational and universal outlook of the world and reality. I refer to this move as my second conversion.

Later in this paper I summarize my experiences with three conversions. The first was when I was baptized and taken into church membership at age 13. The second, which I'm describing here, is a more momentous move affecting the major share of my adult life, which occurred over a period of twenty-five to thirty years. Finally, the third was my conversion to a vegetarian diet which is detailed later.

This second conversion is the one I consider to be most significant in my life. It includes a major reorganization of thoughts and attitudes. My concept of God, the universe and reality could never be the same after this conversion. Naturally it became a real challenge for me to try to define these concepts anew. I admit that the new concepts deal with imponderables. When thinking of the concept "God," it has always been a real challenge to settle on a specific, clear-cut definition.

In one of my earlier views I summarized God in terms of pantheism and naturalism. Pantheism is the doctrine that the universe, taken or conceived of as a whole is God. I have never been able nor did I want to take God out of the picture. Two aspects of naturalism apply here. One, is the notion that many, perhaps all, of the so-called miracles recorded, are natural occurrences which simply could not be explained with the knowledge extant at the time they occurred.

A second aspect is that since God cannot be seen or experienced in a literal way with any of our senses, and since we as humans like to see, hear, see, experience in a real sense, I like to conceptualize God as "something real." So in that context, we might conclude that the "thing" most like God, and still something I can experience with my senses, is "nature".

God in this scenario is "the Whole of Being." It includes a multitude of phenomena, the forces of the universe, the processes of nature, the beauties of nature, the destructive as well as the constructive powers of sunshine, rain cycles, earthquakes, hurricanes and tornadoes, the formation of coal, oil, and mineral deposits, the evolution of life, animals and plants, marine and land life from simple life to the complex human species, and on and on. It includes the known and the unknown. In Marcus Borg's essay "God at 2000," pages 6 and 7, he relates his experiences which are very similar to experiences I have had personally.

He says, "It was utterly crucial in my own spiritual journey to realize that there was another way of conceptualizing God that is another form of theism."

He continues, "In my thirties I began to glimpse this different way of seeing God... I began by putting God in a non-material layer, or level, or dimension of reality... I realized that this form of theism is just as old and just as ancient as supernatural theism....God is not somewhere else, God is all around us... everything that is are in God"

He then explains that "these experiences came about because of a combination of religious experience and reading."

Also, I like the Peace Pilgrim's concept of God. Paraphrased, "intellectually God is truth; emotionally God is love. God is a creative force, a motivating power, an overall intelligence, an ever-present, all pervading spirit which binds everything in the universe together and gives life to everything. I found that I could not be where God is not. You are within God and God is within you. We experience a common unity in the mystery of life."

I have been attracted by the German phrase, "*Ein begriffener Gott ist kein Gott.*" Translated, "a God comprehended is no God." To the best of my recollection this phrase was expressed by a theologian named Ajax, at the University of Chicago some years ago. So God for me is so much, so all inclusive that I cannot possibly comprehend it in any complete sense.

Then some years later, when Anne and I visited the Bethel College church at North Newton, I got a tape and also the script of Gordon Kaufman's sermon he had preached there the week before. I have used that, internalized it, discussed it at some length with our theologically-minded friends, including our pastor who likes to discuss but doesn't agree with Kaufman. Also, I prepared a discussion sheet and led the discussion on Kaufman's theology at our Saturday morning roundtable discussions. I find some genuine reinforcement from Kaufman's theology. He sees God as "ultimate mystery." This is in agreement with the statement above "a comprehended God is no God."

It appears to me that God as mystery can be supported scientifically - scientific in the sense that we can establish the fact of mystery, even though we cannot explain scientifically the contents of the mystery. The intellectual community agrees that there are the imponderables which cannot and probably never will be answered satisfactorily. For example, assuming we accept the "big bang" theory, how did it get started? What caused it to happen in the first place? What were the circumstances before the "bang?" How far out is space? When did time begin? What was before the beginning of time? Or how was the human being made human, that is, how did the difference between humans and lower forms of life, come about?

We have obvious questions for which we have no indisputable answers. If we then define these mysteries as God, we must concede the existence of God. With this assumption, God does without question exist, though admittedly; we can't fully comprehend what God is.

Years ago Martin Luther used the phrase *deus absconditus* which means "God hidden." These notions of God make a great deal of sense to me. And, I summarize my own thinking using the phrase that appeared in an editorial in the Gospel Herald, June 24, 1997, discussing Kauffman's theology, I am one who can "doubt fiercely and believe ferociously" at the same time.

Another recent experience which has contributed to my journey relates to a song that appeared in our local Mennonite Church Bulletin, November 24, 2002. The words express an interesting definition of God:

You are the God of love/hope/peace. You are all there is.
You are all we need. You are all we need.
You are the God of love/hope/peace. You are all there is.

Restated, all there "is," is God. God is the total of all there is. God is the total of all of existence. These words were written by a Mennonite pastor, Chuck Neufeld.

I personally liked the words of this song. If we use up the concept of God in just a small segment of reality, we will have nothing left for the total of all existence. God may not be only the 'prime mover,' as the 13th century theologian Thomas Aquinas stated in his *Summa Theologia*,' but perhaps he/she/it is the total of all movements that take place, but the total of all life, all nature, all forces, all universal laws, the whole of environment. Nothing can be greater than 'all that is.' Also it is easy for me to assume that 'nothing can be greater than God.' Thus we might conclude that since nothing is greater than God, and nothing is greater than all that is, 'all that is, is God.' God then becomes more than I can conceptualize.

To me, the experiences of reading, thinking, discussing, changing and adjusting help to reflect on what this is all about. It's a journey. As the journey continues, I hope I'll continue to get new ideas as long as I live.

My conversion experience alluded to above has not been simple or easy. On the contrary it has been difficult, frustrating and emotionally painful at times. It has definitely not been a sudden experience like the Apostle Paul's conversion from Saul to Paul. In fact it has been a complex process extending over a period of twenty to thirty years. A specific beginning and end is indefinable.

As I analyze this conversion process, I feel that in a general way it began when I went to CPS and was finally consummated, perhaps thirty years later, actually not until in the decade of the 1970s. It was at this time that I could at least try to put my theological concepts into words. It was also at about this time that I was accepted into membership of the Mennonite Church of Normal. This however was not a simple process. In fact it is a somewhat complicated experience in itself.

Church Membership

Although my experience in obtaining church membership is a part of my second conversion, it is an episode in itself, which in my opinion deserves special treatment. I had been refused membership in the Mennonite Church of Normal for many years.

During the time I was considering membership, I had a number of extended conversations with our Mennonite minister in Normal. I attended the Unitarian Church for a period, and discussed my philosophical and theological views with the Unitarian minister. For a period of several years I refused to attend any church regularly. This caused apparent frustration and instability in our family; it affected relations with wife and children. It was neither constructive nor rewarding; in fact, it became seriously disrupting and threatening in our domestic relationships.

In a visit with a sociology colleague from Minnesota, at one of our annual sociology conventions, we were discussing my personal problems. She gave me what I felt at the time, and have become thoroughly convinced since, was sound advice. I had related to her that since I did not attend church regularly, the children were beginning to resist going with mother. Her response was, "Paul, you owe it to your wife and children to spend an hour a week in church with your family. What you do with your mind in that hour is up to you, but you need to be in church with your family." I took this advice seriously and began attending regularly, with the whole family. We became regular church-goers, and even to this day, all of our family has a real appreciation for church.

When our youngest son was to be baptized, Anne and I decided that this would be a good time for all of us to become church members. Anne had a church letter of transfer from her church in Nebraska where she grew up. I could not obtain a letter of good standing mainly because our father had transferred membership of our entire family to the Martins Creek Mennonite Church, Berlin, Ohio, when our family moved, from Protection, Kansas, in 1941. I was in CPS and College, 1941 to 1946. I was never at home in Berlin more than six consecutive weeks at a time after my membership was transferred, consequently the church officials in Ohio did not know me personally, and felt it would be inappropriate for them to give me a letter of good standing.

In correspondence the minister in charge of the Ohio church, indicated that he could state that I had been a member of their congregation, and that membership had never been removed, but at the time felt that he could not comment about my good-standing in the church. And this was understandable to me at the time.

In the next visit with our local minister here in Normal, I requested that he simply allow me to become a member without having to answer all the questions they often asked candidates for membership, questions which seem to me to be trite and meaningless. It appears to me that the issues dealt with, e.g., salvation, Christ's shed blood, accepting Christ as Savior, and the like, are not understood by most of the members accepted into membership. It's a routine formalism, taken in stride and any meaning it may ever have had is probably soon forgotten after the membership process is completed. They answer "I do," "I am," "I will," and the like, without really understanding what is going on. I felt that I could not answer these questions honestly and to the satisfaction of the church officials. After several candid sessions with our minister, and after he had discussed the matter with the Pastoral Committee, he concluded that "we are not ready" to go ahead with my membership.

I indicated to him at the time that I believe some time in the future our church will allow a person to become a member under the terms I requested. At that time I felt pretty well settled in my theology. I had to be honest with myself and live my conscience. I had developed a state of mind and understanding which, even though it continued to be of a dynamic nature, was still beyond returning to the earlier state. I realized that belief is not a matter of the will. It happens to a person. With these experiences it was not really difficult for me to accept the minister's decision.

I did, however, feel badly about the family situation. My wife understandably was upset and questioned whether she should go ahead and join. I encouraged them to just go ahead without me, and that is what eventually happened. Don was baptized, Anne was taken into membership after considerable anguish, tears, and emotional strain and I continued on as a non-member regular attendee.

The issue of me not being permitted to join the church became somewhat divisive among other members of our congregation at the time. I continued to attend church, I had many good friends in the congregation, I was asked to teach Sunday School classes and my relationship with the church continued to move along much the same as if I'd have been a member, yet people were aware that I had not been accepted into membership.

Years later, probably five or six years later, we changed ministers. After the new minister had been here nine months, he approached me and in an informal way, (We were working in our garden at Ropps) he mentioned that he had heard that I had been refused membership earlier and wondered if I were still interested. I assured him that I was if I didn't have to answer all those questions that were sometimes put to the candidates. He indicated that his method was to give the candidate the microphone, allow him\her to state his testimony, tell the congregation why he/she desired to be a member, then let the congregation decide whether or not to accept. So that's the way it happened. When the next group was taken into church, I was included along with five or six others and was accepted into membership.

In my testimony, I explained that I had been reared in a Mennonite home. I had a real appreciation for the Anabaptist principles of community, non-resistance, non-conformity, and so on. I had been attending church here at Normal for several years, I like the people here, have many friends, and would like to associate with them as a member of the church. And, under those circumstances, who in the congregation would have the courage or even want to express opposition. Obviously no one did, so I became a full-fledged member in good standing and have remained so to this day.

People in church know that in my theology I am non-conventional and have some non-traditional ideas. Even so, I continue to serve on committees, teach Sunday school classes, and attend church regularly. In fact, church attendance has become important to me. Church affiliation in the Normal Church is easy for me perhaps because of the diverse character of our members. We have a wide variety of people with a wide variety of ideas and beliefs. We have a strong contingent of college professors and other professionals, doctors, nurses, administrators, farmers, construction workers, and others.

As I analyze my attitude toward the church, I have to admit that the most rewarding aspect is the social relationships, friends, support groups, and interaction in Sunday school and discussion groups. In my mind a major function of human life is to use the mind and intellect we as humans are endowed with, to train and broaden our thinking, and to understand relationships that exist in a universal sense. That, if taken seriously, is the best way to render service to God. From this point then, I accept the project expressed by the Peace Pilgrim, "to live all the good things I believe in." And that is a major life project and an on-going process.

In conclusion and in summarizing my story, I have a very profound appreciation for my home and family background. My parents did their very best to provide for and give their children the kind of background they felt was important. For that, I am deeply grateful. My major learning periods, CPS and graduate school in particular, along with the subsequent college teaching and learning with students and colleagues, along with intellectual and stimulating discussions with friends, and reading the works of some of the world's leading theologians, did something significant to me. This, in my opinion, is as it should be. There is no need for education, for development and growth, if you come out the same place you went in.

In this context, I maintain that I am a strong believer. I believe in God. When one considers the term "Savior," I must ask, "Saved from what?" I cannot believe that a God of love would condemn even the vilest sinner to a circumstance of eternal turmoil and suffering in hell.

M. Scott Peck in his *Road Less Traveled*, (p. 134), makes an important point which I feel applies here. He says, "Growing up is the act of stepping from childhood into adulthood." He continues, "Actually it is more a fearful leap than a step, and it is a leap many people never really take in their lifetime."

In summarizing my development, I analyze it as a move from the simple, and local, fundamentalist approach, to a rational, realistic and universal outlook. In the words of Martin Luther, I say, "Here I stand, I can do no other."

My Third Conversion

My third conversion, while it has been significant in my life, it is not as "soul wrenching" as the second conversion described above. It, however, is sufficiently significant in our lifestyle adjustments, that that I state it as a conversion. It relates to the stewardship of our physical body (the temple of God) and the care of the universe on which we all depend for our very survival.

It is a lifestyle including a vegetarian diet, a program of regular exercise, an attempt to see the connectedness and relationships of all things, along with personal stress management and further social and spiritual development.

I sense a certain responsibility to "pass the word." Some have accused me of becoming "an evangelist" for health and improved lifestyle. Interestingly, when I approach people about this, I invariably encounter opposition. I expect that when the program I advocate includes giving up much of what has become an important part of the lifestyle for most people in our affluent society, the addiction (perhaps I should say a deeply ingrained habit) of the "meat taste," also, suggesting that we come off of our sedentary, soft and easy routine, to include more physical activity, with a regular exercise program, it is only natural that I could expect opposition. Also it is important to mention in this context that we need intentional stress-management and on-going social and spiritual development.

It is important that growth and change continue as we move along in the journey of life. This conversion to a vegetarian diet is a more serious and complex process than might appear on the surface. In fact it has become a spiritual as well as a physical experience for me. Important factors in the vegetarian lifestyle are (1) health, (2) the environment, (3) living lower on the food chain to make more food available for the hungry of the world, (4) animal cruelty, and (5) although debatable, it is probably more economical to eat a non-meat rather than an every-day-meat diet. It is not a taste preference decision. And it certainly is not an easy undertaking in our affluent meat-eating society. Rather it is a serious commitment for reasons stated above. It simply seems right for me.

Probably the most important deciding factor for me was health. I, personally, had no health problems, exercised regularly, competed in Senior Olympics, participated in the PACRACC (220 mile bicycle ride in the three day Labor Day weekend in McLean County, Illinois) for thirteen consecutive years, so I didn't need the vegetarian diet to cure any physical ailments.

Rather I noted the leading causes of death in our society, read results of the many studies being conducted in recent decades by some of the world's outstanding doctors, nutritionists and other researchers, noted what the medical recommendations were for people who experienced a cardiac or cancer problem, or other common ailment, and decided that the only sensible thing for me (and everyone for that matter), was to emphasize prevention rather than cure. In Appendix I, I list the research-orientated publications I subscribe to and read regularly.

Two of my grandchildren were vegetarian. Our granddaughter, Nara McCasland, became a vegetarian at age eleven, and has held consistently to this lifestyle to the present time (2010). Her brother, Darrick, became vegetarian a few years later but has since given up the strict vegetarian diet. Both were motivated mainly by animal rights principles rather than the health factor.

My wife, Anne, who has also accepted the vegetarian lifestyle, has consistently been concerned about serving healthy and balanced meals to her family, grandkids, husband, and others. So when our grandson, Darrick, was planning to visit us for a whole week several years ago, (July, 1990) Anne asked one of her health-minded friends for books with recipes of vegetarian foods. On this occasion she borrowed two McDougall books. She was most interested in the recipes.

The books were lying around so I began reading them. This was the beginning of my vegetarian conversion. I was literally shocked to learn of the many new developments that have taken place in the nutrition and lifestyle research during the past one or two decades, and how important, applicable, and practical this information can be for all of us today.

John McDougall was a young doctor who was unable to accept many things he was taught in medical school. He was unable to fit into the traditional physician's mold of "prescribing drugs or doing surgery." He eventually accepted a position as doctor on a sugar plantation in Hawaii. Here he observed the differences between immigrants from China and other oriental locations, compared with patients on the traditional American diet. While so many of the typical American patients were obese, had heart problems, a high frequency of cancer, and diabetes, the recent arrivals of people from the orient had very little of these same illnesses.

He was agonizing and seriously searching for reasons for these differences. He noticed that the second generation of immigrants seemed to take on the typical American ailments. Since the gene pool was the same for the first and second generation immigrants, he naturally ruled out the genetic factor. Eventually at the suggestion of a friend, he began making record of the food his patients were eating, and as a result became aware that nutrition appeared to be the main difference. From these observation and experiences he became a strict vegetarian, and recommended this lifestyle to his patients with what he insists is much more effective treatment than the traditional medical treatments commonly found today.

Reading the McDougall Program was the factor that caused me to take my "third conversion" really serious. I read and re-read McDougall. Shortly thereafter my daughter Brenda introduced me to John Robbin's, *Diet for a New America*. It was enlightening, inspirational, and contained information with further mental shocks. It pointed out the pitfalls of the "factory farms," raising chickens, pigs, cows, and turkeys, in mass-production, in wire cages, enclosed pens, and feed lots, with growth hormones and antibiotics.

Robbins came out at the same position on nutrition as McDougall. I was "hungry" for all this new information on animal-food-production and nutrition lifestyle, and continued to search. It was opening an all new world for me. I was aware of and had been following Robert Haas' EAT TO WIN program for about eight years prior to my introduction to McDougall, but he was not nearly as strict as McDougall. Haas was the nutritionist for Martina Navratilova when she had her long series of tennis championships. The Haas program was a beginning but I was later convinced that it was not adequate.

In April, 1991, the Physicians Committee for Responsible Medicine (PCRM) came out with the New Four Food Groups (Grains, Legumes, Vegetables and Fruit). This was given a lot of media publicity. We read about it, saw and heard it on press, radio and television. Our local radio station in the farm reports became critical of the new food-group emphasis, because meat and dairy products were not included.

Art Secrist, the WJBC (the local radio station) farm reporter at that time, said in his broadcasts that PCRM was doing false reporting. On one of his reports, he contended that the PCRM was an animal rights group, and the membership was really not physicians as they claimed, but a bunch of animal rights activists.

I contacted Art Secrist, to find out where he got this negative information about the PCRM. He said his source was The Des Moines Register, and that if I wanted more information, I should call either the Des Moines Register, or contact the PCRM directly.

I did the latter and obtained information directly from the PCRM office. I learned that the PCRM was at that time comprised of more than 3,000 physicians, some of them among the most highly respected physicians in the world. At that time the group had a total of over 20,000 members. Today, two years later, that number has increased to more than 50,000. Their major focus is on preventative medicine and lifestyle changes. Their objective is to report current research in an objective manner, they had no vested interest except the health of primarily American society, and eventually the health of the world population, and they welcomed anyone interested in their program, to join.

Annual membership was twenty dollars, for which one received a monthly "PCRM Update." They also had another publication titled "Healthy Eating" for fifteen dollars a year. I subscribed to both, and life has never been the same since.

I reported back to Secrist, told him of my telephone conversation and of my highly favorable impression of the PCRM. He asked me if I'd be willing to come to the station to tape an interview. I was happy to do this, I did, and subsequently he broadcast several excerpts of our interview on his farm-report broadcasts.

As an aside, at the time this was happening, Secrist was suffering from a malignant tumor in his neck and soon he was forced to retired from his broadcasting and the last I heard he was confined to a wheel-chair. At the time however, he had no interest whatsoever in changing his life-style.

Since having retired from teaching my major academic focus has been on nutrition and lifestyle research. This interest seems to continue. I am well aware of conflicting reports one gets from new studies and various vested interest groups. I find, however, that it is usually not too difficult to "sift the grain from the chaff." The conviction of my "third conversion" was supported and reinforced with almost every observation I would make. Consequently, I became more strongly convinced, and committed to this new lifestyle as I continued to read, observe, and to note what it did for me personally.

Later we learned that PCRM was sponsoring a cruise to London on QE2, and providing lectures and seminars on health and lifestyle changes. Anne, another friend from our church, and I, took this cruise and were pleased and inspired with what we experienced. We became personally acquainted with Neal Barnard, a medical doctor and psychiatrist who is president of PCRM (Physicians Committee for Responsible Medicine). We became convinced that he and their entire committee are for real, and that they have no vested interests except preventative health and environmental awareness. In fairness to the committee I should mention that their position does favor the "animal rights" people and they are working to have medical schools discontinue experimenting with animals.

Recently, John Robbins came out with another outstanding book, *May All be Fed.* In it he emphasizes the spiritual aspects of eating lower on the food chain. He notes for example that "it takes 16 pounds of grain to produce one pound of feed-lot beef, and it takes one pound of grain to produce a pound of bread." He points out further that "…today a greater percentage of the human race is overweight than at any other time in history. Meanwhile a greater percentage of the human race suffers from malnutrition than at any other time in recorded history. These two developments stem from a common source."

Succinctly stated, that source referred to above was the transfer of grains from "food" to "feed." That is, rather than humans, even in third world countries, eating the grain; it is fed to animals, the meat of which is to be sold to the affluent countries where it is in turn eaten in their meat diet.

He contends that if we would come off our meat-eating addiction, the whole world could be adequately fed. The world has resources to feed its population indefinitely at the plant level. He presents a very convincing argument.

Let me summarize several important observations and some facts that have been established from recent research, facts that have brought me to my *"third conversion."*

(1) Animal products contain cholesterol; plant products contain no cholesterol. In general the human body manufactures all the cholesterol it needs. Consuming animal products increases cholesterol in the human body, often times resulting in additional health problems.

(2) Plant products contain complex carbohydrates and fiber which should generally be increased in our diet. Animal products contain no carbohydrates or fiber (one exception, milk contains a lactose carbohydrate).

(3) Protein deficiency is a myth. There is no known protein deficiency In a general population, except in cases of" (a) an over-all nutrition deficiency, or (b) where cultural and religious sanctions prohibit eating certain foods, or (c) where cultural influences encourage the non-protein foods.

(4) When the protein content of the diet exceeds 15 percent of the calories consumed, the liver and kidneys are overworked and enlarged, removing excess protein and leaching calcium from the bones into the urine, a major factor in osteoporosis. It also increases the possibility of kidney malfunction in later life.

(5) Evolutionary development of the human body in the past two or three million years reveals more favorable adaptation to plant foods than to animal foods. Some examples are: convoluted intestines that hold fat, excess protein, and the like, in the digestive track, long enough for it to pass into the blood stream, this tends to develop plaques in the arteries and causes other problems.

(6) The human digestive track is on the average 32 feet long; carnivores' (tigers, wolves, etc.) have digestive tracts on the average, 6 feet long. In general humans have alkaline digestive juices; carnivores in general have acidic digestive juices. For carnivores, meat and bones are digested with the acidic digestive juices and passed from the digestive system more quickly than with humans, and without plaque and cholesterol build-up.

(7) Carnivores have canine teeth adapted to capturing and tearing meat. Human canine teeth are diminished and molars more suitable for grinding grains and chewing plant foods, have developed.

(8) It is believed by most physical anthropologists that for most of the human evolutionary developmental period -- two to three million years -- humans were mainly vegetarian. The reason: It is easier for primitive man to "capture" plant food than to capture animal food.

It is interesting to note that what is best for us personally is also best for other life forms and for our life support system, our universe, on which we all depend. When I put it all together, I find no other way. I am convinced that meat and animal products, at least making them the center of our nutrition planning, are silent killers. My recommendation is to limit food intake to the new four food groups, grains, legumes, vegetables and fruit. It is amazing how enjoyable eating seeds, leaves, stems, roots, and fruit, can become once the adjustment is made.

In addition to the nutrition emphasis, and also as a part of my third conversion, I emphasize several other essential aspects of wellness: exercise, stress management, social and spiritual development, and an environmental awareness. Insofar as it is possible to establish a priority, it appears to me that nutrition and exercise should be rated highest. They are basic to physical survival. If these are in order, this in itself becomes a major step toward the stress, spiritual and environmental aspects.

The program for this conversion is not easy to follow. I am never fully satisfied with my performance. To know is not necessarily to do. It is not easy. I always find room for improvement. Probably it should always be that way. To grow and change is part of life. Repeating the Peace Pilgrims statement made earlier, "I am embarked on the lifelong project of trying to live the good things I believe in."

This is my statement made, May, 1993. I made minor revisions 2010. The earlier part of "my journey" was prepared for the CPS Reunion, August, 1992. However, I did some updating and reflecting, February, 1997, changes in theological perspective, particularly in regard to Gordon Kauffman's and Marcus Borg's theology. In February, 2003, I added some comments on the song, "God is all there is."

An Update, 2010

In several instances in my life story, I have stated that life is dynamic. Change is inevitable. Furthermore, that is as it should be. One should always remain open to a new awareness, to new facts, and the realization that it is natural for the human mind to keep striving, to keep searching for truth.

Within that context I must say that I have loosened up on the degree of strictness in my vegetarian diet. Two factors in particular, have played into this change. One, on the recommendation of a medical-doctor friend, I read Michael Pollan's, *The Onmivore's Dilemma* It was recommended reading for a freshman class entering Goshen College several years ago, and highly recommended reading for the general public. Pollan gave me a new perspective on food to be eaten. For him, moderation became an important concept. He suggests that good meat in moderation may be an important part of a good diet.

A second factor is that in 2008, the blood tests in my annual physical examination revealed that I had an iron and protein deficiency. My doctor asked me if I was still on a vegetarian diet. He did not tell me to discontinue the diet, but for me it was, at least by implication, a suggestion that this might be a factor in my blood deficiencies.

We had been eating fish once a week, for several years. Then I added venison to my diet. I have a hunting friend, Kevin Lee, who hunts on our "Rocky Branch" property and has been giving me a deer for our freezer, so it is convenient for me to add venison to our diet. Also, Anne and I both like it, and of all red meat it is probably the most lean, and has certainly not been caged up and fed growth hormones and antibiotics. At my last physical exam (August, 2010) my doctor stated that my blood tests show that the levels are near normal and that he is not recommending any changes in medication. I must admit, also, that it is easier to prepare tasty meals using venison occasionally in my cooking.

Our eating is still largely vegetarian, with the exception of the venison and fish. I eat many vegetables every meal except breakfast and have not bought red meat from a grocery store for probably thirty years. I avoid strictly, any meat that has any hint of factory farm, caged animals, feed lots, and the like.

Since Anne passed away several months ago, and I eat alone, I am still eating the same type of meals we had when I cooked for both of us. I plan to continue moving forward, continuing my exercise program at Shirk Center, and more important, maintaining an open mind, being susceptible to change, and I hope to continue in this vein so long as I live.

Addendum I - Magazines & Publications

This contains a list of magazines and publications I subscribe to in the early stages of my third conversion, perhaps 20 years. By 2010, I have let most, but not all, of these subscriptions lapse.

- Nutrition Action, the health letter of The Center for Science in the Public Interest, founded 1971, advocates honest food labeling and advertising, safer and more nutritious food, and pro-health policies. They accept not government or industrial funding and no advertising.
- Vegetarian Journal, stressing Health, Ecology, Ethics, the publication of The Vegetarian Resource Group, P. O. Box 1463, Baltimore MD. 21203
- Good Medicine, published by the Physicians Committee for Responsible Medicine, 5100 Wisconsin Ave., NW, Suite 404, Washington, DC, 20016
- Environmental Nutrition, published monthly by Environmental Nutrition, Inc., 52 Riverside Dr., New York, NY, 10024
- Health Wise, a monthly publication, Illinois Wesleyan University Wellness Program, Bloomington, Illinois

Addendum II - Important Books

- John A McDougall, M.D., *The McDougall Program*, NAL Books, 1990. (The first three chapters are a "must read.")
- John Robbins, *May All Be Fed*, Avon Books, New York, 1992.
- John Robbins, *Diet For A New America*, Stillpoint, 1987.
- Eric Schlosser, *Fast Food Nation*, Perennial, An Imprint of Harper Collins Publisher, 2001.
- J. Rifkin, *Beyond Beef*, Dutton, NY, 1992.
- Neal D. Barnard, M.D., *The Power of Your Plate*, Book Publishing Company, Summertown, Tennessee, 1990,

Addendum III: Plato's Statement

Plato, the Greek philosopher, makes an interesting statement regarding death and afterlife. Following is a quote from his "Apology" (also known as The Death of Socrates). Socrates has just been given his death sentence.

"He would like to say a few words, while there is time, to those who could have acquitted him. He wishes them to know that the divine sign was never interrupted him in the course of his defense; the reason of which as he conjectures, is that the death to which he is going is a good and not an evil. For either death is a long sleep, the best of sleeps, or a journey to another world in which the souls of the dead are gathered together, and in which there may be a hope of seeing the heroes of old—in which, too, there are just judges; and as all are immortal, there can be no fear of anyone suffering death for his opinions."

"Nothing evil can happen to the good man either in life or death, and his own death has been permitted by the gods, because it was better for him to depart; and therefore he forgives his judges because they have done him no harm, although they never meant to do him any good."

"Those of you who think death is an evil are in error. Either death is a state of nothingness or utter unconsciousness, or as men say, there is a change and migration of the soul from this world to another. Now if you suppose there is no consciousness, but a sleep like the sleep of him who is undisturbed even by dreams, death will be an unspeakable gain. For if a person were to select a night in which his sleep were undisturbed even by dreams, and were to compare this with other days and nights he had passed in the course of his life better and more pleasantly than this one, I think that any man will not find many such days and nights. Now if death be of such a nature, I say that to die is gain. For eternity is then only a single night."

VIII - Believing Man: A Sociological Perspective on the Origin and Development of Religious Behavior

Introduction

The following outline is one I have used for a number of years to explain my understanding of the origin and development of religious behavior.

1. Introduction
2. Man[1] Creates God (Man develops his religious systems.)
3. God Creates Man (Man's religion answers his questions and serves his needs.)
4. The Death of God (Traditional religion becomes dysfunctional as science and new understandings speak to the questions previously answered by religion.)
5. The Rebirth of God (Emerging problems which threatens man's survival, and which he cannot control, cause him to again "look up." Man continues to believe.)

While teaching at Illinois Wesleyan University, my courses of Introduction to Sociology and General Anthropology each had a section on religious institutions. In each of these as well as the

---

[1] Throughout this chapter, the term man means all human beings.

course Sociology of Religion, which I taught occasionally, one was always confronted with a number of questions significant in dealing with social issues scientifically. One, is it possible to be really scientific when considering human behavior? And two, does religious behavior have a quality different from other aspects of human behavior which might make it uniquely impossible to approach scientifically? In my statement here I am making some assumptions which I recognize might be questionable in the minds of some. My answer to the first question is that it is possible to deal with human behavior scientifically. It is observable, thus social science can deal with it. Furthermore (in answer to the second question) I'm assuming that religious behavior is common human behavior and as scientifically observable as other human behavior.

To be scientific one must pull one's self away from all cultural and ethnocentric biases and see the phenomena with a view that can be applied universally. Conclusions in Social Science, regarding religious behavior must be applicable to all faiths, or no faiths for that matter, and be recognized as "to the best of our knowledge, scientifically true."

The scientific method has three qualities:

(1) The sense experience; the observer gains knowledge through one or more of his senses.

(2) Human reason; the observer uses reason and logic to interpret observations.

(3) Finally, agreement among qualified observers. Others who are trained in the area being studied see, hear, taste, smell or feel the same thing. Then if, in using human reason, the social scientist interprets the observations and arrives at the same conclusion, it is considered scientific. Insofar as humanly possible I have attempted to approach the phenomenon of religion in this manner.

I am well aware that some people may question and even object to proposition one in the outline, "Man Creates God." Here I only implore the reader to understand what is intended, along with, associating the intention, with the biological nature of man.

To wit: man is born without belief, ideas, opinions, or even an awareness of his/her very existence. Every normal human being, however, has the potential of developing any, of an almost unlimited variety of cultures, which includes a wide variety of beliefs, ideas, opinions, and the like. And for every individual, what those beliefs, ideas, and opinions actually become depends on the experiences of the individual. The experiences include such things as family influence, Sunday school teachers, general education, interaction and discussions with piers and various individuals, reading, personal contemplation, and the like.

Eventually, beliefs will develop for each person. Part of those beliefs, for most individuals, will include the notion or meaning of the concept "God." That concept has been processed through time, it was developed from personal experiences, it was "made," and in this sense "created." God is to each individual what that individual has accepted in his/her mind God to be. This is what I mean by "Man Creates God."

As far back as we have knowledge human beings have been confronted with the basic questions of (a) how did the universe get started? What is the beginning of things we experience? And (b) how did the specie, Homo-Sapien ever get into the picture? I find that answers to these questions are more profound than appears on the surface. And since it was virtually impossible for early man to find definite and satisfactory answers to these questions they were deferred to religious explanations.

After a number of years of observing, studying, and thinking about religious behavior, I felt that there are some basic observations which would help to explain the phenomenon of religion from either a sociological or anthropological point of view. This challenge motivated me to develop my statement on religion which follows.

My intention has been to keep this treatment on an objective and scientific level. In the process of its development I found it helpful to have one-on-one discussions with colleagues in the religion department at Illinois Wesleyan, and also I have had numerous discussions with interested friends.

It appears to me that the origin and development of religious behavior has very likely followed a general pattern, a pattern that could be applied whether we are considering early man in the evolution of human development, or present-day religious behavior. Also this pattern, in my mind, applies to any religious beliefs or to instances where religious belief is denied. Consequently, I attempted to organize that pattern, develop, and put in writing an understanding as I see it. The outline presented above represents the approach I came up with.

Since man is not born with a particular notion about God and religion, and since most human beings have such a notion, it obviously must start someplace and by someone. Thus, "Man Creates God."

Man Creates God

Some years ago a CBS commentator in covering an eclipse of the sun said, "Men pursue truth as though the truth were something good, important and essential. If he doesn't find it he then makes up something that will do for him what the truth would have done." The commentator then proceeded with some Greek mythology about the sun. How did the early Greeks explain the rising and setting sun?

"It sweeps across the sky drawn by a chariot and four white horses. As it nears the horizon it is swallowed by a dragon. Later, in the course of time it is emitted, things are put back in order and it again comes up at dawn, drawn by the chariot and the four white horses."

Although this is obviously unrealistic for us today, it was an explanation accepted by some people as true in early Greece.

Every man, primitive, ancient, and modern, has created for himself a God or gods. Everyone believes. Every normal person thinks. He may think about what he believes. On the other hand it is possible that the believer isn't aware that he believes. He may simply accept his belief as truth and not think of it as a belief. Sometimes these beliefs are unique and personal; sometimes they are institutionalized and become common to many people. Different persons and different groups of persons have different sets of beliefs.

These beliefs are mental constructs. Each is an image that man has designed for himself. That image will undoubtedly include a god or super-human being. Most people develop their mental constructs really not being aware of what is happening.

It is important to note here, what was alluded to above, that at birth, the human mind is blank. It contains no beliefs, no attitudes or opinions. These are filled in from influences in the environment as time passes. Also it is important to reiterate here, and repeat that in the early stages of the process, people are usually not aware that the development of beliefs is in process. These constructs begin when the person, in childhood, develops awareness, he/she begins to ask questions and get answers. This construct-development process starts in early life and continues indefinitely. Usually then, it is only after the construct is established that the person is able to look back, and if he/she thinks about it, realizes what has happened. This construct has been processed with the teaching of parents, Sunday school teachers, friends, books, the media, personal observations, insights, thinking, contemplating, and any other environmental influences.

Depending on circumstances in place and time such as a person's early religious training, God or the supernatural may be given a wide array of characteristics: all powerful, all knowing, omnipotent, controller of love (cupid), controller of the wind, ocean, tides, rain, death, afterlife. It may be a God of vengeance and a God of love and a host of other things.

John Cobb in his book, *Becoming a Thinking Christian,* emphasizes that it is important to look into the source of our beliefs. The sources, as alluded to above, include experience, tradition, science, discussion, reading, reason, insight, scripture, parental teaching, or personal observation. Obviously these sources mentioned are interrelated. They are cultural, that is, they are designed by man. They are interrelated in the sense, for example, that we reason about scripture, we experience tradition, we read and discuss science, we are exposed to church creeds, and so forth.

Another intriguing thought enters my mind here. Maybe nature is another source. Maybe man is made up so that his very biological nature influences him to create the concept that gives him life after death. Recently I came upon this thought in reading Dan Liechty's book, *Reflections of Faith in a Post-Christian Time.* He speaks of Ernst Becker's "theory of generative mortality anxiety." The human species is, so far as we know, the only specie that understands the fact of death before it actually happens. We know that someday we will die and yet we all have the drive, some say instinct, to survive. We tend to deny death. So in order to live eternally we have created heaven (and hell) which at least in our minds, allows us to live on after death.

Since the sources differ with different people and no two people have identical experiences, it is inevitable that beliefs will vary. God is something different to different people with different sources. Let's remember, however, that each person designs the nature of his/her god in his/her own mind in response to his/her particular experiences.

Obviously, a variety of influences play into the picture. You have been taught or influenced by others, you have read, you have done some thinking, but it is you and none other who ultimately designs the belief that is acceptable in your mind. And, let's think seriously about implications. If there were just one true design, it seems that after all these centuries of contemplating and thinking, and struggling with the issues, the human race would have come to it.

God, the devil, angels, heaven, hell and the like cannot be seen, touched, smelled, tasted or heard in a literal sense. The sense experience does not apply in establishing the nature and existence of these. Insofar as they exist, it is in the mind's eye. The concept has been designed by each person individually with his or her own influencing sources.

The experience of man creating his God is unique with the human being. In all observations it appears to be impossible for any organisms except man to have beliefs, to have a concept of God. Furthermore, from the "nature" source, it appears that the human being possibly could not even survive without belief.

The human capacity to believe is related closely to his capacity to reason, think, organize, plan, anticipate, and remember. The social sciences refer to this uniquely human quality as the ability for symbolic communication. This is the quality that ultimately distinguishes the human being from other forms of life, and it is this quality which we use in being "religious."

An underlying question inevitably emerges. In the long process of human evolution, how did the capacity for belief come about in the first place? How did the idea of spirit creep into early man's head? Lewis Browne (This Believing World, pp. 30-32) says it came into man's head almost unavoidably. Human beings, for example, have the inborn quality to dream. That is a given. Apparently man in his biological make-up is a dreamer.

Lewis Browne says primitive man lies down and falls asleep in his cave. In the morning he awakens and finds himself in the familiar surroundings of his cave where he went to bed the night before. Yet he knows that he had wandered far from that place during his sleep. He vividly recalls fighting wild beasts, hurtling down ravines, devouring mastodons, or flying through the air like the eagle. Even with all this awareness, when he awakens, he is lying in his smelly cave.

The cave man had not studied psychology and the idea of a dream was foreign to the poor primitive. But he did have a human brain; he had human intelligence. He could reason. The only acceptable explanation he could offer was the obvious one, he was dual. I must be two parts, he reasoned, a body and a spirit. At night while my body remained at home my spirit went a-roaming.

Alas, this also explains other things. What happened to man at death? At one instance he is erect, vibrant, and alive. In the next he is prostrate, inert and dead. Obviously the same answer fits here. The soul had fled. In death it never returns. In sleep, with dreams, it flees but returns. Such an observation "gives" man a soul.

Man has two types of needs, physical and mental. His physical needs include hunger, thirst, shelter, sex, an earth to walk on, air to breathe, and so forth. His mental needs include such things as feelings, thought, emotions, reason, knowledge, love, satisfactions, explanations, and other non-material qualities. Spiritual needs are included in this latter age category.

All living creatures have physical needs. It appears that only man has mental or spiritual needs, at least at this level. Religion is an expression of or a response to spiritual needs. It is a mental activity although it may be a response to physical needs. For example, when man is hungry or in danger, if he has no other or realistic way to meet his needs, he prays.

Man's mental activity can be divided further into two age categories. We have (1) rational man, and (2) believing man. Rational man has the urge to know (science) and to act (technology). Believing man takes over where rational man becomes inadequate.

How does it happen that man has beliefs? How does it happen that many people seem to have similar thoughts and go through similar motions, and that these are established in social institutions? They occur for a large number of people and for an extended period of time. How does it happen that man's beliefs, man's religion becomes patterned and routinized? Through group interaction with beliefs, techniques, and other forms of behavior they become institutionalized. That is, they become common to a significant number of people in a relatively organized and permanent fashion.

Someone discovers, invents, or gains an insight. It is shared, it becomes contagious, it satisfies a specific need, it is adopted by others and is eventually recognized by a large number of people as an institution. Eventually man's religious patterns evolve into intricate, complex systems involving vast structures (cathedrals and shrines), programs, memberships, and complex organizations. We can see here how the happenings two thousand years ago have become so important to millions of people like us today. In this connection it is important for us to realize that all organized religions today satisfy some basic needs in the sense that they answer questions or satisfy needs which otherwise would go unanswered or unsatisfied. If it did not satisfy a need it would cease to exist.

In summary, man designs either consciously or unconsciously his mental constructs. These have evolved into his religious systems in response to his needs. After man has created his god, it is then necessary that the god satisfy needs. One important need is an answer to the questions posed earlier: man's origin, and, the origin of the universe. In response, most religious systems throughout history usually indicate where man came from, and how our universe got its start, all of which leads us to our next topic: "God Creates Man."

God Creates Man

How does it happen that God creates man? Any institution must do its job. The questions important to man which are not answered otherwise must be answered by the religious system. Feelings are consoled and answers are satisfying if they can be accepted. For this to happen, the participant must have faith, oftentimes described as "the faith of a little child."

Man never allows himself to be long in a position of not knowing. He needs explanations. That seems to be a given, a biological quality. If he cannot look and see, if he cannot reason to explain it, if he cannot experience it, and if it is important for him to have an answer, he then designs an explanation. This happens probably without his awareness.

We have belief designs for gods, devils, angels, fairies, ghosts, and pixies. We give significance to the cross, holy water, water baptism, communion bread and wine. The Anasazi culture of the southwest Indians has its totem poles and *sipapus*. The *sipapu* is a hole in the ground in front of the fireplace in the *kiva* (their ceremonial chamber), where Mother Earth has given birth to man.

Furthermore, we give belief significance to the good luck charm, horseshoe, broken mirror and the rabbit foot. Some of these involve serious thought, some are entertaining today, some are considered superstitions and not to be taken seriously. Some such as sub-incision of the Australian Aborigines, or other initiation rites are painful but carried out nonetheless. The important thing is that these are symbols associated with beliefs which do explain or provide answers or consolation; it provides the answer for the person who believes. W.I. Thomas, a pioneer sociologist, said, "If men define situations as real, they are real in their consequences."

With such beliefs, symbolic structures and organization, man can live with himself. He can encounter life; face his environment with "truth that has been revealed."

Two big phenomena-explanations alluded to earlier, stand out in history, explanations which speak to perhaps the most important questions religions answer today. One is: What is the origin and nature of man? The other is: What is the origin and nature of the universe?

Human belief systems, virtually all of them in the past or present, have been designed to explain where man comes from, what he is, and how the universe came into existence, how it got organized and how it operates. When present knowledge provides no better answer, when we have no better and acceptable explanation for man's origin and being, the best he can do is to say "God Creates Man." Out of the dust of the earth, or in his own image, or Mother Earth giving birth through the *sipapu*.

Thus we can begin to visualize the overall process. First man creates his god or gods, and then with the god-system (religion) in place, God creates man. The fact that God creates man is satisfying. It answers the question for countless adults, adults teach it to their children; it has met man's needs for many centuries and in many cultures.

If for our purposes we limit our observations to the modern world in the last few centuries, we find that something has happened to this explanation. It has lost ground. Science, new knowledge and technical observation have revealed new explanations contrary to the traditional religious teachings, but which become obvious and cannot be denied. Many of the traditional religious teachings are on the decline. They are weakened, have lost their influence, are oftentimes recognized as false teachings and abandoned altogether.

Countless examples of this are discussed in Andrew Dickson White's *A History of the Warfare of Science with Theology*, (2 volumes, 889 pages) for example, the shift from geocentric to the heliocentric theory, Benjamin Franklin's discovery of the lightening rod, Adam and Eve creation replaced by evolutionary explanation, and many, many others. In this sense we see "The Death of God."

The Death of God

Things often happen to disprove certain religious beliefs, beliefs which had at one time been accepted as truth. New discoveries, new insights and observations prove them questionable or even experientially false. It is sometimes extremely difficult to accept the new knowledge when it conflicts with long established traditional beliefs. For example, more than a century after Charles Darwin's observation on the evolution of man was generally accepted in the scientific world, some state governments, and many church people still refuse to accept it. The literal biblical account of the creation is still the only correct one for them.

Also, in the 16th and 17th centuries Copernicus and Galileo were, on the basis of scientific evidence attempting to replace the geocentric notion with the heliocentric theory, and were persecuted as heretics because their theory was contrary to scripture. The Bible states that "The sun stood still..." (Joshua 10:13) This for the church authorities at that time is evidence that the sun revolves around the earth. Three centuries later the new discoveries, although scientifically documented, were still unacceptable to church authorities. They were on the Index of forbidden books in the Christian church as late as 1825. Andrew Dixon White stated in his *History of the Warfare of Science with Theology*, (p. 375), "Christianity ...arrested the normal development of the physical sciences for over fifteen hundred years."

On October 29, 2002, PBS aired a program on the life of Galileo. At the close of the program the commentator reminded us that in 1992, the present pope, John Paul II, made an official apology for the treatment dealt Galileo in his trial nearly four centuries earlier. He, Galileo, was tried and convicted after he had published his Dialogue on the Two Chief World Systems in 1632, and died impoverished and in prison.

Could it be that we have new insights that are being presented today which might be compared with the Galileo incident? For example, John Shelby Spong's recent work, A New Christianity for a New World (2001) speaks to observations which might well be about as acceptable today as Galileo's work was in his day. One reader wrote in response to Spong's book, "Your words are not just heresy, they are apostasy. Burning you at the stake would be too kind." Could it be that theologians of the more liberal school may be "today's Galileos" which will be reckoned with in the coming centuries?

In history we find a number of major developments which changed man's fundamental outlook. The Renaissance beginning in the 14th century AD and extending into the 17th century saw the revival of art, literature and learning. Novelty was rewarded; new ideas and new explanations were looked on favorably. It was during this period that Copernicus and Galileo were making their contributions. A degree of freedom and independence was emerging which led to the so-called Religious Reformation.

The Enlightenment was a philosophical movement of the 17th and 18th centuries which was characterized by belief in the power of human reason. Out of these developments came the acceptance of Humanism, a movement placing an emphasis on man in this world rather than the hereafter and otherworldliness.

The doctrine of Naturalism came to the fore; it accepted the natural rather than supernatural explanations. This resulted in the burgeoning of science. Science with natural explanations replaced the very need for the supernatural, miracles, myths, magic, and superstitions. Ralph Easton in his History of Civilization stated, "In the 12th century AD., not a soul in all of Christendom dared to doubt the teachings of the Christian church." During the Renaissance and Enlightenment, a few centuries later, this general attitude had changed.

Many phenomena previously explained with gods and miracles and supernatural powers now received natural explanations. Such phenomena as the wind, rain, tides, volcanic eruptions, coal, oil and iron, birth, death, blood circulation, the heart beat and the like, were taken from the category of religious explanations and put into the category of natural and scientific explanations. Dreams and belief in afterlife were given natural explanations. It appears that phenomena such as soul or spirit still do and may very likely remain a mystery.

Although it was and still is commonplace in the minds of many today to believe that the soul leaves the body and goes to its reward after death, there is the tendency for scientists and philosophers to explain such phenomena without getting God involved; e.g., Harlow Shapley, a former Harvard astro-physicist, says, "We no longer need to appeal to anything beyond nature when we are confronted by such problems as the origin of life" (*Of Stars and Men*, page 145). Thus we can see that if we live in the context of the traditional religion, we can readily see why we speak of "The Death of God."

With the development of science, technology and naturalistic explanations, man has gained easier access to most of life's basic needs. Material things became more abundant consequently he did not need to implore his gods to have his food and other possessions supplied. Man satisfied his own needs by the fruits of his labor. He became more and more independent of others, and increasingly self-dependent. He did not need the help of God and consequently prayed less.

This was a real blow to the established and long-standing religious traditions. Religious institutions were becoming dysfunctional. One could hear and read about the church dying. More than one hundred years ago the German philosopher Friedrich Nietzsche made the announcement that "God is dead." To the extent that, in the ensuing years, God was ignored or depended on less, we find "The Death of God" occurring.

Something, however, has happened to this trend in recent decades. Changes of a momentous nature have arisen, situations arise which mankind has never faced before. They become frightening. Because of man's inability to handle some of these developing circumstances, there seems to be a new need for a new religion, a kind of "Rebirth of God."

The Rebirth of God

Developments in the new and technological world have brought on a way of life for modern man which he has never experienced heretofore in the entire history of the world. Along with all the knowledge, science, technical know-how, storehouses of material things, televisions, computers, automobiles, space-crafts, satellites, yachts, homes on the Riviera, round-the-world trips, and other reflections of the affluent society, man begins to recognize the need for something greater than material things, and even something greater than himself. With all this affluence, man has been forced to think seriously about the very survival of the human race.

In many respects man is more fearful today than ever before. In many instances he is unable to cope personally with the impending problems. He has giant monsters to encounter. He has the threat of monsters which are difficult to impossible to deal with today. These are monsters for which he seems to have no, or at least very little defense, for example, nuclear power and no place to dispose of nuclear waste, overpopulation and no effective way to curb it, rampant pollution of land, water and air and our inability to stop it, running out of space to dump our garbage, the constant threat of political and military conflict, bacteria warfare, and on and on.

The very things which cause "The Death of God," when carried further are the very cause of the "The Rebirth of God." Man has lost control. Lewis Mumford has described these developments in a rather simple fashion as moving from the use of tools to the use of machines. Man has the ability to control the tool. He can lay the tool down and when he chooses he can pick it up and use it in his own way. When man uses the machine he must follow the rules of the machine. He must attend to it, and serve it in its operation. In our industrialized world the use of machines runs rampant. Man has moved from the more or less relaxed use of the tool to the stress-causing use of the machine.

A new kind of need emerges. In order to deal with it he must deal with the relationships of the entire universe. He must deal with human values in a different dimension. In order to do this, human attitudes must change, and this change is not easy. He must think about how all of these developments fit into the big system of the natural universe. And it is not easy to put this into the minds of the billions of people who populate the earth.

It must be generally recognized that man is but a little creature in a big universe. Ultimately he does not have control. "The laws of nature grind slowly but they grind exceedingly sure." Somehow, it seems that something bigger than man, the supernatural, the spiritual, must be put back into the picture. And again, this is not an easy matter.

It appears that we human beings must learn to relate to the spiritual world if we are to survive. The dinosaurs failed to adjust to their environment and became extinct. In many respects human beings today appear to be having much the same problem as the dinosaurs. (In saying this I am aware of the various theories regarding the extinction of the dinosaurs.)

Hopefully we will realize the need to adjust and live in harmony with the demands of nature before it is too late. In too many instances human beings still think they should control nature even to the point of making rain, replacing worn-out organs in our body and denying death. It is critical that we learn to live in harmony with nature and that this be done before we reach a point of no return. At this point our charted route is uncertain. At times we reflect some serious concern but most of the time our concern seems to be short range. "Eat, drink and be merry, for tomorrow you may die."

Thomas Aquinas, a 13th century theologian has made a philosophical contribution which may, or may not, speak to the present problems. In his *SUMMA THEOLOGIAE*, he assumes that each event that has happened has an antecedent event that caused it. He reasoned that certain things in the universe are seen to be in a state of motion or change. But something cannot be changed or moved except by another, and yet the series of movers cannot be infinite. Therefore there must be a first or prime mover that is not moved or changed by anything else. This is God.

One might carry this reasoning a step further. Accept the prime mover theory admitting that that mover is neither known nor knowable. If it were known, we would not have to call it God. It is God by belief. God, if experienced through our senses in a literal fashion would, be knowable and eventually known. However, we inevitably return to the unknown God. Yes, God exists but we do not, and cannot know all that this concept entails. Why not think of God as more than just a mover? Perhaps he/she/it is all of existence, perhaps it is, in Gordon Kauffman's terms, "mystery."

As an aside, let me mention a personal observation made just recently in our local Mennonite Church, and has been alluded to other places in my life story. In the bulletin of the Mennonite Church of Normal, November 24, 2002, we find the song of Chuck Neufeld, a Mennonite pastor, which expresses an interesting definition of God:

"You are the God of love/hope/peace. You are all there is.
You are all we need. You are all we need.
You are the God of love/hope/peace. You are all there is."

Restated, all there is, is God. God is the total of all there is. God is the total of all existence. This song was sung twice during the Sunday morning service. The song leader asked the congregation to motion with outstretched hands while singing. After the serviced I called to the attention of both the pastor and associate pastor what the words of the song were saying. It is my opinion that neither had really thought about what the words said or if they did had interpreted it in a non-literal manner.

The song was again used for a series of services, October 12, October 19, and October 26, 2003, in the Mennonite Church of Normal.

I personally liked the words of this song. If we use up the concept of God in just a small segment of reality, we will have nothing left for the total of all existence. God may be the prime mover, but not only that. God may be all the movements that take place, the total of all life, all nature, all forces, all universal laws, the whole of environment, the whole of all things real, and the total of even that which we cannot conceptualize.

Another view sees God as "Mystery." In this framework, every thinking person realizes there are the imponderables, things we are aware of but do not have nor can we find the answers. For example, how did the universe get started? Who, what,

caused the "big bang?" Or how did life get started? We are
aware that it did, but not aware of how. These are mysteries
which we will probably never find answers to. The Bible tells us
"No man has seen God at any time" (I John 4:12). This
statement appears to be good support for considering God as
Mystery.

Now, let's move away from the issue of defining God. We
must understand that no one has a moral right to insist that his
definition of God is right and must be accepted by all. So let's
summarize, and draw some conclusions.

As we view the big picture, all humankind in the whole
universe, through all ages, appears to believe. Some may view
and believe about the big picture, and others may think smaller.
Degrees and levels of thinking and believing vary. However, it
appears that beliefs are inevitable. They cannot be avoided. If
we are human, we believe.

As alluded to earlier, in order to understand how beliefs come
about in the first place we must look for the source of beliefs.
The source is inevitably human experience. And this principle
would apply universally. Influence from social interaction is a
universal principle. Tradition, reason, insight, inspiration,
socialization, and the like, develop inevitably among all
humankind.

The belief is developed first; then it serves its need. It goes
back to the summary of the cycle beliefs must go through. First,
Man Creates God; Second, God Creates Man; Third, The Death
of God; and finally, God is Reborn. Man continues to believe.
Beliefs vary but do exist in all normal human beings. Belief is a
given.

This is a statement I make today. I continue to search for
truth. I hope the process of arriving at theological and
philosophical decisions is dynamic. It changes from time to time
and occurs in varying degrees with new experiences, new
observations and insights. Hopefully my search for truth will
continue as long as I live.

A New Revelation: Nature Offers a Dilemma

These next few pages, "A New Revelation," reflect my thinking that resulted from the discussion in our Wednesday morning Book Study Discussion Group, when we discussed Dan Liechty's, "Reflecting on Faith in a Post-Christian Time." I realize that it doesn't exactly fit here but I feel that it is sufficiently thought-provoking and insightful that I have decided to include it in my "story," and I'm not sure of any better place than here.

Combining and relating some of these experiences cause me to arrive at some new meanings relating to my major philosophical/theological insights. Building on the discussions alluded to above, then building on my Believing Man thesis that I also describe in this chapter, I relate the concept Liechty makes of the Ernest Becher's notion, "the flight from mortality is the root of human evil," (p. 45). I, along with a number of the fellows who expressed themselves in our discussion group here, questioned the Liechty/Becker notion quoted above. However, at this point in my thinking, I feel that we did not get the real meaning of what Liechty was saying. Furthermore, at this point I am saying that I agree with the statement, that "the flight from mortality is the root of human evil," and that, in fact, is my new "revelation" that I'd like to share here. (I gave each of our discussion group members, a dozen men, a copy of this "revelation," and interestingly, I received very little response, either positive or negative from any of them.)

My objective in this statement is to explain how I come to my new conclusion. In so doing, I have to start with the premise I've held for some years. That is, in order to have a society with a way of life that could endure indefinitely in the world, one would have to go back to the hunters and gatherers of prehistoric times. This was a way of life that existed prior to the agricultural and pastoral revolutions ten thousand years ago, and could very likely have continued indefinitely without doing damage to, or destroying the environment. Man was basically using nature in a very simple fashion rather than trying to control it.

Prior to these revolutions, Homo sapiens accepted nature, as nature presented itself. In those days they were not involved like today, in that "flight from immorality." Food, clothing, shelter, and life's basic necessities were taken from nature just as nature offered them, in raw form, taking nuts, berries, fruits, roots and stems from the wild, and hunting animals for food, clothing, and tools.

Reproduction and stability of population was maintained naturally, and without any advanced measures to prevent death. Life and death were natural occurrences. Mortality was understood to be simply a natural and inevitable part of being alive. Death was a common occurrence, it was expected and accepted. Population numbers with this lifestyle were held in check and at a level which did not over-tax the space and resources that the earth provided. Consequently, there was less "evil" (of the Liechty/Becker type) then, than exists in today's world.

At this point in our discussion, it is important to introduce a basic gift to mankind, a gift that is responsible for the dilemma. It is responsible for a contradiction and many frustrations that have permeated the human social order through centuries. That gift is advanced intelligence, a brain unlike that of any other animal. With this intelligence Homo Sapien could perform in ways that were not possible with other forms of life. To illustrate, with this intelligence he has an acute awareness of the past, can anticipate and plan for the future, he has a memory, the ability to communicate symbolically (language), he has the ingenuity to make complicated tools, he could make and control fire, and do a host of things that were not possible in other forms of life.

These forms of human behavior occurred with early man and the intelligence that makes them possible was put to use. That "use" takes the form of, or results in, what M. Scott Peck refers to as "man's original sin." That sin is the tendency to be lazy; we want to make it easier for ourselves. We take the short-cuts. We seek the better life, we want promotions, and we refuse to be satisfied with things as they are. We have the ability to, and we

VIII – Believing Man

naturally take the line of least resistance. For most people today it would seem unwise for us to not express and put to use that quality (Peck's "original sin") which is provided us "naturally."

Herein lays the dilemma. On the one hand it appears as (and actually is) a genuine contradiction. We need to, and we know we will eventually die, yet we strive to survive. Human intelligence with a rational mind tells us that we need to stabilize population. Also, we are forced to observe nature's laws, and with our natural sex drive, reproduce in order for our specie to survive. This aspect of human activity means taking nature's offerings just as nature offers them. And at the same time we have the natural urge to develop new ways to make life easier and better for ourselves, we want to control nature.

On the one hand our "original sin" comes into play and with our "natural" intelligence and ability, goes to work playing the one-upmanship game with nature. That is our attempt to escape mortality. In this escape, rather than simply accepting nature as is, we humans seek to "improve" it (nature) with all kinds of scientific developments and technology, medical advances, hospitals, organ transplants, seat belts, and the like, which helps us in our "flight from mortality." Then we define this as creative expression, as wholesome and constructive activities, and as progress. Within a given value system that is what it really is. Is it, however, the value system we should accept? I say "no." We can go back to our rational awareness and realize that our "progress" cannot continue in this manner indefinitely. And with this acceptance we are headed for a dead end. Society is preparing the noose for its own hanging. That is why this "evil" ("flight from mortality") is, according to Liechty, the root of human sin.

We are denying mortality. We do this because of the natural urge (some say instinct) to survive. This urge is inevitable; it is "natural." At least it could be avoided, but only with great understanding then conscious effort to minimize it regardless of whether or not it is a major sin. It appears to me that Liechty and Becker are saying that denying mortality is a fundamental evil. That is, denying death is fundamentally evil. The implications I'm referring to don't necessarily come out just this way in Liechty's book (I think for a good reason, the book must be acceptable to a given public), but the "root of evil" seems to me to be the violation of nature's laws, yet this, we view as progress.

A second natural gift which needs to be considered in this equation and eluded to above is the sex drive. We have the urge to biologically reproduce. By the exercising of this "gift" we do the "honorable" task of "replenishing the earth," which means (so we think) further and better survival of mankind, all of which, however, is further "flight."

So let's summarize. Historically, it began with domesticating animals and cultivating the soil. We domesticate animals, and cultivate the soil because it is easier to provide life's essentials with animals in our control than it is to go out and run them down in the wild. If we cultivate the soil and specialize in only those plants, which we can use for our sustenance, life is made easier so we do it that way. We are only observing that natural human quality of wanting to survive which is exercising Peck's "original sin."

So the dilemma blares out loudly. The very fact of being alive involves a contradiction. We accept mortality (see Liechty, pp. 35 & 36) yet we want to survive, all of us, forever. We have the urge to reproduce. We want to propagate our specie. We want to live an easy life. And I think we naturally want to be good, kind, helpful, live a life of service, loving, but in so doing, we are perpetuating the conditions (over populating and polluting the earth, which, if continued long enough, mean inevitable extinction of, probably not only humans but possibly all life on earth.

In our rational mind we want the best for mankind to happen in the long-run. In our emotional mind and in the short-run we want everyone to survive and live the good life. It's impossible to have it both ways so here I can only submit, "the laws of God (nature) grind slowly but they grind exceedingly sure."

All of this is not necessarily a pleasant thought, not a joyful conclusion but that's the way it seems to me. "Eat, drink, and be merry, for tomorrow you may die." (Ecclesiastes 2:24, also 3:13, tells us, "There is nothing better for a man than that he should eat and drink and that his soul should enjoy the good of all his labour. It is the gift of God.")

In 2010, I present this brief epilogue to the "revelation:"

So, since we are still here, and aren't volunteering to leave this world, let's stop all this nonsense of intellectual pursuit and philosophizing, and keep on trying to improve our state of being and enjoyment. Let what happens, happen. Yes, "eat, drink, and be merry," eat healthily, drink moderately, and enjoy life.

IX - My Concluding Statement

To some extent this project has been in progress for many years. As a whole, it includes activities in my personal experience, and also a statement of my philosophical/theological positions that have developed over the years. The unfamiliar reader would very likely see this whole project as a hodge-podge. It obviously is not a continuity of events. However, it is my story. It's all a part of my life. It is the way it happened to me. And after all, that's what I intended from the beginning. So, as Walter Cronkite used to say as he concluded his news reports, "That's the way it is."

As I consider the nature of some of the chapters, particularly, chapters VI and VII that deal with my religious views, I realize that some readers will question what I've done. Some of the statements I make, and conclusions I have arrived at will probably surprise, even shock, some readers. We need to keep in mind that the workings of the mind, like beliefs, opinions, decisions, judgment, and the like, are dynamic. They are constantly open to change. I do not state these as final. It is where I am at present. I do not present them with a closed mind. I questioned even up to the time I submitted the manuscript for printing, whether or not I should perhaps include some of my more controversial material. But I am encouraged by some knowledgeable friends who have applauded me for stating some of the unconventional views and experiences as I do here. Also, I am convinced and have stated on numerous occasions, a person doesn't go out seeking certain beliefs and attitudes, but these things, simply "happen" to a person.

So here I can only say, if anyone takes offense at what I say, or if someone realizes how far I have strayed from my childhood teaching, and feels I've gone astray, I can only apologize. It's the way it happened. I do not wish to cause any offense to anyone. I repeat, it's just the way it happened, and I'm choosing not to dodge or deny what has become a sincere part of me. I've always felt that communication is important and in communicating, one should be honest and truthful. My intention is to understand and be understood.

As I view my, so called, conversions described in Chapter VI, I am aware of a number of changes that have occurred in my thinking in recent years. And I vow to keep an open mind, and hopefully continue to think, and be open to change, as long as I live.

As my story ends and as this goes to press, I am ninety three years old. I am still in reasonably good physical health. I go to the Illinois Wesleyan University fitness center usually five days a week, early morning, 5:00 to 7:00 am. I bicycle to Lake Evergreen, almost twenty-five miles occasionally, and am a "modified" vegetarian. I am less "hard-nosed" about my diet than I was twenty years ago. I have recently taken to eating fish and occasionally venison.

I am registered to compete in the Illinois Senior Olympics, bicycling, track and field this year. 2010 is the qualifying year for the National Senior Olympics. I am confident that if I compete in the State Meet, I will qualify for the Nationals. I do not have much, if any, competition at my age level. First or second place qualifies for the Nationals. They will be in Houston in 2011, and I hope to be there.

I also have a good garden, and am involved in Timber Stand Improvement (TSI) programs at Rocky Branch and Hedgewood, working with my State Foresters. I cook most of my meals, do my launderings and general household duties. I admit that my hips, back, and knees seem to ache more and more as time passes. I say reluctantly that this will probably eventually cause me to quit running in the track events. I say reluctantly because these are events that in the past have been the most enjoyable. And let's face it, sooner or later; all rigorous activity must come to a close.

My wife, Anne, passed away February, 2010. She was quite dependent on my care for more than three years. I miss her. I miss the opportunity 'to do things' for her. It was actually rewarding for me to do what we did together. It was especially rewarding to me that she was always so appreciative. She disliked the thought of ever going to a nursing home and I could not see her going to professional care so long as I was physical able to provide care. And by her admission, she enjoyed life more when she and I could do things together.

However, since she's gone, I am making the adjustment of living alone. And it is not easy, however, even in my times of loneliness, I have no difficulty keeping busy. And in conclusion, I say, it is gratifying for me personally to finally finish and get "My Story" to the printers.

I have a final up-date before going to print: I indicated earlier that I am qualified for several events in the Nationals to be held in Houston in June, 2011. Receiving the schedule, I find that the events I'm qualified for are: cycle races, June 18-21; 100m dash, June 22; race walk June 25.

Then I note my family schedule, Nara's wedding, June 18, in Colorado Springs, and the D. D. Miller reunion in Berlin, Ohio, June 24, 25, 26. Both of these events are important to me. Considering the long-run significance of these events, along with the fact that I'm in the upper years of my age category in the Senior Olympics it didn't take me long to decide to give up Senior Olympics, and plan to attend both family events. So that's what I plan to do. And considering my physical condition, I plan to continue with Senior Olympics in the future as long as I'm physically able.

Appendix I - List of Pictures

Appendix I – List of Pictures

Appendix II - List of Tables

Appendix III – "The Crusaders" Male Quartet Itinerary and Program, CPS, from 1943 to 1946.

Table 7: "The Crusaders" Male Quartet Itinerary & Program, CPS - 1943 to 1946.

Date / Event	Program
April 14, 1943 Farnhurst Chapel	Phil Frey, speaker 2 numbers
April 16, 1943 Farnhurst Chapel	Phil Frey, speaker 2 numbers
April 25, 1943 Farnhurst Chapel Delaware State Hospital Easter program for patients.	2 numbers
April 29, 1943 Farnhurst Chapel Rev. Caldwell visiting Methodist	Minister speaker 2 numbers
May 1, 1943 Zion Mennonite Church Souderton, Pennsylvania	Wm. Stauffer, speaker 4 numbers ($10.00)
May 18, 1943 Delaware State Hospital Graduating Exercises Farnhurst Chapel	2 numbers "Adoration by Beethoven "Finlandia" (the home port) by Sibelus
June 6, 1943 2 numbers Richardson Park, Delaware	2 numbers
June 20, 1943 Hockiesson Methodist Church Hockiesson, Delaware	Rev. Caldwell in charge Complete program ($5.00)
July 26, 1943 Farnhurst Chapel	Rev. D.D. Miller, speaker 2 numbers
September 10, 1943 Hockiesson Friends Meeting House Hockiesson, Delaware	Complete Program ($5.00)
September 17, 1943 Dunwoody Convalescent Home Media, Pennsylvania	Milton Brackbill in charge Complete Program

Appendix III – The Crusaders Quartet Program

Date / Event	Program
September 18, 1943 Youth Center, After-broadcast Service Delaware Avenue-Bethany Baptist Church	1 number, "Faith of Our Fathers"
September 25, 1943 Youth Center Broadcast Station WILM, Wilmington	2 numbers: "Faith of Our Fathers", "The Glorious Gospel"
October 3, 1943 Grace Baptist Church Oakmont, Pennsylvania	Ed Ferguson in charge 35th Anniversary Program 4 numbers
October 13, 1943 Anniversary Celebration, CPS Unit #58 YMCA Auditorium Wilmington, Delaware	2 numbers
October 18, 1943 (on furlough) Central Mennonite Church Elida, Ohio	Menno Troyer in charge Complete Program ($40.00)
October 19, 1943(on furlough) Lockport Mennonite Church Archbold, Ohio	Phil Frey in charge Complete Program ($179.51)
October 22, 1943 (on furlough) Walnut Creek Mennonite Church	Paul R. Miller in charge Complete Program ($60.43)
October 23, 1943 (on furlough) Martins Creek Mennonite Church Millersburg, Ohio	D.D. Miller in charge Complete Program ($61.01)
October 24, 1943 (on furlough) AM - Berlin Mennonite Church Berlin, Ohio	D.D. Miller in charge Complete Program ($56.59) 2 numbers
PM - Coschocton CPS Camp Coschocton, Ohio	
Evening - Kidron Mennonite Church Kidron, Ohio	Rev. Hofsteter in charge Complete Program ($100.00)
October 25, 1943 (on furlough) Stahl Mennonite Church Johnstown, Pennsylvania	Sanford G. Shetler in charge Complete Program ($28.41)
November 3, 1943 Bull Session, CPS Unit #58 Kent Hall, Farnhurst, Delaware	Quartet gives each CPS man a five-dollar bill from tour proceeds.
November 9, 1943 Methodist Youth Convention Marshallton, Delaware	Complete Program with exception of a solo number and announcements
November 13, 1943 Youth Center Broadcast Wilmington Station, WILM	2 numbers

Date / Event	Program
November 14, 1943 Church of the Brethren Ephrata, Pennsylvania	Complete Program ($22.00)
November 20, 1943 Youth Center Broadcast Radio Station WILM Wilmington, Delaware	2 numbers
November 21, 1943 Friends Meeting Media, Pennsylvania	Complete Program ($10.00 plus transportation)
November 25, 1943 Delaware State Hospital	Thanksgiving Program for Patients, 4 numbers
November 28, 1943 Farnhurst Chapel	Sponsored by Religious Life Committee, CPS Unit #58 Complete Program
December 4, 1943 Youth Center Broadcast Radio Station WILM Wilmington, Delaware	
December 5, 1943 Church of the Brethren Richardson Park, Delaware	3 numbers at the mortgage burning service
December 25, 1943 Youth Center Broadcast	3 numbers, last Radio Broadcast
Radio Station WILM Wilmington, Delaware January 16, 1944, 7:00 pm - Graced Baptist Church Young People's Meeting Oakmont, PA 9:00 pm - Radio Broadcast, WIBG, Philadelphia, Pa Ardsley Community Chapel, Baptist Ardsley, Pennsylvania	2 numbers
January 23, 1944 Westtown Friends School Westtown, Pennsylvania	Complete Program
January 30, 1944 Friends Meeting 4th & West St., Wilmington, Delaware	2 numbers
March 5, 1944 Delaware Avenue-Bethany Baptist Church Wilmington, Delaware	3 numbers

Date / Event	Program
April 7, 1944 Delaware State Hospital Auditorium Between Acts of Play "Great Dawn"	
April 27, 1944 Commencement Exercises Delaware State Hospital Farnhurst Chapel	2 numbers
June 10, 1944 High School Alumni Banquet Newark, Delaware	Numbers
July 23, 1944 Delaware Avenue-Bethany Baptist Church Wilmington, Delaware	3 numbers
July 30, 1944 Dunwoody Convalescent Home Media, Pennsylvania	Complete Program (transportation provided)
August 6, 1944 Farnhurst Chapel CPS Service	2 numbers
August 20, 1944 8:00 P M, Delaware Avenue-Bethany Baptist Church Wilmington, Delaware	3 numbers
August 27, 1944 PM - Ft. Wayne Mennonite Mission, Ft. Wayne, Indiana	Rev. Ebersole in charge Complete Program ($19.78)
Evening - Leo Mennonite Church, Leo, Indiana	S. J. Miller in charge Complete Program($48.05)
August 30, 1944 Ohio Conference (Mennonite) Walnut Creek, Ohio	Special Music of Evening Session "Faith of Our Fathers" AM, l number PM, 2 numbers
August 3l, 1944 Ohio Conference Walnut Creek, Ohio	AM - 2 numbers PM - 3 numbers Evening - 3 numbers ($113.00)
September 17, 1944 Presbyterian Church Kennel Square, Pennsylvania	Betty Russell's home church 4 numbers ($5.00)
September 30, 1944 Stanton Methodist Church Banquet Stanton, Delaware	5 numbers and talk ($10.00)

Date / Event	Program
October 7, 1944 Graterford Brethren in Christ Young People's Conference	AM - 2 numbers PM - 3 numbers Evening - 4 numbers ($20.00 plus transportation)
October 14, 1944 CPS Anniversary Celebration Hospital Gymnasium	4 numbers
October 19, 1944 Norristown CPS Unit State Hospital Norristown, Pennsylvania	Complete Program Keller & Bucher giving talks (transportation)
October 29, 1944 Farnhurst Chapel	CPS Service, Roy Roth, speaker 2 numbers
November 8, 1944 Wilmington City Mission	"Bigfred" Ingersol, evangelist 4 numbers
November 10, 1944 (8:00 P M) Banquet at the Hockiesson Meeting House	Dr. & Mrs. Maris, speakers 4 numbers ($5.00)
November 10, 1944 (10:00 P M) Mother A U. M. P. Church Williams Gospel Singers Wilmington, Delaware	Second Anniversary Celebration 2 numbers
November 12, 1944 East Lake Methodist Church Wilmington, Del	6 numbers ($10.00)
November 17, 1944 Farnhurst Chapel CPS Service	E. M. Yost, speaker 3 numbers
November 19, 1944, 3:30 P M Presbyterian Church Kennel Square, Pennsylvania	Dr. Bob Jones, Evangelist 4 numbers
November 19, 1944, 8:00 P M Faggs Manor Presbyterian Church Faggs Manor, Pennsylvania	Dr. Bob Jones, evangelist 5 numbers ($20.00)
December 25, 1944 CPS Christmas Program Farnhurst Chapel	T. Books, speaker 2 numbers: "While Shepherds Watched Their Flocks", "Low How a Rose 'Ere Blooming"

Date / Event	Program
January 7, 1945 Grace Chapel Upper Darby, Pennsylvania	Ed Ferguson in charge "God is our Refuge" "Hear My Prayer O God" "O Sanctissmo" "I'd Rather Have Jesus" "Nearer My God to Thee" "Have Thine Own Way Lord" "Climbin' Up the Mountain" ($10.00)
January 20, 1945 CPS Camp #45 Luray, Va MCC Deputation to Represent Hospital Work	Complete Program of Talks and Singing "Faith of Our Fathers" "God is Our Refuge and Strength" "The Glorious Gospel" "Shine, Shine" "Roll Dem Bones" "Sophmoric Philosophy" "Have Thine Own Way Lord" "At the Close of the Day"
January 21, 1945 Luray, Va, CPS Camp Church Service, A M	"Get on Board" "Climbin' Up the Mountain" "Nearer My God to Thee" "Hear My Prayer O God"
January 21, 1945 Farnhurst Chapel CPS Service	
May 17, 1945 Commencement Exercises Delaware State Hospital	"Prayer Perfect" "Sophomoric Philosophy"
May 19, 1945 Delaware Avenue-Bethany Baptist Church	Two quartet numbers with chorus program "Some of These Days" "Nearer My God to Thee"
June 9, 1945 Roy Bucher's Wedding Hostetler's Play Barn Bird-in-Hand, Pennsylvania	"Hear My Prayer O God" "O Promise Me" "O Perfect Love" "O Father Lead Us"
At Reception	"Have Thine Own Way Lord" "The Glorious Gospel" "My Love's Own" (Pie-Maker's Song) "The Harlem Goat" "Sophomoric Philosophy" "At the Close of the Day" "Roll Dem Bones" "Shine, Shine"

Date / Event	Program
August 15, 1945 Farnhurst Chapel	Service After V-J Day
August 19, 1945 Farnhurst Chapel Sunday Evening Service August 26, 1945 First Baptist Church Berwyn, Pennsylvania	"Hear My Prayer O God" "Nearer My God to Thee" "From Every Stormy Wind That Blows" "God is Our Refuge" "Faith of Our Fathers" "The Glorious Gospel" "From Every Stormy Wind That Blows" "O Father Lead Us" "I Want My Life to Tell For Jesus" "Some of These Days" "Climbin' Up the Mountain" "Nearer My God to Thee" "Hear My Prayer O God" "At the Close of the Day" ($20.00)
September 2, 1945 CPS Camp #52 Powellsville, Md.	Half a dozen or so numbers at M. Brackbills after the Service ($10.00) "Spirit of the Living God" "God is Our Refuge and Strength" "From Every Stormy Wind That Blows" "The Glorious Gospel" "O Father Lead Us" "Now Look Away to Heaven" "Some of These Days" "Climbin' Up the Mountain" "Nearer My God to Thee" "Have Thine Own Way Lord" "The Doxology"
September 6, 1945 John Martin's Wedding Mrs. Wise's Residence, Wilmington, Delaware	"O Promise Me" "O Perfect Love" "O Father Lead Us"
At Railroad Station	Half a dozen or so secular numbers

Date / Event	Program
September 8, 1945 At Burkharts near Lancaster, Pennsylvania	Corn Roast, Informal Four or five numbers, informal Recordings at Erbs Lititz, Pennsylvania
September 9, 1945 Christian Missionary Alliance Church Wilmington, Del	"Spirit of the Living God" "God is Our Refuge and Strength" "The Glorious Gospel" "Nearer My God to Thee" "Have Thine Own Way Lord"
November 4, 1945 CPS Service Farnhurst Chapel	"Spirit of the Living God" "Hear My Prayer O God" "At the Close of the Day"
November 11, 1945 Wilmington Youth for Christ Rally Playhouse, DuPont Building	Capacity Crowd, estimated at 1500 2 numbers, "Nearer My God to Thee", "The Glorious Gospel"
November 11, 1945 CPS Service Farnhurst Chapel	"'Tis Midnight" "From Every Stormy Wind That Blows"
November 17, 1945 Marcus Hook, Pennsylvania Men's Banquet, Baptist Church	"Spirit of the Living God" "The Glorious Gospel" "The Sophomoric Philosophy" "Pie-maker's Song" "At the Close of the Day"
November 18, 1945 Berwyn Baptist Church Berwyn, Pennsylvania	Chorus and Quartet Rendered Program; Quartet, 4 numbers
December 21, 1945 Zell & Messick's Apartment Wilmington, Delaware	Crusaders entertained with about half a dozen mostly secular numbers.
January 6, 1946 Music Studio Delaware State Hospital Farnhurst, Delaware	We sang for nearly four solid hours. Really exerted ourselves with that final spurt. Got record of about 13 songs. John Burkhart, Lancaster, PA was the recorder. Very good job.
January 6, 1946 CPS Service Farnhurst Chapel	Our last public appearance before parting ways because of discharges.

Appendix III – The Crusaders Quartet Program

Date / Event	Program
August 4 & 5, 1979 Farnhurst Reunion Messiah Bible College Grantham, Pennsylvania	Quartet had not been together for 33 years, 7 months.
Bull Session Meeting, August 4	"Bill Grogan's Goat"
Church Session, Morning, August 5, 1979	3 numbers, "Spirit of the Living God" "Get on Board"
Playhouse, DuPont Building Capacity Crowd, estimated at 1500	2 numbers "Nearer My God to Thee" "The Glorious Gospel"
November 11, 1945 CPS Service Farnhurst Chapel	"'Tis Midnight" "From Every Stormy Wind That Blows"
November 17, 1945 Marcus Hook, Pennsylvania Men's Banquet, Baptist Church	"Spirit of the Living God" "The Glorious Gospel" "The Sophomoric Philosophy" "Pie-maker's Song" "At the Close of the Day"
November 18, 1945 Berwyn Baptist Church Berwyn, Pennsylvania	Chorus and Quartet Rendered Program Quartet, 4 numbers
December 21, 1945 Zell & Messick's Apartment Wilmington, Delaware	Crusaders entertained with about half a dozen mostly secular numbers.
January 6, 1946 Music Studio Delaware State Hospital Farnhurst, Delaware	We sang for nearly four solid hours. Really exerted ourselves with that final spurt. Got record of about 13 songs. John Burkhart, Lancaster, PA was the recorder. Very good job.
January 6, 1946 CPS Service Farnhurst Chapel	Our last public appearance before parting ways because of discharges.
August 4 & 5, 1979 Farnhurst Reunion Messiah Bible College Grantham, Pennsylvania	Quartet had not been together for 33 years, 7 months.
Bull Session Meeting, August 4 Church Session, Morning, August 5, 1979	3 numbers, "Spirit of the Living God", "Get on Board", "Faith of Our Fathers"

This concludes the itinerary of the Crusaders Quartet during their service in CPS at Farnhurst, Delaware.

Appendix IV - Constitution of the CPS Unit Council

Table 8: Constitution of the Unit Council

Constitution of Unit Council Preamble

We the assignees and wives of CPS Unit #58, in order to promote unity, harmony, and a spirit of Christian fellowship, do hereby adopt the following constitution.

Article I, This organization shall be known as the Unit Council of CPS Unit #58.

Article II, Members
Section I. The Council shall consist of seven members. The chairman of the Religious Life Committee and the chairman of the Recreation Committee will serve as members of the Council. The unit director shall be an ex-officio member. The married couples will elect two representatives, and the single fellows shall elect two. Section II. The elected members shall serve a term of six months, while the committee chairmen shall serve on the council as long as they are chairmen of their respective committees

Article III, Officers
Section I. The officers shall consist of a chairman, a vice-chairman, and a secretary elected by the members of the Council. Section II. The chairman shall preside at all meetings and perform such other duties as ordinarily would be assigned to that office. Section III. In the absence of the chairman, the vice-chairman will assume the responsibility of the chairman. Section IV. The secretary shall keep an accurate record of the minutes of all meetings of the council.

Article IV. Duties of the Council

Section I. The Council shall decide on definite time for meeting, and meet regularly once each month. Special group or council meetings may be called at any time when deemed necessary.

Section II. The Council shall serve in an advisory capacity in all matters pertaining to the welfare of the unit it represents. It will be the business of the unit director to carry out the advice of the council after it has been approved by a general meeting of the membership of the unit.

Section III. The unit director shall conduct all elections.

Section IV. All Council and general meetings will be conducted according to generally accepted parliamentary procedure.

Article V.

Section I. This constitution may be amended by a 2/3 vote of a quorum. A quorum shall consist of twenty-five unit members.

Appendix V - The Politics of Conscientious Objection in World War II

Most of the following information has been gleaned from the Congressional Records and was compiled by the National Service Board for Religious Objectors, Washington, D.C. in a pamphlet titled "Congress Looks at the Conscientious Objector." A great deal of testimony and debate transpired in Congress, much more than I am including here. I have selected the portions which, in my opinion, reflect representative portions of the testimonies and debates. These portions represent the various aspects of debate related to the conscientious objector issue. They represent wherein opposition to the conscientious objectors laid, the churchmen and also government officials who favored recognizing the principle of conscientious objection to war, along with many other details which should help us to understand how the whole CPS program in World War II was under-girded by political provisions of the United States Government. Before looking at the actual testimonies and debates, it is important for us to be aware of the national and international events which were current at that stage in history.

In the summer of 1940, the war, later to be known as World War II, was waging ferociously. Germany had conquered much of Europe. France fell to the German forces. It appeared that Britain was doomed. The United States was supplying aid but since war had not been declared, the U.S. was not an active participant in military activity. The Lend-Lease proposal was making the Neutrality Act appear increasingly meaningless. It was obvious that sentiment in America was building, in support of the allied forces. The American Army was drilling with trucks masquerading as tanks, but was having difficulty keeping its troops to the 280,000 target through this volunteer program.

Recognizing the pending involvement, Congress raised the troop limit to 375,000, and talk of conscription was in the air. President Roosevelt called for increased interest in "Government Service" to remove the stigma of the word "military." Congress saw the public attitude toward peacetime conscription change. A Gallup poll that summer showed 67 per cent of the American public favoring conscription although America was not officially in the war, and also recognizing the fact that America had never before conscripted a military force during peacetime. With the European allies being seriously threatened, and Japan having warned the world to keep hands off French Indo-China, the American sentiment continued to heat up.

The Selective Training and Service Act of 1940 had been written by a New York attorney, Greenville Clark. It was introduced into Congress by Senator Burke and Representative Wadsworth, known as the Burke-Wadsworth Bill. Congress was holding committee hearings on it during July and August, and along with the consideration of conscription the problem of the conscientious objector also came to the front.

The original bill provided the same consideration for conscientious objectors as was given conscientious objectors in World War I; that is consideration for members of the historic peace churches to serve in noncombatant service, if judged sincere. The questions regarding conscientious objectors were not high on the priority list of the Congressional committees debating the bill. However, a few religious groups and some of the more liberal minorities concerned themselves directly, and it consequently became an issue of prime importance. Some of these groups passed resolutions and sent spokesmen to Washington.

In the hearings on the Selective Training and Service Bill, July 10 to August 2, Congressman John J. Sparkman stated,

I was reading the provision about the conscientious objector, and it appears to me that he is required to be a member of some religious group which has as its doctrine objection to participation in war. Do

---

you not believe that the bill ought to be changed so as to take care of the individual conscientious objector?

Major Lewis B. Hershey replied,

In the World War by administration they did that. You are speaking of something that I have a great deal of sympathy with, but I have not arrived at, perhaps, the best solution. Unquestionably if we could find the man and know that he is, in fact, whether he belongs to a creed or whether he does not, a conscientious objector, we should try to the utmost to do something about it. We have had quite a little dealing with several of these people that have met us and discussed the matter with us and I think that they are very honest about it. Of course, on the other hand, you have this great group of people who are not honest, that are trying to run in under the tent if someone else puts it up, and somewhere in there I think that we should contrive a solution, but it is a little difficult.

During the same hearing, Dr. C. S. Longacre, general secretary, Religious Liberty Association of America, and representative of the Seventh Day Adventist Church, testified before the same House Military Affairs Committee, as follows:

Mr. Charles I. Faddis (PA): "As I understand you, Doctor, you do not object to registration."

Mr. Longacre: "Oh, no."

Mr. Faddis: "And you do not even object to compulsory training so long as the individual who has religious convictions against killing somebody is placed into a non-combative branch of the service."

Mr. Longacre: "We believe every American citizen should help protect his country. Christ said, "Render unto Caesar things that are Caesar's.""

Mr. Faddis: "That is a very fine attitude."

Mr. Longacre: "We believe that. We believe that as noncombatants we should share to the best of our ability."

Mr. Faddis: "So long as that man is not placed in combative service you have no objection at all."

Mr. Longacre: "No objection at all..."

Mr. Faddis: "... In the army on the line would you construe non-combatant service as hauling munitions to guns, cleaning guns, taking care of horses connected with guns, driving tractors connected with pulling guns, if tractors were used, or carrying the ammunition up and handing it to the man who fires the gun and so forth?"

Mr. Longacre: "Some of those things you mentioned, handing the ammunition to the fellow, come pretty near the same as working in ammunition factories..."

Mr. Faddis: "There must be someplace to draw the line as to your suggestions. We will have to draw the line somewhere."

Mr. Longacre: "Yes."

Mr. Faddis: "And we might as well start now and have some understanding where we are going to draw that line. Everybody recognizes in the service, both on board a battleship or in the army that there are certain types of service where men do not actually resort to lethal means to assist in conducting whatever engagement may be on hand."

Mr. Longacre: "Yes sir. Our denomination has appointed a war service council and in that council we have laid down certain lines of work."

Mr. Faddis: "All right, we will be glad to have them."

Mr. Longacre: "They are medical, nursing, cooking, first aid, dental, embalming, band music, accounting, secretarial, printing, electrical, mechanical, carpentry, surveying, tailoring, shoe repairs, and so forth. All of these lines are suggested but there are many other lines of noncombatant service which we could engage in consistently beside those."

Mr. Longacre: "I might say during the World War quite a few tried to get in under our colors and get the same privilege we had who were not in our church. For instance up in Camp Lewis in Washington, 800 of our boys went to General Clark and asked him for that privilege, asking for the privilege of being exempted from bearing arms, and also from Sabbath duties on their Sabbath, which General Clark granted to them. And some of the other fellows came along and said we do not believe you should grant that privilege to the Seventh Day Adventists unless we have the same privileges that are granted them. The General said, "All right, are you willing to work hard every day on bread and water in order to live up to your convictions?" Then he asked them, "Are you willing to be lined up and be shot down rather than give up your convictions?" They said "No" Then he said, "Then you have not any religious convictions, you are simply contrary."

Mr. Thomiason: "I am very glad to hear you say that".

Mr. Longacre: "He said, that is the best way to test them out, put them on bread and water," and he also told them that they were going to be shot. And he said, "Then we know they are sincere."

The following is an excerpt from the testimony of Raymond Wilson, Philadelphia, PA

Mr. J. Joseph Smith (Conn.) "... the Friends have in the past, while maintaining their opposition to military service as such, been willing to serve in dangerous positions, and sacrifice their lives if necessary."

Mr. Wilson: "Yes, I think that there were 16 men who died in the unit in Poland and in the work in Europe from typhus and other efforts right after the World War, in trying to combat the effects of the war. The American Friends Service Committee built villages and they did construction work in a great many of the devastated areas of France, and they were the first group to go into Germany after the armistice; they supervised the feeding of 1,200,000 children in Germany; and they were active in Poland and Austria and Russia, and I submit the Society of Friends has seen more of the devastation of war and have tried to do what they could to meet it than any group of its size in the world... The sincere conscientious objector is not afraid of losing his life; he doesn't want to take anyone else's life"

The following is part of the testimony of Abraham Kaufman, executive secretary of the War Resisters' League, New York City.

Mr. Kaufman: "... those who oppose war must also oppose conscription. We are for defense because we have deep affection for our country and what it stands for. This is a question of deep interest and we wish to make it clear that we reject, not defense, but military defense. The type of defense we advocate is a type which we believe in not for idealistic reasons alone, but because we believe it is practical. Where tried it has worked. In India, by Gandhi, in the Ruhr Valley in 1923, and in Pennsylvania 300 years age, we find evidence of the success of this method of defense."

Mr. Dewey Short (Mo.):"If you will pardon the interjection, those methods saved neither Czechoslovakia nor the Orient, did they?"

Mr. Kaufman: "These countries all had compulsory military training. But it was only after losing out with the method of military defense that those people resorted to that in desperation, and not deliberately the way Gandhi did, refuse to use arms. They are doing this in desperation,"

Harold Evans, Philadelphia, Pennsylvania, representing the Religious Society of Friends, made the following statement in his testimony:

Mr. Evans: ".... We respectfully voice our conviction that democracy cannot be preserved by coercion; that modern war annihilates democracy; and that freedom can be maintained only by self-discipline, by contagious enthusiasm for service, by devotion to a great cause. May it not be that the true defense of the things we hold dear in American life will be found in a rekindled enthusiasm for democracy, in a rebirth of religion, and in new avenues of voluntary service at home and abroad? If our people could again catch the crusading spirit of a great constructive cause, could we not tap the spiritual forces that surround us and prove ourselves good neighbors in word and in deed to all people? If God be with us, who can be against us?"

The following is a part of the testimony of Frederick J. Libby, representing the National Council for the Prevention of War:

Mr. Libby: ".... I am a Quaker, but I am secretary of the National

Council for the Prevention of War and I am speaking in its behalf; but I am familiar with the situation in the churches on this issue of conscientious objectors throughout the country."

"Now, you are exempting from combatant service only the members of well recognized religious sects which in the World War, I think, were Quakers, Mennonites and Dunkards; However, there are going to be many of them that will not be willing in peacetime to enlist in the army because that is what is still required under Section 10, in the army, but for noncombatant services, and to my mind that is going to be offensive to the consciences of many members of those sects; but as Mr. Evans explained today, the Quakers are not willing to accept special treatment. They do not believe that there is just ground for them to be treated differently from conscientious objectors who are Methodists, or Baptists or Episcopalians or Congregationalists or Catholics or Jews."

Senator Minton: "Has not your religion always taught its people that war was wrong and that they should not associate themselves with wrong; and now then you have taught them that from childhood, while in many other religions we are not taught that? Do you not think there is a difference between that group whose conscientious objections are based upon a religious belief that they learned at their parents' knees and just some idea that he has that he does not want to serve?"

Mr. Libby: "Senator, I think that the opposition of most young people to war is really on the basis of its futility as a method. They feel ..."

Senator Minton: "I will grant you that. I will grant that it settles nothing; but we do not have any choice as to whether we will have war."

Mr. Libby: "I know your position; but there are at the same time a great many ministers in the country..."

Senator Minton: "A great many what?"

Mr. Libby: "Ministers; churchmen who have been preaching the gospel of Christ in substantially the same terms as the Quakers. Now, Dr. Harry Emerson Fosdick has said on a national hook-up over the radio, that under no circumstances will he take part or have anything to do with another war. He is one of our outstanding preachers. There are many that have taken that position; and there are young people who have been taught that same point of view and hold it now as firmly as the Quakers."

Senator Minton: "It is not in the tenets of any regular religion, except perhaps the Quakers, Mennonites and Dunkards, and they have it in their canons of faith, do they not?"

Mr. Libby: "Yes, but there is a tremendous..."

Senator Minton: "Yes, and they have learned that from their childhood up; their mother's knees."

Mr. Libby: "True".

Senator Minton: "That this thing is wrong in the sight of God. It has been taught them as a religious thing."

Mr. Libby: "Yes, but 20 years..."

Senator Minton (continuing): "I have sympathy for the youth that is brought up with that teaching; but I was not brought up that way, and I have not any sympathy for the youth of the country that are not willing to stand up in defense of this country in its hour of need."

Mr. Libby: "Now, Senator, let me say a word about that."

Senator Minton: "I do have some sympathy for these young people who have had training in their churches and in their religious training against war. I have some sympathy for their conscientious objections, but I haven't any sympathy with youth who just simply says "I am not going to fight for my country, whatever you say about it. I am not going to war, whatever the circumstances are."

Mr. Libby: "I know if that is all, Senator, you will have wide support in that condemnation of that type of youth; but there are thousands and tens of thousands of young people who are just as conscientious in their rejection of war methods as they understand the Christian religion as the Quakers are."

"Now I heard Gen. John F. O'Ryan speak to a thousand pastors of the State of Ohio some years ago. It was the pastors' convention. And it was such an extraordinary address that I took notes of what he said. He said this: 'You may ask me how I reconcile war with Christian principles. Frankly, I don't. You can't.' He went on, "I have not always seen it that way. It came to me first at camp; when my wife--who is a Methodist, I am a Catholic--came by the bayonet room, which we had set up. The boys were there driving bayonets into dummies representing human beings and stamping on them with their hob-nailed shoes, and my wife when she got where I was, was speechless with horror; but finally she burst out. How can you reconcile that with your Christian principles?" And he said, "I never thought of it before." On the spur of the moment I said, "I don't."

And he continued, "I don't today..."

The Selective Training & Service Bill was first discussed before the House Military Affairs Committee, July 10 to August 2, 1940. Since that time the subject of conscientious objectors has been officially discussed either in committee or on the floor of the House or Senate, thirteen different times. Some of the hearings extended through several weeks with a number of lengthy testimonies. Twenty-eight different witnesses appeared before House or Senate committees between July, 1940 and June, 1943. Five of these appeared on repeated occasions. The major share of these witnesses testified in support of the provision for conscientious objectors. Some, particularly the military officers who were called in, testified mostly in an informational role. Senator Elmer Thomas, (Oklahoma) on February 17, 1943, presented a resolution representing the American Legion, attempting to eliminate completely the section of the Selective Training and Service Act which made provision for conscientious objectors, Section 5 (g), Senator Thomas, appearing before the Senate Military Affairs Committee stated that he had "requested the Senate drafting department for a bill to seek the effectuation of the resolution... received the draft, introduced it into the Senate and it has now been referred to this committee... and is known as Senate 315."

The resolution Senator Thomas received from the American Legion contained the following words, "... all men subject to the draft shall do service in the armed forces of the United States."

Some disagreement arose between the House and Senate Military Affairs Committees regarding what constitutes "good faith." This concept, "good faith," was a part of both bills reported out of the House and Senate. Both the House and Senate Committees originally reported out identical bills providing that the Register of Conscientious Objectors remain in the hands of the Department of Justice, which was to conduct hearings "with respect to the character and good faith" of all objectors. On September 6, 1940, however, this provision was struck out on the floor of the House, taking the determination of "good faith" out of the hands of the Department of Justice and putting it back into the hands of each local board. Congressman Jerry Voorhis, of California, raised objection and attempted to get it back into the hands of the Department of Justice. His efforts failed. The House language prevailed and as it was finally approved that "good faith" was to be determined by the respective local boards, and allowing that the person being considered be entitled to appeal to the appropriate appeal board which was in turn to refer the case to the Department of Justice.

The Selective Training and Service bill became law September 16, 1940, and provision for conscientious objectors to engage in alternative service was included. At that time, the war in Europe was at its height and public anti-German sentiment was mounting as the war progressed. A month after the Law was enacted; President Roosevelt proclaimed that more than sixteen million adult American men between the ages of 21 and 36 were registered in the peacetime American Army. At the time of this Proclamation, the length of service was limited to one year.

The attack on Pearl Harbor struck December 7, 1941, and war was declared. From January to August, 1942, approximately eight months, any discussion of conscientious objectors did not come up in Congress. The German forces were pushing deep into Russia. Russia was pleading for a "Second Front." U.S. was stepping up the military tempo, women's auxiliaries were added to the armed forces, draft deferments, rations, and prices were being tightened, the registration was extended to cover men ages 18 to 65, and the number in Civilian Public Service increased to more than 4,000.

On August 19, 1942, the Senate Subcommittee on Military Affairs began an interesting debate regarding a proposed amendment to the Selective Training and Service Act of 1940, which was to extend the benefits of employees' compensation to conscientious objectors. The chief witness before this committee was Col. Lewis F. Kosch, Chief, Camp Operations Division, Selective Service System. He was strongly in favor of extending employment compensation to the CPS men. He reported some strong arguments in favor of the amendment, it was reported out of the Senate Military Affairs Committee favorably, and eight days later brought up on the floor of the Senate for debate. It was passed by the Senate; it then went to the house but was never brought up, before the 76th Congress adjourned. Selective service resolved to try it again the following session, however, as the war waged on without any solution, and new threats on some of the European fronts emerged, priorities changed. Greater demands were placed on manpower for the army. Increased demands were made by our arsenal factories and other industries essential to war, all of which increased the demand for labor. Of the many bills introduced into the new Congress, the extension for employment compensation for conscientious objectors was not high on the priority list.

Before dropping the discussion on the employment compensation for COs, however, I think we should relate some of Col. Kosch's testimony and the interaction that took place between him and some members of the Senate Military Affairs Subcommittee. Some excerpts include the following.

"My job is the administering of the camps under the Selective Service to which men classified as 4-E are sent for work of National Importance. ... Our object in sponsoring this bill is to protect the government in future cases of claims that might come up."

Senator Styles Bridges (N.H.) asked,

"Do you think, Colonel, that in time to come in our lives, the Government of the United States will look very kindly toward a claim by a person who has refused to fight for the country in its direst hour of need?"

Kosch replied, "Well, I don't think it is a question of how we are going to look at it, but it is a question as to what the man's rights are. Under this law as it is set up, he can do work of national importance in lieu of service in the army. The government requires him to go to camp and do work, and the only reason he is not subject to compensation is the fact that he is doing this work without any pay." Senator Bridges then asked, "Colonel, how much of an obligation do you think the citizens of the country have to a man who refuses to fight for his country when his country is in jeopardy and everything is at stake?" To which Col. Kosch replied, "I don't think my personal opinion on that would have anything to do with it. Under the law as set up there are certain rights for this man and certain places to which he is allowed to go; it is considered service to his country and he is just complying with the law. I am not a conscientious objector, myself. In fact, I have had 32 years of service, and this is just a job that has been given me to do, and I feel I have to look after the rights of the people that I am representing here and the things I am running, and try to protect the Government in every way we can in the future."

A discussion then that ensued focused on the nature of the work done, who furnished clothing and food and at what cost. Senator Edwin C. Johnson (CO) then (reading from the "Conscientious Objector under the Selective Training and Service Act of 1940."), said,

"It will cost $35 per month per boy to operate the program, and the various religious groups involved are assuming that the individual, the family, the local church or denominational group will desire to help finance his stay in camp."

He then read further the section which points out the difference between financing the military man and the CPS man,

"Persons drafted for military service, whether combatant or noncombatant, will be provided with clothing, food, and shelter and all necessary medical, dental and hospital care. In addition they will receive regular army pay of $21 a month ... for the first 4 months of their service and $30 per month for the remaining 8 months. Persons, who perform a year's service under the Civilian Public Service program will receive no pay and in addition either they, or their religious group, will pay for their own maintenance and the general administration of the camps as an expression of their willingness to make sacrifices for the things they believe in."

After some intermittent discussion, Senator Johnson asked, "What denominations predominate, Colonel?" To which Col. Kosch replied,

"The Mennonite group accounts for about 37 per cent of them, and two-thirds of them are in the Mennonite, the Brethren, and the Friends, which are the 3 old-line peace churches. The other third comes from all other denominations and at the present time we have 114 different denominations of religious groups represented."

Col. Kosch then discusses the geographical distribution. A great many come from the Bible Belt, the farming class, particularly the Mennonites and Brethren, starting in Pennsylvania and New York, and work west into the farming areas of Ohio, Indiana, Illinois, and across the Mississippi into Iowa, Nebraska, Kansas and Missouri. These, he states, are the heavy groups, only one other state would rank in the top ten, California. He was asked whether any of the COs leave the camps and decide to join the army. His reply, ".... we have tried to be fair and have found that about one out of eight--in other words over 500 of the 4,000 we have gotten who were originally classified as IV-E--have changed their minds and have gone into the army."

Some discussion arose among the committee members as to the difference between a conscientious objector and a slacker. Major J. T. Coatsworth, who was representing Selective Service System explained,

"... (M)any of these boys have been confined in their early lives to such an extent, having been under the influence of their church and their elders, that they do not have worldly knowledge and experience as other people have; so instead of their being slackers they are the result of this rather isolated life. .... If we were to take a young boy and bring him up as many of these boys are brought up, without the influence of newspapers, without the influence of the radio, without the influences that we normally have, the natural result would not be so much a slacker as an entirely different person. We are dealing with a different type of person generally."

Col. Kosch then adds,

"We have one group of these people here in Pennsylvania, which is the most conservative element, that believes that the ideal mode of life was the year 1870 and that you should never get beyond that. They don't use rubber tires on their buggies ... Whether they want to or not, they are helping the government conserve rubber now. But they live in these valleys up there; they buy everybody else out; they get everybody else out but themselves and they stay to themselves; they don't have automobiles. If a man buys an automobile, he is kicked out of the church. We have had cases of that, where these boys have bought automobiles and were kicked out of the church, and the boards said they could not be conscientious objectors because they had left the church. They won't have radios in their places; they won't have telephones; they won't have electric lights. If they buy a farm that has electric lights, they tear them out. All they have in their places is their church papers. The ministers tell them what is going on in the church. The father is the head of the family as long as he lives. In other words, his son may be grown up and married and have children of his own, but the old man tells him what to do. We feel that if we could get these youngsters out from the influence of these older people we could do something with them."

Other discussion followed, and then Col Kosch made a statement comparing the CPS men with the CCC men. He said, "We have mature men and men who know how to do the work and how to handle tools, while in the CCC, we just had boys that didn't know a shovel from an ax when they started...."

Finally, Senator Johnson asked, "Do you find these men do very much missionary work?" To which Col. Kosch replied,

"We try to discourage that.... We are not setting up programs which put them in a position where they can do it, like social-welfare, teaching in schools, and so forth. We have had pressure put on us to put them in teaching schools where they are short of funds, and so forth, but we have refused to do it, because we do not believe that the government should be a party to helping these men spread their pacifist propaganda..."

With the convening of the 77th Congress, the big push was for the enactment of the Tolan-Kilgore-Pepper bill (S 2871) which was designed to establish an Office of War Mobilization which could in turn enable the government to make work assignments to areas considered essential in the war effort. Naturally, church leaders and other groups concerned with protecting individual freedoms, became concerned. Various witnesses again appeared before the respective congressional committees. The problem was resolved without much fanfare. Most of the conscientious objectors who were not yet drafted, and consequently not yet in camps, were assigned to farm or dairy work, which was considered of national importance and essential for the war effort.

In February, 1943, some senators were still irritated with and working against the conscientious objectors. One bill, H. R. 2142, was introduced by Representative Carter Manasco (Ala.) which would have denied employment "in the Federal Government to conscientious objectors and persons refusing to subscribe to an oath to uphold and defend the Constitution of the United States."

As indicated earlier, Senator Elmer Thomas (OK), took a similar position in the senate, and would go even farther, he advocated denying voting in public elections, running for public office, or being employed by the government in any position for all conscientious objectors. In a hearing before the Senate Military Affairs Committee, February 17, 1943, after Senator Thomas had presented the resolution he had received from the American Legion in Oklahoma, and had had a bill drafted and had just presented it to this committee, he stated,

".... I trust you will be successful in securing this amendment..... Mr.

Chairman and gentlemen, that is the record I desire to make..... I will leave it for such consideration as this committee may see fit to give it, and I hope you will give it your full attention. Thank you very much, gentlemen." The chairman responded, "You are quite welcome Senator. We are very glad to have had you with us this morning. We will in due time give that consideration. Now, gentlemen, I have some twenty-odd letters here in reference to this bill, S. 315, which the reporter will copy into the record."

At this point in the hearing, thirty-four letters to the Senate Military Affairs Committee, all opposing the bill, were included in the record. The discussion then moved on to S. 675, the proposal to extend employment compensation to conscientious objectors. The latter is the bill that expired with the adjournment of the 76th Congress. General Lewis B. Hershey, Director of Selective Service System was a strong proponent of this employment compensation bill. He and Col. Kosch both felt it was important as a protection for the government against possible claims in the future. After another round of testimony and debate, the compensation bill was reported out favorably on April 2, 1943, and the Thomas amendment to eliminate conscientious objectors was tabled.

The final focus on conscientious objectors by Congress was regarding a program for COs to engage in Foreign Service. Some congressman discovered that hidden in the depth of an unprecedented 72 billion dollar War Department Appropriation Bill was a paragraph aiming specifically at providing funds for Foreign Service for COs. A rather devastating letter written by Frank C. Waldrop, appeared in the Washington Times-Herald, May 6, 1943, claiming that the relief-reconstruction program for conscientious objectors to China, which was under consideration at the time, would give the conscientious objector unfair and undue attention. His letter concludes with the statement this project will be viewed as "the biggest, permanent world-saver of them all; Nice spot for a man with a poor future otherwise." The House amended the War Appropriations Bill to read, "...no appropriation contained in this Act shall be available for obligation or expenditure or for any expense whatsoever, directly or indirectly, for or on account of any person in a civilian status listed as a conscientious objector ...."

In the Senate debate considerable support was afforded the conscientious objectors, particularly in regard to the various experimental programs they were engaging in, for example, two men submitted themselves to malaria research, seven men submitted themselves for toxicity of sea-water experiment, four men took an altitude experiment, twenty submitted themselves to a cold and heat research experiment, one on cancer growth and metabolism study, several fellows submitted to a louse control program getting 200 lice on each, kept on their clothes for three weeks and experimented with different types of insecticide sprays, 75 to 100 men were sprayed with influenza germs and attempted to kill the germs by the use of different sprays, also 60 men are parachute fire fighters. These experiments were related to the Senate Committee by Col. Kosch and Col. Keesling. Even with these testimonies, however, the Senate Military Affairs Committee eliminated the amendment providing funds for conscientious objectors. A Conference Committee appointed from both the Senate and House to reconcile the differences, changed the measures to contain the following,

"...no appropriation contained in this Act shall be used for any expense pertaining to (1) the instruction, education or training of Class IV-F Conscientious Objectors in colleges, (2) the service of such conscientious objectors outside the United States, its territories and possessions, (3) the transportation of such conscientious objectors to or from any college or any such service,..." so foreign service for conscientious objectors was dead.

This concludes the discussion of the conscientious objector in Congress. The major source for this discussion, The Politics of the Conscientious Objector in World War II, is taken from the booklet titled "Congress Looks at the Conscientious Objector," published by the National Service Board for Religious Objectors, Washington, D.C., December, 1943. The individuals who compiled the booklet are not indicated. The book, however, does include all congressional activity that transpired during the period under consideration. I think I am safe in saying that most COs in service during this period had at best, only a vague notion of what was happening in Congress. The objective in such a report is to provide information for the layman, for those who served in the military perhaps because they didn't know, to church people, former CPSers, and to anyone else with an interest in historical information. After all, the first step in the solution of a problem, is an awareness of the problem itself.

Appendix VI – Original Deed for the Family Farm; 1908, Protection, KS

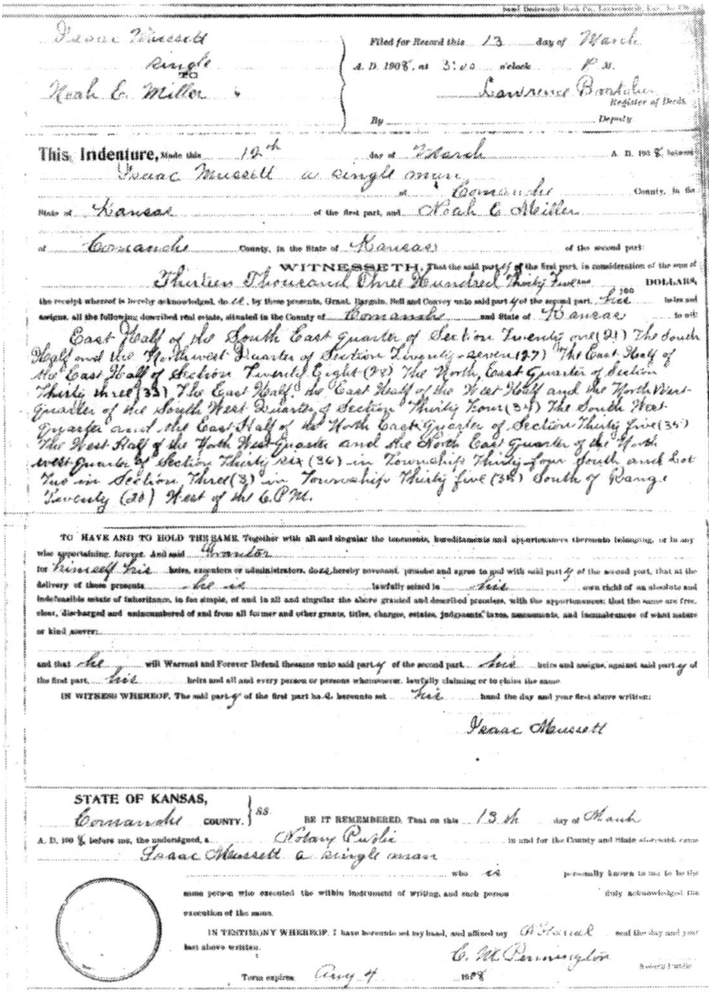

Isaac Mussell
single
TO
Noah E. Miller

Filed for Record this 13 day of March A. D. 1908, at 3:00 o'clock P. M.
Lawrence Bortolus
Register of Deeds.
By ______ Deputy

This Indenture, Made this 12th day of March A. D. 1908 between Isaac Mussell a single man of Comanche County, in the State of Kansas of the first part, and Noah E. Miller of Comanche County, in the State of Kansas of the second part:

WITNESSETH, That the said party of the first part, in consideration of the sum of Thirteen Thousand Three Hundred Thirty Five and 00/100 DOLLARS the receipt whereof is hereby acknowledged, do es, by these presents, Grant, Bargain, Sell and Convey unto said party of the second part, his heirs and assigns, all the following described real estate, situated in the County of Comanche and State of Kansas to wit:

East Half of the South East Quarter of Section Twenty one (21) The South Half and the Northwest Quarter of Section Twenty-seven (27) The East Half of the East Half of Section Twenty Eight (28) The North East Quarter of Section Thirty three (33) The East Half, the East Half of the West Half and the North West Quarter of the South West Quarter of Section Thirty Four (34) The South West Quarter and the East Half of the North East Quarter of Section Thirty five (35) The West Half of the North West Quarter and the North East Quarter of the North west Quarter of Section Thirty six (36) in Township Thirty four South and Lot Two in Section Three (3) in Township Thirty five (35) South of Range Twenty (20) West of the 6 P.M.

TO HAVE AND TO HOLD THE SAME, Together with all and singular the tenements, hereditaments and appurtenances thereunto belonging, or in any wise appertaining, forever. And said Grantor for himself his heirs, executors or administrators, does hereby covenant, promise and agree to and with said party of the second part, that at the delivery of these presents he is lawfully seized in his own right of an absolute and indefeasible estate of inheritance, in fee simple, of and in all and singular the above granted and described premises, with the appurtenances; that the same are free, clear, discharged and unincumbered of and from all former and other grants, titles, charges, estates, judgments, taxes, assessments, and incumbrances of what nature or kind soever:

and that he will Warrant and Forever Defend the same unto said party of the second part his heirs and assigns, against said party of the first part, his heirs and all and every person or persons whomsoever, lawfully claiming or to claim the same.

IN WITNESS WHEREOF, The said party of the first part ha s hereunto set his hand the day and year first above written:

Isaac Mussell

STATE OF KANSAS,
Comanche COUNTY. } SS.

BE IT REMEMBERED, That on this 13th day of March A. D. 1908, before me, the undersigned, a Notary Public in and for the County and State aforesaid, came Isaac Mussell a single man who is personally known to me to be the same person who executed the within instrument of writing, and such person duly acknowledged the execution of the same.

IN TESTIMONY WHEREOF, I have hereunto set my hand, and affixed my Official seal the day and year last above written.

C. M. Pennington
Notary Public

Term expires Aug 4 1908

Entered in Transfer Record in my office, this 13 day of March A. D. 1908
Jay T. Botts

Figure 1 - Page 1 of deed giving 169.76 acres to David D Miller, D. Paul's father.

Sophronia Miller et al,Plaintiff vs. Ursula Miller et al,Defendants,	State of Kansas,County of Comanche,ss. Filed for record this 3 day of June at 2:00 P.M. 1915. F.R.Campbell.,Register of Deeds

JUDGMENT AWARDING PARTITION.

CASE No. 2508

IN THE DISTRICT COURT OF COMANCHE COUNTY,KANSAS.

Sophronia Miller in her own right and as guardian of Tuscon,
Nora,Billy,Levi,Christina.and Harold Miller,minors,   Plaintiff.

VS

Ursula Miller and her husband E.Enos Miller,
Elias Miller and his wife Nettie Miller,
Alfred Miller and his wife Lovina Miller,
Lewis C.Miller and his wife Susie Miller,
David D.Miller and his wife Maggie Miller,
Howard Miller,single,   Baldwin Miller,single,
Mary Miller,single, ...   Defendants.

JUDGMENT AWARDING PARTITION.

Now on this 21st day of May 1915,the same being one of the days of the may 1915 term of the above named Court the above entitled matter came on to be heard on the application of the Plaintiff to have the report of the commissioners confirmed and judgment rendered accordingly.

And the Court after being fully advised finds that there are no exceptions on file and that the commissioners have made partition as directed ,Except a change in the ten acre tracts in West 20 acres of NE NW 36-34-20 and have found that said divisionwas fair and equitable so far as the minor defendants are concerned.

IT is therefore by the Court ordered and adjudged that the lands asked to be partitiond in the petition of the plaintiff be and the same are hereby divided as by said commissioner reported,to wit:

To Ysula Miller E½ SE¼ 21 and E½ NE¼ 28-34-20,160 acres,

Alfred Miller NW¼ 27-34-20 ,160 acres,

Howard Miller the SW¼ 27-34-20,160 acres.

Elias Miller the E½ SE¼ 28 & N½ NE¼ 33-34-20,160 acres.

Mary Miller North One Third of the 480 acres of land described as follows.

E½ W½ & E½ 34-34-20,160 acres

Tuscon Miller the middle one-third of the 480 acres of land described as follows.

E½ W½ & E½ 34-34-20,and in addition thereto the west eight acres of Lot 2 of 3-35-20, 168 acres,

David D.Miller the South one-third of the 480 acres of land described as follows.

E½ W½ & E½ 34-34-20,and the east 9.76 acres of Lot 2,3-35-20,169.76 acres,

Nora Miller the SW¼ 35-34-20,160 acres,

Billy Miller the NE¼ NE¼ 35- and East Ten acres of NE¼ NW¼ 36-34-20,containing 50 acres

Levi Miller SE¼ NE¼ 35 & West ten acres of east Twenty acres of the NE¼ NW¼ 36-34-20, containing 50 acres,

Christina Miller the SW¼ NW¼ and the East ten acres of the West Twenty acresof the NE¼ NW¼ 36-34-20 containing 50 acres ,

Harold Miller the NW¼ NW¼ and West ten acres of the West twenty acres of the NE¼ NW¼ 36-34-20,containing 50 acres,all of said land in Comanche County,Kansas

According to The N.E. Miller Family History by Lewis (Lew) Miller all of the fourteen children but two received portions of the land outlined on the accompanying map. Each portion was valued at approximately $2000.00. The other two children had received their inheritance in cash at an earlier time. The two not listed on this legal document are Baldwin and Lewis so apparently those were the two he was referring to.

Figure 2 - Page 2 of the same 1908 deed.

Appendix VII - Detailed Table of Contents